Praise for *The Pa*

"By writing *The Path of Presence*, Synthia Andrews has given us access to exceptional guidance for living more meaningful and satisfying lives. By including her own life experiences in the book, her principles for becoming more fully present burst into light. While reading, I found myself smiling that involuntary smile that comes to reassure me of the rightness of whatever I'm focusing my attention on at the time. Being particularly concerned with how our society is moving away from real time person-to-person contact, I was comforted by her ideas on how we can counter our own feelings of isolation."

—Arthur Strock, PhD, school psychologist,
author of *Live By Your Dreams*

"In a hectic world, *The Path of Presence* gently guides you to a natural way of being. For anyone committed to serving humanity with heart, this book is compassionately practical and will resonate with your soul."

—Anne Black, PhD, psychologist and founding director
of The Warrior Connection

Path of Energy

"*The Path of Energy: Awaken Your Personal Power and Expand Your Consciousness* is a powerful blend of spiritual philosophy and scientific principles woven into the perfection of a practical formula for everyday life. If you've always known that there's more to you than you learned in Biology 101, but find yourself intimidated by the technical language of science, this is the beautiful book you've been waiting for!"

—Gregg Braden, *New York Times* best-selling author of *The Divine Matrix and Fractal Time*

"We congratulate Synthia Andrews, ND, for beautifully and skillfully writing a one of a kind book, on energy awareness, for the 21st century. As we collectively move into realms of higher frequencies, being able to discern the delicate differences between energies becomes imperative. *The Path of Energy* is without a doubt the ultimate sourcebook for developing this vital ability."

—Dannion and Kathryn Brinkley
Best-selling authors of *Secrets of the Light: Lessons from Heaven*

Path of Emotions

"Dr. Andrews shows how we can use our emotions to make ourselves miserable or happy. Then, more importantly, she shows us practical and effective ways we can channel that energy to take charge of our health and happiness and rid ourselves of our human barriers to love."

—Henry Grayson, PhD, author of
Use Your Body to Heal Your Mind and Mindful Loving

THE
PATH of
PRESENCE

8 AWARENESS-EXPANDING ENERGY
PRACTICES TO IGNITE YOUR PURPOSE

SYNTHIA ANDREWS, ND

THE PATH OF PRESENCE
EDITED BY PATRICIA KOT
TYPESET BY PERFECTYPE, NASHVILLE, TENNESEE
Cover design by Ian Shimkoviak/ thebook designers
Assorted cover image composition copyright © Shutterstock 2016
Printed in the U.S.A.

To order this title, please call toll-free 1-800-CAREER-1 (NJ and Canada: 201-848-0310) to order using VISA or MasterCard, or for further information on books from Career Press.

The Career Press, Inc.
12 Parish Drive
Wayne, NJ 07470
www.careerpress.com

Library of Congress Cataloging-in-Publication Data

CIP Data Available Upon Request.

This book is dedicated to Erin and Emerson.

"You don't necessarily have to believe in higher
powers to develop Presence; you have to believe in
higher principles of kindness, compassion and love."
—Synthia Andrews

ACKNOWLEDGMENTS

There are many people to thank for all that went into writing this book. So many have contributed so much to this outcome that thanks must be given by first name, in alphabetical order. Thank you all!

A Place Called Hope—raptor rehabilitators and friends Todd and Christine, who provided the tips for nature lovers in the appendix. Good friends and good people. Check out their incredible work at *www.aplacecalledhoperaptors.com*.

Adriel Infantino—my younger daughter, who brings light to the family through the sweetness of her Presence, keeps us laughing, and reminds me that I don't have to leave my brain at the door in order to engage spirituality.

Barry and Lil Levine—owners of Willoughby's Coffee & Tea and Erin's employer at the time of her accident. Barry and Lil treated Erin like family, keeping the lunchtime vigil and continuing to pay her salary and health care insurance through the crisis. In addition, they provided me with endless free coffee, and I can say, as a long-time coffee connoisseur and world traveler, Willoughby's is the best coffee anywhere. Fortunately, they sell their self-roasted coffee by mail order! Check them out at *www.willoughbyscoffee.com*.

Colin Andrews—my husband, who accepts with equanimity my rousing the household every morning at 5:00 a.m. as I rise to write before going to work. He is my constant support and holder of my heart. For efficacy, he is not included in much of the writing of Erin's journey, but he was there throughout, always being of service (*www.colinandrews.net*).

Erin Infantino—my older daughter, who opened her heart and let me in. We healed together.

Johanna Sayre—my very best friend, who nourishes the seeds, edits the words, and sees the deepest parts of my heart. Thank you, always.

John White—my agent, still trying to retire, but rising to the need of every new book.

Joyce Logan—the heart-centered social media wizard helping me emerge in electronic form. *www.joyceloganmarketing.com*

Meredith Young-Sowers—author and spiritual leader who wrote the Foreword to this book. I can't thank Meredith enough for her encouragement, understanding, and willingness to give of her time and expertise. Her generous spirit touched my heart and gave me a boost along the way. *www.stillpoint.com*

Michael Pye—acquisitions editor at New Page Books. When I stared writing the proposal for this book in July 2015, Michael e-mailed. We had not talked in two years. He asked if I had a book for them, which I did. Then came the accident and the book was forgotten. In November, the week I returned to writing, Michael again called out of the blue to ask if the proposal was ready. His psychic percipience let me know I was on track. Thanks, Michael, I really needed that!

Susan Rosati—my favorite kundalini yoga teacher whose Presence permeates this book.

Pillar Gonzales—who brought her willing spirit and her horse, Annie, to the farm. I don't know where we would be without them!

Tiokasin and Jadina—friends whose in-depth conversation helped fine-tune concepts in this book.

The Ramsby clan—my family of origin. In my parents, siblings and their spouses, and gorgeous nieces is the essence of Presence I try to write about. Each, in their own unique way, brings integrity and intent into struggles in which it is easier to leave them at home.

The team at New Page Books—a fabulous group of people to work with who hold the best of intentions.

The women of Soni's Cottage Workshops—the extraordinary group of spiritual explorers assembled by teacher Soni Masseur who let me impart the Pillars of Presence for the first time. Their sweet hearts light the path.

CONTENTS

Foreword: The Path of Presence 11

Introduction. 15

part i: journey into the eight pillars

Chapter 1: In the Light of Presence. 21

Chapter 2: The Pillar of Being 33

Chapter 3: The Pillar of Connecting. 53

Chapter 4: The Pillar of Grounding 75

Chapter 5: The Pillar of Centering 97

Chapter 6: The Pillar of Balancing 117

Chapter 7: The Pillar of Aligning 139

Chapter 8: The Pillar of Clearing 159

Chapter 9: The Pillar of Honoring 181

part ii: stepping into presence

Chapter 10: The Eight Pillar Process. 203

Chapter 11: Being Me. 213

Chapter 12: Foundations of Creating Your Vision 223

Chapter 13: Opening to Nature's Design 237

Chapter 14: Presence in Conflict Resolution 249

Chapter 15: Walking a Path With Heart 257

Conclusion 263

Appendix: Emotional Meaning Chart 269

Glossary 273

Notes 281

Index 285

fOREWORD:
THE pATH Of pRESENCE

The first thing I turned to in Synthia Andrews's new book, *The Path of Presence*, was the heart-stopping story of her daughter Erin's accident. As a parent, I read Synthia's words as if they were my own, and what she was experiencing was so vividly told that it felt like my own story with my daughter. I was immediately invested in this story and the book.

I wondered what would follow the telling of the various episodes of Erin's experience. I soon discovered, as I turned the pages, that Synthia was taking us along a powerful heart-centered path into the very essence of Presence by demonstrating the attributes of Presence through each of the Eight Pillars. Each Pillar came to life for me as I realized she was teaching what she had come to use and understand through her experiences with Erin but also from her many years as a healer and teacher.

In Chapter 2, for example, Synthia follows the telling of Erin's accident and the call in the night with meaningful and practical understandings of how to survive such an experience mentally, emotionally, and spiritually and what to learn to navigate the treacherous waters of any challenging life experiences. While Synthia was forced to draw on inner strength and knowing from the experience with her daughter, still this book is for all of us in any circumstance in which we seek to manage life in a better way.

She teaches us about "awareness of present time," for example, and the challenge of holding our attention in the present. She offers us an explanation of how staying in awareness of present time sharpens our senses and wakes us up to opportunity. She writes:

◇ *There is a deeper level of reality that is accessible when you are awake in the present moment.*

◇ *Your Presence dynamically interacts with this level of reality to work for the higher good in concert with your inner truth.*

◇ *You have inner resources and abilities that can only be accessed in present time.*

◇ *Your attention is a force that can be turned into a laser beam of perception that takes you below the surface and beyond the obvious.*

This is no abstract discussion of Presence, but a profound journey into the depths of what is needed when the extraordinary and the ordinary hit our lives and we struggle to find meaning, support, grace, and endurance.

Presence is difficult to grasp because it is a way of Being that defies description. Yet Synthia does a masterful job of guiding us through the varied ways we can understand Presence and live in that sacred space.

From the very first chapter, I found myself reading slowly and carefully, not wanting to miss any of her finely crafted phrases or thoughts. As I read the various chapters dealing with Being, Connecting, Grounding, Centering, Balancing, Aligning, Clearing, and Honoring, I found a renewed appreciation for Presence and her gentle but on-point discussion of how to recognize Presence and claim it within our own hearts.

In today's world, in times of stress and in times of joy, we look for ways to find that special inner space from which to manage our emotions, to find balance when there is only challenge, and to discover love and caring for ourselves when others are too busy surviving their own lives. As I explored the various Pillars in Synthia's book, I quickly realized that Erin's story was but one story of the many we each have in our lives when we need to have something within our own mind and heart to rely on—and that something is the connection to spirit.

Spirituality isn't about understanding the power of love in an abstract way, but where the rubber meets the road and we need to have guideposts to mark our way through uncertainty into a place of peace, joy, and acceptance.

I've known Synthia for a number of years and have enjoyed her books. But I felt such a strong resonance with this book because I recognized the truth of her elegant words and her genuine awareness of Presence. She was writing from knowing Presence rather than just speculating about it—and that makes all the difference.

This is a book I knew immediately that I would return to over and over to rediscover its wisdom and practical tools for staying steady in Presence. *The Path of Presence* is a gift to all of us, and I know it will travel through many hands, helping, healing, and teaching the real way to experience Presence. Well done, Synthia!

Meredith Young-Sowers, DDiv
Author of *Agartha: A Journey to the Stars*,
The Angelic Messenger Cards, Wisdom Bowls, and *Spirit Heals*
Founder and director, Stillpoint School of Integrative Life Healing

INTRODUCTION

There are two sides to me: the side that is curious about the nature and mechanisms of life and studies physiology and medicine, and the side that connects with and perceives subtle energy. For me, they are different sides of the same. My path has been to explore life while looking through both lenses.

As a result, I have done a lot of apologizing. Half my time seems spent apologizing to my science-based family and naturopathic colleagues for my "woo-woo" eccentricity. The other half seems occupied apologizing to those who also perceive subtle energy for my desire to put the underpinnings of science in the discussion, and my compulsion to create discernable steps to achieve awareness.

Perhaps apologizing has helped me find balance between science and mysticism, but at this time, apologizing for being different is finished. Now each of us is asked to embrace our truest expression of self and together create a new relationship with reality.

Events in the world today ask that we show up as all of who we are. This may not be comfortable or popular, but it is necessary. In this book, I have tried to find my authentic expression on topics that can be demanding to describe. Sometimes I have been successful and other times, not so much.

I started thinking about Presence and the energy elements that uphold Presence around the time my friend Richard, a Native American from the Osage lineage, died in 2013. In my mind's eye I saw an image of a sacred lodge supported by the eight lodge poles, two in each direction. Each lodge pole became the Pillar of an energetic practice that upheld Presence. My undertaking has been to understand and convey clearly the Pillars and the energy practices that maintain them without falling into jargon and cliché. No small task, at least for me.

I write what has meaning to me and do not assume it has meaning for anyone else. If it does, I am honored. Finding my voice in this book has been challenging. To speak from the perspective of "I" and own the practices feels egocentric and self-important. To speak from the universal "we" sounds presumptive. To speak directly to you sounds like lecturing. There is no perfect voice. In the end, I chose to make this a conversation and speak directly to you. My hope is to validate your internal truth. If this feels overbearing, forgive me. In truth, I am teaching myself.

I have authored two other books with New Page Books: *The Path of Energy* (2011) and *The Path of Emotions* (2013). During the writing of both books, synchronistic life experiences required that I live the truth of the principles discussed. While writing *The Path of Energy*, my husband and I were subject to intense, soul-level interference whose energetic elements were objectively verified. As I wrote *The Path of Emotion*, my mother died. My writing did not cause these events; however, everything I was writing about was tested. In those two books, I chose to leave out the personal side-story.

Once again, during the writing of *The Path of Presence*, life demanded I live through and verify the book's principles when my older daughter was in a near-fatal car accident. Because each of the Pillars is so perfectly encapsulated within my daughter's story, with her permission I have included details of the accident and subsequent events at the beginning of each Pillar chapter. I hope by doing so the truth and utility of the energy practices described within the chapter are made evident.

Finally, words mean different things to different people. It is challenging to find words that express deeper concepts. If I have used words that stiffen your resistance, it is unintentional. Try to look beyond to the heart of what I seek to convey and let the word dissipate in the ethers. Thank you.

My lifelong journey into subtle energy and emotions has been passionate, joyful, and wildly fulfilling. I offer this book in support of each reader's expanding awareness of his or her energy path. I hope to see you in my Facebook group or in one of my courses. You can visit my Website at *www.synthiaandrews.com*.

Synthia Andrews
May 16, 2016

Journey into the Eight Pillars

How you use your feelings and intuitions, the manner in which you pursue your dreams, is determining the quality of the present and future of Earth. Conscious participation in the process is the reason to develop your Presence.

The Eight Pillars are aspects of awareness that help you live more consciously. Conscious living frees your innate abilities and opens your perceptions. Your Presence interacts with the ambiance around you to draw out a deeper experience of life.

The questions arise: What happened to just Being? Why can't we just enjoy being alive? Do we have to be aware of everything?

"Just Being" is the primary experience in developing Presence. Practicing with the Eight Pillars helps you to "just be" free of your preconditioned training. Otherwise, you are "just Being" with all of your habitual responses, unprocessed emotions, fears, and addictions. The Eight Pillars opens the door of awareness to live fully and freely awake, aware and alive.

Although the Pillars are presented in linear fashion, one is not necessarily more important than another. The Pillars are the support poles that uphold Presence; each bears equal weight. You will never master any one completely or develop all of them equally. You will move into and out of awareness of them. You are never done. The exploration is a journey throughout life, with the opportunity of always going deeper.

Each chapter in this section is preceded with a personal vignette of my and my daughter's journey through her near-fatal car accident. They are included because they so perfectly encapsulate the Pillar under discussion. As you read, you may be reminded of such events in your life and realize within your story are examples of how you developed Presence. I offer these glimpses into our story to help you hold onto yours.

All you need bring on this journey is a willingness to explore and a desire to manifest more of your authentic self in your life. The tools you will use are carried in your body and accessed through your breath. You have everything you need.

in the Light of presence

Awakened Perception

Awakened Perception

Occasionally, and without warning, the world around me changes: The light is brighter and more alive, streaming in a multitude of colors, shades, and densities into, through, and around objects, trees, animals, people, and me. I am incorporated into this stream of light that is all-that-is. In such moments, I am home.

The change can happen on an in-breath and be gone on the out-breath. The experience is both fleeting and eternal. It does not need repeating to be imprinted in my memory, yet several times I have been graced: once in a yoga class, once in a copse of pine trees, once looking into the eyes of the man who would become my husband, and once as my world fell apart. Twice more it occurred as a prolonged interaction.

In her TED talk, titled My Stroke of Insight, Jill Bolte Taylor eloquently describes a similar experience that occurred during her stroke. Watching her talk, I wondered whether my flashes of self-realization were the result of mini strokes. I concluded they were not. Rather, they were flashes of awakened sight. In those nanoseconds of sentience, seeds were planted whose need to grow directs the course of my life.

These moments of clear sight are not unique to me. Many people have such experiences or feel them just beyond the edge of their consciousness. Perhaps you have had a similar event and appreciate that there is a part of you, outside of your everyday awareness, that operates within this arena of light. That part is your Presence, a reflection of the deeper totality of who you are. It orchestrates your life, instills you with purpose, and works toward your highest good. When you develop Presence, your path is illuminated as your inner self shines.

The conventional view of Presence is that it is a set of qualities you project that influence people to perceive you in a certain way. In this book, Presence is a spiritual force within. It is developed through your relationship with eight specific aspects of being alive: a reflection of how consciously you use the precious force of life.

The Power of Presence

Presence is the canvass that conveys your essence to the world. It communicates the turmoil or serenity of your thoughts, the turbulence or coherence of your emotions, and the conviction of your truth. It reflects how you process, integrate, and use life-force. Presence carries the force of your spirit to interact with the whole of reality.

As your inner self is reflected outwardly through your Presence, you draw to you everything needed for the lessons and achievements of life. If you pay attention, Presence guides your path and gives you the conviction to pursue your dreams. When tragedy strikes, as it will in every life, Presence provides the grace to meet the challenges with strength, calm, and courage. Through Presence, the continuity between internal and external reality, the continuous flow from one to the other, is experienced.

Since the reality you perceive is filtered through your Presence, the more developed your Presence, the greater your awareness of deeper layers of existence. It's your choice whether your awareness is based within the single layer of the material world or it expands into the spirit within everything and further into the dimension of light. Developing Presence is a process of developing awareness. As you do, the richness of life increases exponentially.

The flow between internal thoughts and feelings and the creation of external experiences can sometimes be obscure, and you might not see the connection. Then it can be a struggle to manifest your dreams and live from your inner truth. You may have difficulty rising to the ever present challenges of life and feel obstructed in being your authentic self. Obstruction is usually due to learned limitations that are reflected in your Presence. Here's how it works.

The essence of who you are, along with what you came to achieve in this life, exists at the very core of your being: in your heart, which is the throne of your spirit. Your heart is fed and enabled through life-force, which streams to you from the heavens, the Earth, the air, and the food and water you eat and drink. When you were young, your core self radiated unimpeded into the world. Inevitably, criticism, judgment, perceived failure, and other inhibiting experiences created beliefs that overlaid your radiance, causing distortions. To hide these perceived imperfections, defenses were laid on top of the distortions. As a result, not only is your perception filtered through limitation, your life-force is spent sustaining this very complex arrangement. Using your life-force to uphold limitation and defense restricts the emanation of your core, essential self, hampering the quality of your life.

Restoring the light of your Presence is a process of letting go of distortions and false beliefs. It is a renewed appreciation of the radiance that is your true self. You can address distortions through talk therapy, bodywork, meditation, and many other practices. It can take a very long time, or no time at all. It can be as simple as awakening.

This book reflects my path as a naturopathic doctor, energy intuitive, and mother into eight energy-based practices centered on eight unique levels of awareness. I call these the Eight Pillars of Presence. These practices magnify Presence and ignite purpose. Purpose is not some grand and monumental task you assume for this life. Rather, purpose is a natural extension of who you are. Your purpose is to be all of yourself as fully, completely, and lovingly as you can. Practicing the Eight Pillars enables your authentic self to shine.

The purpose of your life is to be your true self. Freeing your essence to shine is the purpose of developing Presence.

The Eight Pillars of Presence

Your energy is tied up in relationships with everything around you. You have relationships with people, governments, organizations, your inner self, Earth, plants, animals, ideals, goals, and more. Everything you give your attention to results in an exchange of energy that creates a relationship. Quantum physics calls this entanglement. Each relationship requires you to look at the world in a slightly different way. Some relationships distort reality; others clarify.

The Eight Pillars are Being, Connecting, Grounding, Centering, Balancing, Aligning, Clearing, and Honoring. Each Pillar reflects a specific relationship based in an essential awareness that supports the uncovering and expression of your authentic self. Being, for example, reflects your relationship, or lack of, with death and your ability to engage present-time awareness. When death becomes your ally, you are enough, just as you are, and able to be present in the moment without running to hide in the past or the future.

You are in constant internal and largely subconscious dialog with the relationships within the Pillars. In this book, these dialogs are brought to light and interacted with. Practices of self-reflection and energy exercises guide you inward for the encounter. The growth of doing so is reflected in your Presence and vitalizes your dynamic, creative engagement with life.

The benefit of developing and using the Eight Pillars was dramatically demonstrated to me when my daughter was in a near fatal car accident while I was writing this book. My world was rocked as I struggled to rise to the turmoil and pain that unfolded. If any of the Pillars had seemed theoretical to me before, they revealed themselves as fully relevant, multi-layered, and beautifully functional. Consequently, I can say with certainty that the Eight Pillars can carry you beyond your current limits to connect with a deeper reality. The journey they take you on provides meaning, joy, and empowerment. They will help you overcome challenges, yes, but also help you to live you light and share your brilliance with the world.

Using the Eight Pillars and developing Presence transforms your awareness and changes the nature of your reality. You become part of the healing and transformation of a world that is out of balance. You become part of a new wave traveling through Earth.

Tools for Developing Presence

Your access into the Eight Pillars occurs through your body-mind in the integration of your physical, mental, emotional, and spiritual perceptions. Access to the body-mind is achieved using conscious breathing and felt-perceptions. Conscious breathing leads your awareness into the exercises, while felt-perceptions, also called felt-senses, provide the feedback necessary to chart your path.

These are not complicated tools that you need to learn. They are natural, innate functions of your body-mind. You use them every day, sometimes consciously, most of the time unconsciously. All you are doing now is becoming aware of how you use them and doing so on purpose.

Felt-Perception: Speaking With the Language of the Heart

Felt-perception is awareness based on a combination of mental insight with body sensations, emotions, and feelings. Felt-perceptions are the basis of intuition, gut feelings, hunches, and deeper insights that reveal your inner truth. They represent the language used by your heart to communicate with your conscious mind.

Although you may have forgotten it, you were born knowing this language. It is a method of communication using your body-mind that engages in a conversation where words aren't necessary. Body sensations, feelings, emotions, and unique perceptions are the vocabulary.

Here is some of the vocabulary of this language:

◇ Sensations such as goose bumps, shivers, hot, and/or cold that arise in response to situations.

◇ Emotions that come from deep within, arriving with no apparent stimulation during conversations, activities, or meditation and shift your energy.

◇ Gut feelings about people, places, or choices.

◇ Sensations such as feeling pushed away, feeling weak and lacking energy, or feeling disconnected and detached are signals that something is wrong.

◇ Sensations such as feeling drawn forward, feeling stronger and more energized, or feeling more engaged are signals that something is exactly right.

◇ Feeling a sense of connection, opening, or flow when your actions or thoughts are in sync with your vision, the flow of the universe, and present-time information.

◇ Visions or images that produce deep feeling and have a profound sense of reality that guide your direction.

◇ Pulsations, waves, and flow within the body.

◇ In situations where the body's wisdom has been ignored for a long time, the body might be forced to speak with pain, dysfunction, and possibly disease.

◇ The arrival of new thoughts, ideas, or concepts that seem to come from nowhere.

Using this language, truth is recognized when information you receive is accompanied by body signals. Deeper understandings are found with unexpected images that impress on your awareness. Directions are made clear when you sense a flow within your body as you make your choices.

There are myriad ways to speak with a dialect for each person. The nuance of the vocabulary of this language is uniquely yours. To understand it, you need to attend to the signals you receive, notice what they relate to, and start a personal dictionary. Perhaps you have already begun to pay attention and to chart your personal vocabulary. However, if you would like, there is more information in my book *The Path of Energy* (New Page Books, 2011).

On the journey into the Eight Pillars, felt-perceptions are your constant guideposts. It will soon be second nature to assess life using these tools.

Conscious Breathing: Accessing Your Attention

Your attention is the most powerful tool you have for perceiving the world and engaging intention. Being able to direct your attention opens the gate for living with full engagement, accessing all parts of self and bringing your fullness to the situations you encounter. Attention rides on the vehicle of your breath which leads your awareness into the felt-perceptions of the body-mind. Becoming aware of your breath shifts your internal state of Being and frees your attention to explore life.

The breath is the link between the body and the mind. When the breath is shallow and limited, attention is kept in the head or outside the body. This pattern develops in order to avoid uncomfortable feelings. Taking short, shallow breaths or holding the breath for short periods of time protects you from feeling uncomfortable emotions and sensations in your body. It also keeps you from feeling what is real. Bringing your breath more fully into the body allows you to feel and engage your felt-perceptions.

Conscious breathing is nothing more than becoming aware of the breath and using it to direct your attention inward. This shifts your state of Being, opens new levels of awareness, and accesses felt-perceptions. Conscious breathing is your vehicle to contact deeper parts of self and shift into deeper levels of awareness. Each of the particular aspects of awareness within the Eight Pillars is accessed through conscious breathing.

Take a deep breath right now and notice how your mind is instantly calmer and your awareness of your body instantly increased. If you want to intensify this awareness, deepen your breathing even further. Deep, relaxed, unforced breathing draws your attention down, out of your mind, and inward to your heart. When you deepen your breath, it's impossible for your body-mind not to change. Within a few minutes of such breathing, you will be in a different place from before you started. Your mind will be calmer and clearer, your muscles more relaxed, and your attention more focused. This is inevitable.

Combining conscious breathing with felt-perceptions is used throughout the journey into the Eight Pillars. Conscious breathing opens your awareness, and felt-perceptions guide the journey.

The Culture of Confusion

Everyone has Presence: you, I, people on the street, leaders, celebrities, everyone. Only the degree of expression differs. You may wonder, if Presence is the key to a rich and meaningful life, why isn't it being cultivated by more people? The answer is confusion. Our culture has a way of confusing one thing with another. Sometimes it's difficult to see what Presence truly is.

The first time I presented the Eight Pillars in a workshop, I was startled at what happened when participants were asked to think of a person with Presence. Expecting examples like Nelson Mandela or Mother Theresa, I was surprised that many attendees named people who either projected an aura of glittering glamor or who were intimidating in their behavior. Needless to say, neither of these were what I had in mind.

In the first instance, where people provided examples of glittering personalities, Presence was being confused with charisma. It's easy to see why. Charisma projects energy. It draws people's attention and gives the impression of mastery. It embodies the fine art of presentation and first impressions. Casting a spell with the subtleties of body language, communication, and style, charisma can mesmerize people.

However, despite the importance of first impressions, charisma can only express one aspect of who the person is: the persona he or she is presenting to the world in that moment. Charisma tends to fall apart when sufficiently challenged. Charisma will not see you through tragedy. It is based on what the person wants to project, rather than who the person truly is: presentation, not essence.

Presence is not the same as how you present yourself. Although Presence is conveyed through what you say and do, also included is the vibe you give off while you do it. You can control your expression and how much grip to give your handshake, but it is impossible to mask the energy you radiate. While charisma polishes your veneer, Presence reveals your true self and ignites your purpose. Existing beyond will or reason, Presence cannot be manipulated into Being. You can only open to it and let it shine.

In the second instance, where people who were overbearing and intimidating were named as having Presence, self-importance was being confused with personal power. Because Presence does increase personal power, it's fair to question the distinction. After all, con men, dictators, politicians, and false gurus all have both charisma and very powerful projections, enough so that people become followers in a personality cult.

Self-importance projects power either through intimidation or by saying what followers want to hear. In both cases, power is derived from the energy others give them. Remove the belief of others, and the projection of power crumbles. When confronted, self-important people tend to get mean. They fear the exposure of inner lack when outward power is removed. They have no inner ground to stand on. The energy the overbearing personality uses is not generated from personal source and does not carry the conviction of truth. Power exists only in the mind.

Self-importance is associated with the need to dominate and is easily corrupted and abused. The belief in the need for dominance is prevalent everywhere in our society: politics, corporate structure, sports, and advertising. It is the cause of Earth's current state of imbalance. Working in the arena of false power, even in a desire to use it for good, perpetuates the social, economic, and environmental crises in which we currently find ourselves.

Given the confusion, it's no wonder so many people sabotage their own success. Do you want to have more impact in positive world change, grow your ideas, and share more of your story and wisdom but are afraid of the consequences of being too visible? No wonder! You are likely to be attacked just for being yourself or, worse, be mistaken for someone who only seeks self-importance.

The truth is, because Presence aligns you with your essence, it moves you into the flow of something bigger. The type of power that radiates from Presence is different: softer, rounder, more pervasive, and unstoppable. When you feel it rising within, it is not to be feared or shunned. It is being called forth to help you be more of who you truly are so you can help consciously create the world.

Qualities of Presence

Putting aside charismatic people and those who project domination, recall a person who exudes true Presence. How does his or her Presence express itself? Invariably, these people stand out from the crowd and make good leaders. They exhibit kindness. They carry conviction. They are genuine and are able to sit in the silence of not knowing. They have dignity.

All of this translates into one understanding: They are comfortable in their own skin. They know who they are and have finished fighting with themselves over whether or not to express it. They have achieved a level of wholeness most people do not know they are missing or don't believe is possible to attain.

You may have tried techniques for developing Presence in the past and even been happy with the results, yet recognize that what is being defined in this book is different. Most of the time, developing Presence is approached by suggesting you adopt the qualities that people with Presence possess. You are told to wear certain colors, to be stylish in your clothing, and to practice specific types of body language. You are given tools to communicate with your target audience. These techniques work well to project an image. They can be effective in getting you comfortable and providing confidence. They can get you started, but can they create a Presence that is established in the voice of your essence?

Developing the characteristics of Presence without developing the relationships they are based on leaves you with no foundation. Everything is great until you are challenged by a circumstance you don't understand and can't control or by someone with a more powerful projection than yours. Then the qualities you have dressed yourself in either collapse, sinking you into self-doubt and unworthiness, or they become ridged and drive you to engage in ego-battles. Either way, Presence is reduced to the dominion of dominance.

Truthfully, trying to exhibit specific qualities doesn't create Presence. It is the other way around: Presence engenders specific qualities. This is why Presence is unaffected by circumstance. People can agree with you or not; it doesn't change who you are. People can follow you or not; it doesn't change where you're going. And when you feel overwhelmed, you have a resource that will reestablish your foundation and revitalize your Presence. The Eight Pillars will always restore and rejuvenate your Presence.

The Paradigm of Wholeness

A Native American friend of mine, Richard, is a person of Presence. When he enters a room, he carries more weight than a single person. An entire lineage walks alongside him. He is grounded, centered, and holds his vision in the forefront of his actions. Aligned with something larger than himself, he moves within its flow. When he speaks, even if he says the same thing as the five people before him, his words convey greater meaning. His Presence has impact, awakening something in those who listen and calling forth a response.

Richard is as human as you and I: He makes mistakes, he enjoys a pint of beer, and he doesn't always live up to his ideals. His humanness does not take away from his Presence, nor does his Presence mean life is easy. No one can say Nelson Mandela and his family, or Mother Theresa, had easy lives. At the same time, they lived with purpose, their Presence had impact, and they achieved their goals.

Though few are called to a life of sacrifice, being alive does include sacrifice. Life is sacrificed every time you eat, breathe, or clothe yourself. In every choice you make, one outcome is sacrificed for another. How often do you sacrifice your essential self in your decisions? What percentage of your decisions allows your true self to shine? What would you have to sacrifice to improve this percentage? You may find your need for security, your fear of rejection, your belief in competition and dominance, your certainty of your own failure, or some other limiting belief may need to be sacrificed in order to magnify your Presence.

When events aren't working the way you imagined, or affairs of the world make you feel helpless, you're being called to dig deeper; you're being asked let go of assumptions and everything you think you know about life and how it works. Einstein observed that a problem cannot be changed from the same mindset that created it. Every assumption predetermines an outcome. Enter the development of Presence empty. Surrender, and let your heart be your guide.

Here is the crux: Everything you need, you have; everything you will become is already inside of you. In the words of Michelangelo, "Every block of stone has a sculpture inside of it; it is the job of the sculptor to discover it." Developing Presence is releasing the sculpture from within the stone, letting go in order to free the final form.

You are part of an awakening. You are realizing that relieving the problems in your life and in the world require that you shift more than just your way of thinking, but also your way of Being. How you use your feelings and intuitions, the manner in which you pursue your dreams, is determining the quality of the present and future of Earth. Living fully in the beauty of the present and consciously participating in the creation of the future is the purpose of developing Presence.

Right now, the Earth is shifting out of the existing paradigm of dominance and competition into wholeness. People are being called to Presence. You don't need this book to participate; you are participating simply by being alive. Practicing the Eight Pillars engages your awareness to participate even more consciously. The Pillars will help you establish the fullness of Presence as you walk a Path with Heart.

2

The pillar of Being

PILLAR: Being
AWARENESS: Present Time
CHALLENGE: Lack of Attention
RELATIONSHIP: Death
GATEWAY: The Body
GIFT: Free Attention
EMOTION/ATTITUDE: Awe
QUALITY BROUGHT TO PRESENCE: Force

The Midnight Call

The shrill sound of the phone rouses me from the deepest sleep of the night. I am instantly awake, reaching to seize the receiver before the first ring ends. My heart is pounding. What, other than bad news, arrives before the sun? I strain to decipher the name on the caller ID: Yale Hospital. My grip tightens as I bring the handset to my ear. A friend was admitted to the hospital the previous day; perhaps her housemate is calling with bad news.

"Diane?" I ask tentatively.

A confused-sounding female voice stumbles into a reply, "What? Hello? Is this Synthia Andrews? Has someone already contacted you?"

Not Diane. I shrink. "No. No one has contacted me." My voice is reluctant. I don't want to hear anymore. I don't want to be on the end of this call.

I brace for bad news. It arrives: My older daughter has been in a car accident. She is alive, she wasn't driving, and no one has died. Before relief has a chance to touch me, an avalanche of fear-filled facts descends. The full extent of her injuries is unknown: Her head, her neck, her back, and her leg are all damaged. She needs immediate emergency surgery. The woman's voice walks me through the procedures. My brain is skipping; I can't keep up.

"Do you agree to this surgery? Do you agree to a blood transfusion if it will save her life? Do you agree to resuscitation in the event . . ."

"Yes, yes, yes!" Of course, I agree; who wouldn't agree? And why do they need my agreement when she's an adult? I clutch the phone, pacing, sitting, standing, and pacing again. It's happening too fast. "Wait," I say, expanding with hope. "If she needs a transfusion, can I give her my blood?"

There is a pause. My husband has risen from bed and started to dress. He gathers his cell phone, wallet, and car keys.

"No, we don't do direct blood donation," the woman responds.

I deflate. My blood is all I have to offer; giving it is all I can do to join my daughter in her fight for life.

"Do you have any questions?" the voice asks.

"No. I'll be there as soon as I can," I say, reaching for pants and shoes. "I'm leaving now."

The line seems to go dead, but I can still hear soft breathing. The woman resumes, her voice gentle now, concerned, "That's good. As soon as you can."

The unspoken hangs in the silence. Oh shit. Oh shit. Hospital personnel are trained not to say such things.

My husband drives. I have already told him what was said, and now neither of us speaks. The 20-minute ride seems endless. Death sits next to me and prickles my skin; its nearness awakens my life-force. The console blows cold air on my toes, bare in sandals. The cold rolls across the top of my feet, bounces off my ankles, spreads across the floor, and escapes under the seat. The sun rises. Pink light filters through branches, gilding the edges of the leaves.

I am suspended in this distinct slice of reality, intensely alive, acutely aware of every breath and sensation, and completely present in this moment.

Suddenly, panic. Snatches of the phone conversation hammer at my calm. My mind pitches itself out of my body, out of the present moment forward to what awaits. My imagination races ahead to pain and fear, to the struggle we will surely face, and to the possibility my daughter is already dead. Why is my husband driving so slowly? Why doesn't he hurry? How can he be so damn deliberate?

The desire to jump out of the car, to run as fast as I can, threatens to overwhelm. I force my attention to return from the future, to let go of the urgency of the phone conversation. I bring it to the present, to the happenings inside the car. Breathe in; breathe out. I follow my breath into my body. I anchor in the beat of my heart, the rhythm of my breath. My body holds me in the present where I am connected to all-that-is.

With my feelings, I reach toward my daughter and find the stream that is her. She fills my heart. She is alive. I can feel the pulsation that is her, and I know with utter certainty—it is not her time.

I disappear into the song of the road under the tires. I am restored in the single-pointed awareness of life that death provides. A yoga mantra repeats inside my head: Breathe in the breath of life, the breath of God. Breathe out the breath of life, the breath of God.

Anchored in my body, there is no time. There is only now. This is the Pillar of Being.

Pillar: Being

Being wakes you up where you are: in the present moment. You have heard the saying that the point of power is in the present: You can't go back and change the past; you can't go forward and act in the future. Action takes place only in the here and now. If you are asleep to what is around you, wrapped up in thoughts that take you somewhere else, how can you use the moment for meaningful action?

Emergency situations such as the midnight call alerting me to my daughter's accident have the power to shock you into being fully present. However, the intensity of such moments can be so frightening to experience that you numb the feeling by jumping backward or forward in time, thinking about what happened or what is yet to come to avoid the overwhelming feelings of the moment. Achieving the Pillar of Being requires that you train your attention.

Through Being, you awaken to the mystery of life, to the unknown possibility of each moment. Imagine there are other levels of reality that exists alongside you. Access to these other levels is through the doorway of Being that focuses your attention on the magical flow of energy streaming within and around you all the time. That flow connects you to all-that-is. It can guide you into the felt-perceptions of a new way of knowing.

There are immense challenges in the world today. By accessing different parts of your consciousness, Being provides new insights and paths. Whether you face personal trials in your finances, health, career, and relationships, or are addressing the larger struggles of the Earth, Being in present time increases discernment and makes it easier to sort through the layers of information and misinformation. Through Being, you are connected to what is real, where the basis of balance and sustainability can be found.

Being in present time reflects how you show up in the world and what your Presence offers others. How much of yourself do you bring to each moment? Are you fully present and awake to the world around you, or missing all this moment holds because of the to-do list in your mind? Do you give people the gift of your full attention, or is half your mind somewhere else? To attain Being, you experience life, rather than do life.

Being provides your Presence with power.

Awareness: Present Time

Being is achieved through present-time awareness, the *moment-by-moment simultaneous awareness of your thoughts, feelings, and bodily sensations alongside the events occurring outside of you.* Through present-time awareness, the world is revealed directly via the senses rather than reflecting what the mind imagines or projects. Although used as a technique to manage stress, present-time awareness is much more. Through present-time awareness, your attention is a fully focused force of perception that is aligned with your inner truth.

The focus of present-time awareness opens your perceptions, increases your intuition, and guides purposeful action. There are certain assumptions in present-time awareness that impact and expand your Presence:

⬥ There is a deeper level of reality that is accessible when you are awake in the present moment.

⬥ Your Presence dynamically interacts with this level of reality to work for the higher good in concert with your inner truth.

⬥ You have inner resources and abilities that can only be accessed in present time.

⬥ Your attention is a force that can be turned into a laser beam of perception that takes you below the surface and beyond the obvious.

⬥ You are exactly where you're supposed to be, doing exactly what you're supposed to be doing.

The perception and purposeful action gained through present-time awareness can impact all aspects of life, especially relationships. Recall the intensity of your attention at a time when you were in love. How does it feel to be in the light of someone else's complete attention? In such moments, you are seen and valued. There is no doubt that thoughts of other things are not intruding. You are all that matters, the center of the world. Contrast that with the image of a little kid in a restaurant whose parent is trolling a smart phone. It hurts not to have the attention of the people you love. It's painful to realize you aren't always present for the people who matter the most to you. Your attention is a gift. When it is offered to the people you are with, relationships flourish; intimacy deepens, and links of love, loyalty, and commitment become stronger.

Being in present-time awareness is essential to showing up in the world as your true self. The ability to self-reflect, relate your current situation to past experience, and adjust for the best future outcome happens through present-time awareness. When you can align with a higher vision in the present moment, the world is transformed, and so are you. Using felt-senses to explore the world, you find things are not as you were taught. Instead, there is dynamic interconnection, a flow between internal and external reality.

Perceiving through present-time awareness, the present moment reveals the essence of reality and opens the door to your true potential.

Challenge: Lack of Attention

The biggest challenge to present-time awareness is the lack of command over where your mind is. The here and now seems mundane. Interesting things happen over there, in the future, or in rehashing the past. People often misunderstand what living in the present really means, imagining it as a justification for irresponsible behavior. However, Being in present time does not mean living hedonistically for the moment, ignoring past mistakes, or not planning for the future. It does mean that you need to develop a different relationship with the past and the future.

Recent discoveries in neuroscience reveal that when you remember, you are not simply accessing information stored in the brain. Rather, you are re-creating your memories each time you recall them. What took place does not change, but the parts you remember and the way you connect the dots to create meaning are re-formed in relation to what you know and who you are in the present. In other words, memory is a creative process. Your memories evolve as you evolve. Remembering, then, is much different than living in the past. Memory is bringing past events into alignment with the present moment.

In contrast, living in the past keeps you a victim to what has already happened and blinds you to present options. Perhaps you wallow in previous mistakes, obsess over past grievances as you continually rerun old arguments, or refuse to let go of lost happiness. You spend your time engaged in what can no longer be changed, repeating refrains of what if, if only, should have, would have, or could have. And nothing ever changes.

The challenge is to alter the dialog with your memories and recreate that part of the past that serves your growth. Live in the present and turn the past into an informational resource. How do you do that? By processing the emotion held in the past event. Grief, anger, betrayal, whatever the emotion, ask yourself: What does that emotion give me? How does it feed my energy, self-concept, or direction in life? What belief about myself or about life does it sustain?

If you can sit with the emotion lodged in past events and allow your body to discharge its energy, you will be able to accept past challenges and integrate your experiences into the present. Your memories will become a source of power that helps you move forward, rather than a source of pain that holds you back, as you will see in Chapter 8. Additional information is in my book *The Path of Emotions* (New Page Books, 2013).

Living in the future is as disempowering as living in the past. In the future, you lose yourself in wishful thinking, always waiting for the right time, the perfect person, or the best means to move forward. Hoping for a better future can lead to ignoring opportunities available in the present and turn you into a victim. Having hope is not the problem; not taking action in the present toward manifesting what you are hoping for is.

Do you give more weight to future desires than to the needs of the moment? Do you spend time making lists instead of taking action, worrying instead of addressing potential problems? The present moment is lost when you maintain the focus of your attention on what you're going to do, rather than what you are doing. Instead, make the future a conscious extension of the present by staying in the present moment while taking action toward a future vision. You don't need to plan every step and think through every possibility; you can stay present and hold the vision loosely, and let it breathe and grow. You cease to live in the future when you create a vision to work toward. It's time to stop wishing for things to be different and, in the words of Jean-Luc Picard, "make it so."

Relationship: Death

Coming face to face with death shifts present-time awareness from an intellectual exercise to a way of life. In the presence of death, tomorrow and yesterday fade. Time is suspended. Life occurs in the eternity that exists in the space between the inhale and the exhale. Suddenly, each breath becomes a gift; the next one may not come. Even in the presence of someone else's death, you are confronted with your own mortality. The present moment is all you can truly be sure of. It is all that exists.

This acute sense of being alive is the appeal of extreme sports and other thrill-seeking activities in which the rush of facing death can be addictive. Equally addictive is the desire to run from death in fear, to act as though death can be permanently avoided; as if, through denial, there will be a different outcome to the end of being alive.

Living in fear of death keeps you focused in your head, thinking about the future or the past. You are trapped in time and space, hurtled forward, and driven by a relentless clock, one second, one minute, and one hour closer to dying. Hurry. There is so much to do before then, so much to prove and experience. You won't hear the ticking and will probably deny that the clock is even there, and yet it drives you. The dysfunctional relationship with death must be mended to fully live in the present.

I am not enough. This is the message the fear of death conveys. In the time available to you before you die, you are pressured to do more, have more, express more, and be more. The pressure can make you afraid to make choices, reluctant to establish boundaries, and hesitant to commit to one path because . . . what if you choose wrong? What if you don't pick the door that the prize is hiding behind? What if you say no just as all your dreams are about to come true? Or what if the path you're on doesn't go anywhere? *What if you waste your life?*

In facing my daughter's death, all the things I spent my life rushing to do, all the ways I justified my value, had absolutely no importance. All that mattered was bathing my daughter in life-force, a force made purely of love. Facing death alongside my daughter, I found that death is an illusion. Misunderstood entirely, when accepted as an ally, death offers total transformation.

Death as an ally exists between the two extreme reactions of thrill-seeking and denial. Accepting death as an ally does not mean escaping problems by dying, and it does not mean that courting death will give you a greater sense of being alive. It doesn't even mean that the awareness of death will help you sort your priorities.

When death becomes your ally, it declares that you are enough. It declares that life is enough. You can stop running. You are here, exactly where you are supposed to be, doing exactly what you are supposed to be doing. Death reveals the present moment in its entirety with no barriers between internal and external reality. You are freed from the grip of an unanchored mind and the treadmill of circular thoughts, instilled with the joy of life. You return to the spiritual center within that is home.

The relationship with death changes with time. Before you have children, it is one thing, after, quite another. In the elder years, it comes as a friend or tormenter. But one thing is certain: Death is a constant in life. Developing rapport is essential.

The awakening that comes with accepting death frees your attention and brings you into present time. The transformation reveals that the purpose of Being on Earth is in Being. You are here as an experiencer, each breath an invitation to the present moment.

Your relationship with death determines how fully you participate in life.

Gateway: The Body

How to master attention is the first issue that arises when reaching for present-time awareness. How do you keep your focus in the here and now? The answer is through your body.

The physical body anchors the mind. In fact, sensations and feelings are so essential to Being that present-time awareness can be considered a close cousin to body awareness. Your body is a finely tuned instrument that instantly receives, processes, and responds to information, making your body the gateway into the present moment.

In everyday consciousness, there is a split between the mind and the body. Focused on the information in your mind, you ignore the massive amount of information being presented by the body in the form of sensations, feelings, and emotions. Once this split occurs, without physical Grounding, your mind loses the nuanced perceptions obtained via your body; without the illumination of your mind, your body loses its directional compass. When your mind is brought into your body, your attention is focused and your heart automatically opens to spirit. This is the natural state of being human.

Your body speaks the language of the spirit living within your heart, as discussed in Chapter 1. Sensations, feelings, and other body events are signals that validate what you are thinking, saying, or doing. They pinpoint the significance of information being received. For example, when you're listening to someone telling a story, sensations might signify a particularly important point. Or a stroke of insight might be accentuated with body sensations to confirm its significance.

When the heart is closed and the mind unanchored to the body, you are outside present-time awareness, and the dialog with spirit is missed. Even when you are listening, you may have trouble understanding. Remember the vocabulary of the language of the heart in Chapter 1. Then, right now, as you continue reading, pay attention not only to the words you are reading and the thoughts they generate, but also to the sensations, resistances, openings, and gut feelings being presented to you via your body. Let present-time awareness speak to you through your body. Does it deepen your understanding of the concepts discussed?

There are many reasons why a mind-body split occurs making present-time awareness difficult. Two are obvious. First, the mind gets bored; it doesn't like to stay quiet. It likes to impress itself with the mental gymnastics of its own brilliance. As a culture, we have been trained to undervalue the wisdom of the body as less important and less real than the wisdom of the mind. Only recently do neuroscientists understand the unique contribution to intelligence that comes from the body.

The second reason for the split is the desire to avoid the body's uncomfortable feelings and incessant demands. The body complains of physical and emotional pain, craves pleasure, and is driven by hunger and thirst. It is a subconscious strategy to close down awareness of the body to avoid feeling the overwhelm of strong emotions such as desire, grief, anger, or fear. However, when you close down your feelings, you lose connection to the body and miss the unique contribution the body makes to your perceptions.

Splitting the awareness of your mind from your body is an act of denial. Suppressing uncomfortable feelings and emotions sends the mind into the past, the future, or any place other than where you are. Present-time awareness encourages you to process your feelings as they occur. Otherwise, the tendency is to push difficult feelings aside and stuff them into the body, which turns them into inner land mines. Then when you seek to be in present time, you run smack into those uncomfortable feelings that have been waiting for your attention. When you process things as they arrive, or as close as possible, your body is free to be alert and awake in the here and now, and you can experience what it is to be fully alive.

Living in times and places other than where you bodily reside is the realm of the disembodied. It is not possible to feel tomorrow's headache; it is not possible to re-experience yesterday's broken leg. In contrast, the here and now is experienced, not thought about. It is lived, not planned. The present is occupied by bodies filled with breathing, moving, and doing. There is no room for uncertainty or doubt, which are emotions based on hoping for future outcomes. The present is certain and complete. Like it or not, it is here, now. All you can do is deal with it. With your mind anchored inside your body, perceptiveness is naturally heightened. Attending to the moment, you are at your most powerful.

Consider the experience described at the beginning of the chapter. When I reached to find my daughter to know if she was alive or not, I was using an extension of my senses that could be accessed only through focused attention in present time. When I directed my full attention on her through my body, her feel was distinguishable from every other sensation. Receiving information from felt-senses is natural. It happens all the time through the subconscious. With the heightened perceptions evoked by present-time awareness, subconscious information is available consciously. My daughter was easily recognizable and her vitality measurable. Accessing perceptions of this kind is a function of the heart, which, when they are used in harmony, is the balancing place for mind and body.

Take a minute to consider how the people in your life are distinguishable by the way they *feel*. Think of someone you love and extend your senses toward them. What do you notice?

Gift: Free Attention

Present-time awareness positions you at the point of infinite possibility and gives you the single most valuable tool with which to explore: free attention. Unfettered from places, people, things, and times other than when you are in the moment, free attention is available. You can use it to explore the hidden depths of the present moment, focus on understanding a situation, or follow the threads of your own abilities. Present-time awareness and free attention have a reciprocal arrangement: The more you have of one, the more you automatically have of the other.

With the full attention of your body-mind and with death as an ally, you lose the fear of being fully alive. Mistakes are simply another type of experience and have no power to make you feel like a failure or less than anyone else. You no longer need to prove your worth; you are enough, free to act and create, to see and be anything. This is a powerful place to be. In the face of disaster, this is where you draw courage and Presence of mind. In the face of unexpected opportunity, this is where you find the assurance to say yes.

Free attention is your the faculty that expands awareness. Opening to the present moment, your felt-senses reveal that the world is more than it seems. This awareness instills a sense of awe, an emotion that opens your mind to unknown possibility. Under, above, and within you is a deeper level of reality that infiltrates and transcends the purely physical. This is the formative level whose essence is light. The light can be called energy, life-force, or simply consciousness. It is all three.

Perceiving in the light level of reality is a profound experience. Most startling and difficult to describe is the aliveness of the light, the realization that it is conscious and aware, enveloping, warm, and receiving. Light interacts. It is the essence of love. The feeling upon encountering light at this level is one of incredible familiarity and safety. While in thrall to it, all things, animate and inanimate, are imbued with life. After the light recedes, the stark emptiness of the world is shocking.

Interaction with light provides an inkling of what mystics of all ages have asserted: Love is the glue that holds the universe together. Whether you are aware or not, this is the substance of your Presence. Even while you engage physical reality, your Presence interacts within this realm.

The Practice of Being

As discussed in Chapter 1, the breath is the link between the body and the mind. Being in present-time awareness is achieved by using the breath to bring the mind back into the body. Deep, relaxed, unforced breathing draws your attention inward, and with that small amount of change, you have freed some attention from your mind for present-time awareness.

Now use that free attention to observe the felt-sensations within while simultaneously paying attention to events in the world around you. There is nothing more to it than this: no magic formula or esoteric practice. The difficulty is that you have to practice breathing and paying attention every day in order for present-time awareness to become your natural state.

As you engage life and encounter different situations, bring yourself out of your mind and into your body-mind to free your attention. Here are the basic steps:

◇ Pause, then take three deep, cleansing breaths. Inhale all the way into the bottom of your lungs, breathing in peace and breathing out tension. Even if you only have time for one breath, it will be enough.

◇ Become the observer and notice what you feel as you are engaged in your situation.

◇ Check for the felt-senses that were discussed earlier, such as,

   ✦ Tingling, as if your body is just waking up.
   ✦ A sense of opening and relaxation.
   ✦ Pulsations or waves.
   ✦ Flow or resistance.

◇ Pay attention to how your felt-senses change with different thoughts or with actions you are engaged in.

◇ Maintain awareness of thoughts, feelings, and body sensations while external events unfold.

Paying attention can be difficult. Most people are easily bored, and before you know it, you are no longer an experiencer; you are a director, a controller, and at the mercy of circular thoughts that lead you into the past or the future. Being requires that you break the habitual self-talk that directs your mind and energy. This begins with making a decision. You have to decide that present time awareness is important. You have to choose to engage life as it unfolds, letting go of control and expectation, of living anywhere but the present.

Starting this practice is easiest in a controlled environment such as in a sitting meditation. Here, the first obstacle you might encounter is the persistence of unwanted thoughts. This is the thing: Thoughts, in and of themselves, have no power. They are only thoughts. When thoughts are invested with emotion, then they have power. If a thought comes into your mind, acknowledge it and let it be. Investing it with your frustration or disappointment, and trying to push it out only keeps it longer and makes it bigger. Acknowledge it, say hello, and then use it. Notice how it feels in your body-mind. Make it part of your practice of awareness. It will soon leave and if it comes back, fine. It's only a thought.

Although present-time awareness is part of every spiritual tradition, old and new, Being is still the most challenging Pillar to achieve. Sometimes, a shock provides the thrust necessary to shift the filters of everyday awareness and allow the nuances of the present moment to take precedence. Present-time awareness is enhanced through practices that bring your mind into your body such as massage, yoga, Tai Chi, and meditation. Using the following self-reflection and energy exercises will also help you develop and use your attention and discover what gets in your way.

Being in present-time awareness magnifies your Presence so you are fully engaged, awake, aware, and able to act. What you are able to do when you are fully present goes beyond what everyday awareness suggests. You have extraordinary abilities you have only begun to tap. Being provides the raw force needed to engage.

Self-Reflection

In what ways do you express that you are not enough?

Pretend the feeling of "not being enough" is a coat. Put it on. What does your body feel like? What happens to your posture and your body language? What happens to your mood? How does the coat of "not being enough" change your perceptions of what's around you? How is your Presence impacted? How is your creative spirit impacted?

When do you forget to breathe? Are you breathing now? How deeply? Don't change a thing; just notice.

Have you ever experienced a close call with death? What feelings do you remember from that event? How were you changed? What does it mean to you to have death as an ally? When someone dies, how do your feelings about that person change? Stay in your body as you consider these thoughts. Notice what you feel: what parts of you becomes tense, what becomes open.

What percentage of engagement do you have with life right now? What would it take to have 100 percent?

What percentage of your attention is spent thinking about places other than where you are or carrying on conversations in your head with people who are not with you?

What percentage of time does your attention transmit love? What percentage is anger, worry, or resentment? Do you feel you have a choice?

How do you feel about shifting into another level of awareness? Do you feel fear, disbelief, or longing? What will it take to let all of these feelings go?

How much space do you leave open for mystery?

Do you get in the car and focus on what you will do when you get where you're going rather than on the world you are driving through?

What are the actions of today bringing to you?

Right now, as you read, pay attention to the sensations, resistances, openings, and gut feelings being presented to you via your body.

How are the people in your life distinguishable by the way they *feel*?

How much of your potential are you using?

Do you give more weight to future desires than to the needs of the moment, spend time making lists instead of taking action, and worry instead of addressing potential problems?

Where are you aimed?

How do you feel about the idea of light-based level of reality? What do you notice in your body when you think about it?

Energy Exercises

Exercise 1: Breath of Life

1. Take five deep breaths.
2. Imagine that the air you are inhaling is filled with hundreds of tiny stars.

3. Over the course of these five breaths, scan your body from your toes to your head or from your head to your toes. Notice:

   * Where do you have discomfort?
   * Where do you have ease?
   * Where are you supported?
   * Where are you holding?
   * Where is there space?
   * Where is there no space?
   * Where are you empty?
   * Where are you filled?

4. If you notice a discomfort, resistance, or lack of support or if your attention is drawn for any reason to an area of your body, offer that area the gift of your attention floating on your breath.

5. Your breath is Prana, the breath of life.

6. Breathe life into every cell.

7. There is no need to direct your cells or change a thing; just offer your cells life-force in the form of stars. Your body knows what to do.

8. Continue whatever activity you are involved with as you scan your body. Paying attention to your body at the same time as you are paying attention to other things is part of present-time awareness.

9. Dual attention is the natural state of balance between internal and external reality. Dual attention is an essential aspect to being in present time.

Notice how you feel.

Exercise 2: The Breath of Opening

Make it a practice throughout your day to stop and notice the relationship between your body and the present moment using the steps described earlier. Here is simple exercise to unite your body and mind into awareness of the moment:

1. Take three deep, cleansing breaths, inhaling peace and exhaling tension.
2. Let the mind follow the breath inward.
3. Bring your attention into your body.
4. Nothing needs to be changed or regulated; just follow and observe.
5. Give your attention to every sensation.
6. Imagine that each sensation carries a message: Pressure, pain, hot, cold, pleasure, touch, and emotion are all lifelines into the current moment.
7. Let every sensation travel inside to your core, bringing what is outside, inside.
8. Allow yourself to be the gathering point of all this exact moment has to offer.
9. Take a walk. Notice what you feel in your body as you move from one space to another.
    *   Can you feel changes of light in your body?
    *   Can you feel birds in the trees?
10. Just notice with no attachment or expectation.

Exercise 3: Bridging Inside With Outside

Use Exercise 1 or 2 to unite your mind and body.
   Now:

1. Notice your body-mind as part of the landscape of the room or the setting around you.
2. Feel your feet as an extension of the ground; feel your body as a continuation of the chair you are sitting on.
    *   How much pressure does the chair exert on your body?
    *   Where is the boundary between you and it?
    *   Is there a boundary?
    *   Is this comfortable or uncomfortable?

3. Experience your mind as part of the thought field of life.

4. Notice yourself as an integral part of the continuum.

5. Reverse the awareness that rides on your breath. Let your attention flow out on your exhale. Extend your sense of self as far into the room as you can. Notice how you feel:

   + What is the natural limit to your extension of self?

   + Do you feel stronger or weaker as you extend?

   + Do you fill all the space around you equally, up, down, and all around?

   + What changes internally as you expand externally?

   + Are you comfortable or uncomfortable?

   + Can you maintain a point of connection between this external extension of yourself with your internal center?

   + How balanced or unbalanced do you feel?

Whatever your experience, know that you can return to everyday awareness any time. You can also return to present-time awareness at any time.

The pillar of connecting

PILLAR: Connecting
AWARENESS: Holographic Awareness
CHALLENGE: Isolation
RELATIONSHIP: Ego
GATEWAY: Emotions
GIFT: Authenticity
EMOTION/ATTITUDE: Compassion
QUALITY BROUGHT TO PRESENCE: Clarity

Inside the ER

The emergency room is hushed, suspended in the quiet between episodes of chaos. Three slumped forms fill the seats near the reception desk. My niece sleeps soundly in one, my brother shifts restlessly in another, and the third is occupied by a family friend, Paul, who was first on the scene of my daughter's accident.

Paul jumps up as my husband and I walk in. He is agitated as he recounts his experience of rounding the corner to find a car upside down on the road, the occupants spewed across the asphalt. He stops to help, running toward an inert form seemingly trapped beneath the car and panics when he sees it is my daughter, apparently dead, blood streaming in rivulets from her head.

Paul stops talking, emotion overwhelming him. My husband soothes him; I am numb to the story, absorbing the details with disembodied calm. A refrain runs in a continuous loop in the back of my mind: alive, not dead. Alive, not dead . . .

We are taken as a group into the treatment area, winding along the narrow corridors to the cubicle that holds my daughter. She lies on blood-soaked sheets, enclosed in a cervical collar and leg brace. I touch her shoulder and stroke her cheek. She opens her eyes and smiles. Tension flows through my body into the Earth. I squeeze her hand; she squeezes back. Not paralyzed. It becomes part of my mantra: alive, not dead, not paralyzed.

We all talk at the same time: My brother makes jokes and my husband offers assurances. It's hard to know whether she hears. Suddenly, the atmosphere in the emergency room changes. Overhead loudspeakers call all hospital personnel not involved in emergency procedures to report to the ER. Nurses, technicians, and doctors immediately begin to appear. An attendant escorts us hurriedly back to the waiting area.

"Multi-car pileup on 95 in Old Lyme," he says. "Injured are being airlifted to several hospitals. If they come here, this will soon look like a war zone."

I hang back, wanting to stay with my daughter, not sure why I must leave. Will she be lost in the chaos? I ask to stay but am ushered out.

Thirty minutes pass and still I am not allowed back. My husband, brother, niece, and Paul all leave, anxious to do something useful: take care of her dog, locate her personal items that were in the car, or talk to the police. I wait another fifteen minutes, then ask to go back again.

The attendant is angry at my repeated request. "No one's going back," he admonishes. "There are too many casualties."

I have a hard time understanding why he thinks it is acceptable for my daughter to be alone. "So other people are being put in my daughter's treatment room?" I ask with terse sarcasm. My anger is born of worry.

The attendant scowls and shakes his head. "Of course not, but it's too busy."

"I won't bother anyone. I'll be inside the room with my daughter, keeping her company. I won't be out in the aisle."

I imagine the fear and pain my daughter is experiencing, how she must be anxious to know the condition of friends in the car with her. She needs someone to be there. She needs information and comfort. She needs an advocate. My anxiety ratchets up another notch.

The attendant shakes his head. "No one is going back," he proclaims.

The hairs on the back of my neck rise. "I am her mother," I growl between clenched teeth. "I want to see her."

He looks at the computer screen and shrugs. "Well, she's 32 . . ." he lets the sentence hang and lets me finish it in my head: She's 32, an adult; you have no rights.

My fingers grow talons and my mouth fangs. I had rights enough to authorize her treatment, but not enough to be with her in her pain and fear. Anger heats my face. I restrain from leaping across the counter and ripping him to shreds. The part of my attention that has been absorbed with my daughter slams back into my body. I am now fully present.

I focus on the short, muscular man in front of me, examining his stance and translating his body language into words.

His head is tilted to the side, eyes narrowed and looking at the screen: you can't tell me what to do. His lower jaw is forward and his chin juts out: one more word and I'll have you tossed out. His shoulders are pulled back and his chest is puffed: I'm in charge; don't push me. His hand is clenched in a tight fist: this is my job, and I'll fight to do it right.

Now, I understand. He is defending his job. I know my body mirrors his exactly as I, too, am defending my job. However, the aggression I display is not how I feel. How I feel is afraid, uncertain, and on the verge of collapse.

We are at an impasse. To move forward we have to connect, something we can't do through layers of defense. One of us has to step down. I inhale deeply and exhale the tension from my body. I pull in my talons and fangs, let go of my protections. I leave myself utterly vulnerable.

I haven't moved away from the desk, but the attendant refuses to glance from the computer screen to meet my eye. I reach toward him from my heart, searching beyond his role for the place inside him where we are both just people. When I finally feel him, I speak.

"Yes, she is 32. And she is hurt, alone, and afraid. Can you help her?"

My words flow along the lines of connection forged moments before. They reach him. He tips his head sideways, grimacing. His fist unfolds. His chest softens. He compresses his lips. He has the grace to appear embarrassed.

He doesn't speak to me but swivels in the chair and calls to one of the volunteers. "Show her to trauma 19," he says and then turns back to me. "Your daughter is on the way for a CT-scan. You'll have to wait in her treatment room."

"Thank you," I whisper as I hurry to follow the disappearing volunteer.

We arrive at the cubicle just as my daughter is being wheeled out. I reach forward and squeeze her hand. "I'll be here when you get back," I assure her as she is whisked away.

The room is dark, empty, and quiet. My purse slides to the floor as I sink into the single straight-backed plastic chair and close my eyes. Tiredness permeates every muscle. My chin drops to my chest.

I think about the attendant, about connection, imagining the fine gossamer threads that weave us all together. How easy it is to forget and to act as though what happens to one of us does not affect us all.

Suddenly, an image of my daughter's horse, Emerson, is impressed in my mind's eye. Emerson chose my daughter. He loves her. Four weeks before, something was unaccountably wrong with him. He was in obvious distress, walking with a crabbing motion, moving forward while curled sideways. The vet diagnosed a neck injury, but no neck injury had occurred. Anti-inflammatories took care of his symptoms, and the episode was forgotten. Until now.

I shiver. Are the connections between us even more substantial than I had thought? I remember Dean Radin's research into precognition described in his book Entangled Minds. *He explains that coming events are preceded by a bow wave of energy: the greater the emotional impact of the event, the greater the weight and velocity of the wave.*

Possibility swirls in my mind. Did Emerson receive the force of the bow wave of my daughter's accident? Can the energy of an event that has yet to occur have physical impact? It sounds ridiculous. How is such a connection possible? And if it is, what is the purpose?

Later, after I have seen the CT-scan, after I understand that the first two vertebrae in my daughter's neck are exploded outward, fragments floating freely, after I realize she is still in danger of being paralyzed, after the day is over and she is in a drugged sleep, I go home.

It is after midnight. The stars are bright in a velvet sky. I walk through the barn and stand at the open door to the paddock. The horses, dark lumps along the fence line, break away and move toward me. Emerson stumbles forward, curled to the side and barely able to walk.

He reaches me and puts his head against my chest. Tears stream down my face. I rest my cheek on his forehead. My mind can't embrace the greatness of this mystery and doesn't believe the impact of such connection or the power of such love. But in my heart, there is no doubt: This horse absorbed the force of my daughter's accident. Through their connection, he helped her survive.

I stroke Emerson's muzzle. What is there beyond thank you?

Pillar: Connecting

The Pillar of Connecting is mysterious. Does the apparent link between my daughter and her horse seem far-fetched and romanticized? To the rational mind, of course it does. In the current worldview, people are unconnected, individual entities motivated by self-interest whose actions are, by nature, intended to serve their own purpose. This concept of separatism gives birth to assumptions of limitation and competition that affect the way community is created, how business operates, and how money, resources, and opportunity are allocated. The impact is most evident in politics, yet even scientific studies are designed with the inherent bias of separatism.

Separatism gives the illusion of duality: us and them, right and wrong, or a force of evil confronting a force of good. The Pillar of Connecting makes no sense in this worldview. Thankfully, concepts of reality are shifting. Connecting happens within the realization of oneness, of experiencing yourself as a distinct part of a larger whole from which you cannot be separated. In this view, there is only one force: You can be open or you can be closed. Like a water tap, you can decide how open or closed you are at any particular time and how much force you want to allow.

Awareness: Holographic Awareness

Oneness is more than the idea of interconnection in which you are a separate entity connected to others through the ecosystem of life. Oneness is understood through holographic awareness. Since they were first created in 1962, three-dimensional holograms have become so commonplace their significance is often neglected. Surrounded by three-dimensional images on key fobs, in celebrity pictures, and within sculptures where the eye of the inner image follows your every move, they are familiar. In their everydayness, it is easy to overlook what they reveal about reality.

Holograms are created with beams of coherent light—light whose wave patterns are in phase with each other. Every part of a hologram holds the information of all parts. For example, imagine tearing an ordinary picture in half. What do you have? Two pictures, each containing one half of the original. However, if that were a holographic picture, tearing it in half would create two complete and identical pictures, each exactly the same as the original, only smaller. Each half can be torn again, resulting in four entire images. Each time they are torn, the image remains intact, only losing size and clarity.

When holograms were first available for marketing, they seemed magical, a feat of scientific genius. However, holography was not created by scientists: It was discovered by scientists. The principles already existed in nature. Scientists discovered what nature revealed.

The idea of natural holograms might change the way we view reality. For example, neuroscientists suggest the brain works as an advanced hologram. Quantum physicists suggest the universe is holographic, explaining such things as non-locality and entanglement of subatomic particles. Non-locality is the observation that two particles can exchange information without being in the same place: They can be in different rooms or different continents and still interact. Entanglement is the manner in which these particles are connected. In a hologram, concepts such as my daughter's horse absorbing the impact of her accident are understandable.

If science is the study of nature and technology the application, then the principles of holography reflect a deeper layer of reality. Perhaps you've had experiences of connection similar to my daughter with her horse that you discounted as impossible. Maybe you felt the significance but had no explanation. Holographic awareness provides a model in which this level of connection makes sense. The challenge is to look at the events of your life with this awareness and connect the dots to find deeper meaning and purpose.

The basic assumption of holographic awareness is that we are all part of the same fabric, the same whole. In spirituality, the whole is given many different interchangeable names: God, universal consciousness, the supreme being, the universe, the creative spirit, the source, the divine, and the light are a few. I like the saying that there is a face (and name) of "God" for every person who looks. Here are some beliefs that arise from holographic awareness:

⬥ You have access to all of reality from within. This access is natural, innate, and automatic.

⬥ Access is gained through coherent thought in the same way coherent light creates a hologram.

⬥ The part of you that is in resonance with the whole is your essential, authentic self.

⬥ You are a unique and individual part of the whole, and your perceptions co-create the entirety.

◇ You are essential to the whole and equal to every other part within it.

◇ You are exactly where you are meant to be.

◇ Your job is to be yourself as fully, completely, and totally as you can and to fulfill your unique part in co-creation.

◇ The whole is evolving, and each of us is part of that evolution.

◇ The universe and all parts of creation are conscious. Because the type of consciousness is different from that of Being human, this does not mean it isn't present.

◇ You are not alone.

At first glance, there is an apparent conflict. How can people be unique individuals, yet also be at one with everything? Working with an image can help. Imagine a globe. Each person (also, of course, each animal, plant, spiritual being, and all of creation) sits at a unique vantage point on the globe, providing vital information along pathways of exchange from that particular vista back to the whole. These unique vantage points are not separate; they form the matrix of the whole.

If the visual you created is similar to that of the World Wide Web, it's not surprising because science and technology reflect nature: The World Wide Web is a reflection of the energetic underpinning of reality in which information is transmitted through vibration. In holographic awareness, each vantage point affects the vibration of the entirety, creating a continual flow of awareness. If you are unsure how vibration can carry information and change the degree of flow, check out the field of Cymatics. YouTube has some spectacular videos demonstrating the organizing effect of vibration on matter.

In holographic awareness, your perceptions are not simply observations of what is; they are part of what forms the shape of reality. You are a co-creator of the whole, impacting the direction of evolution.

The part of you that is at one with the whole is your essential, authentic self. Surrounding your essential self is simply perspective, belief, and expectation. You can access all of reality from within through the Pillar of Connecting. Rather than creating a link between two separate things, *Connecting brings into alignment the essence within each that is the same.* The importance of this awareness provides the key to living with ease in the material world, which is explored in upcoming chapters.

If you are enmeshed in pain, limitation, and suffering, connect with your authentic self and find the essence of your connection to the whole. Shift your awareness from limitation to flow, and by changing your perspective, you are changing the whole. Evolution is not the slow process that is taught in schools. Reality is formed through awareness, and awareness can shift in the blink of an eye.

Challenge: Isolation

Isolation is at the root of all disease. Cells isolated through lack of blood supply or nerve innervation die. Babies wither away without touch. Ecosystems in isolation collapse. People isolated from each other lose their minds and, isolated from their spiritual center, become lost and lose joy.

Isolation causes so much psychological pain and suffering that it is the most effective means of controlling people. Shunning members of the community who act outside of agreed norms and putting prisoners in isolation are extremely effective punishments. Even torture and abuse are twisted forms of connection, easier to withstand than isolation.

Despite the many tools of communication in today's world, in general, people are feeling more isolated. Many work in cubicles, live in concrete surroundings separated from nature, relate to other people through electronic screens, and are kept too busy to nurture relationships. The increasing occurrence of depression and suicide is not remedied by all the communication devices advertising connection. Facebook, Twitter, and other social media platforms create instant contact without content. They provoke quick response with little connection.

This is not to suggest that electronic media isn't exciting and doesn't have benefit. Like most people, I rely on its immediate convenience. The bottom line, though, is that living beings need face-to-face connection, touch, and exchange. When these are replaced by electronic contact, many people feel isolated, misunderstood, and unimportant.

Each person I have spoken with who has thought about suicide or attempted it says the same thing: *I felt completely alone and, by my mere Presence, a burden to those around me.* This is not the statement of someone who is connected within a larger whole: unique, essential, and loved.

For many people, isolation is self-imposed. The fear of being fully seen and then rejected fosters fear of being visible. Because visibility equals vulnerability, you might hide your true self in a persona you think people want to see. The love you receive and accomplishments you achieve don't feel real. "If only they knew who I really am, they wouldn't love me" is the refrain you might play in your head. Stop and ask, "What do I gain from being isolated? What am I protecting? Would it really be more painful to be seen?" Kevin Hines jumped off the Golden Gate Bridge and lived. His story is one to consider. Google him on YouTube.

A friend from the Lakota Nation, Tiokasin Ghosthorse, says that in his language there is no word for loneliness. He explains that everything in creation is a relative, so wherever you go, you are with family. Sadly, reservations and boarding schools have tried to demonstrate to Native people why Western culture created the word. In the Western paradigm, humans are separate from the rest of creation right from the start, meant to either master it or, at best, steward it. Imagine being raised to know you are an integral part of creation, connected to each and every other life form. Imagine embracing that awareness right now. Imagine the safety and comfort of belonging.

Relationship: Ego

The relationship that needs to be developed to allow the Pillar of Connecting is with the ego. There is no doubt that the ego can disrupt full engagement with life and diminish your Presence. However, the reason this occurs is usually because the ego is treated as an enemy and considered a lower aspect of self that must be suppressed or eliminated to attain higher awareness. This is another aspect of duality thinking; only "us and them" exist within. The truth is that nothing is created outside of the whole. Even the ego has function that needs to be honored. When the ego is balanced, it supports your spiritual growth; when it is unbalanced, it creates chaos.

A healthy, well-developed, and balanced ego is connected to your spiritual center and provides strength, resolution, and will power. Rather than getting in the way of awareness, it motivates exploration and supports the ability to take risks. Great advances in science, social revolution, and even spiritual awakening make it into the world through the strength of someone's ego. Only a healthy ego can endure the pressure and isolation of standing against social pressure and of living in a world based on separation. *When connected with your spiritual center, the ego supports your ability to stand in your truth.*

Think about the most difficult situations you have experienced in your life: bullying, betrayal, and loss. How did you get through? You might find your ego gave you the strength, purpose, and resolution to grow.

Ego causes problems when it is unbalanced. An out-of-balance ego is afraid of the world. It believes the myth that it is bad and reacts in one of two ways. Either the ego builds defenses and protects itself by trying to prove its superiority, or it accepts its own awfulness and collapses into despair. The first leads to self-importance and the behaviors usually associated with an egotistical person: boasting, one-upmanship, arrogance, entitlement, and cruelty. The second leads to self-hatred and debased, equally cruel behavior.

I am bad is the message of an unbalanced ego. To correct itself, it tries to be perfect and then boast about it. The ego wonders why no one else notices how well it has overcome being bad and mastered being perfect. This would be funny if it wasn't so tragic. All the ego really wants is to do its job; trying to be perfect ensures this never happens.

Perfection isn't achievable or desirable. The best growth often comes out of mistakes. If you are afraid of making mistakes, you can't grow. Even at its most unbalanced, the ego helps your growth by providing a reflection of your growth-edge. The unbalanced ego, driving you toward perfection, shows you where your fear and self-loathing reside. Self-acceptance and compassion are the tools for a healthy relationship with ego. Being kind and fair to self and others is enough.

Through self-compassion, the ego can remember itself as part of the whole. It can step up and provide its unique contribution. Then defensive attitudes can be dropped and Connecting can occur.

If you are starting to wonder why the whole ever separated into individual points of perception that can become isolated and confused, that is an excellent question, which, of course, is not possible to answer. Some spiritual traditions call the separation of individual souls from source the out-breath of God: sort of like the Big Bang of the spirit. Souls return to source on the in-breath, bringing with them all they have learned in the experience of individualization. Interestingly, astrophysicists theorize that the universe will eventually stop expanding and begin contracting. Imagine a breathing universe!

Why separate at all? Maybe creating is simply a joyful act and all of creation is an expression of love infused joy. Find the essence of that concept to align with, and the ability to fully embrace life will be yours! The point of individualization seems to be to take the God force within into as many experiences as possible and engage each experience as fully as possible. So rather than rushing past being human to be at one with the all-that-is, maybe it would be more meaningful to engage the experiment: experience the creation with as full an awareness of oneness as possible, generating as much love as possible, and see what happens.

When the perspective changes from trying to become perfect to experiencing the joy of creation, the ego suddenly remembers its purpose: to help you carry out the dreams of your soul, connected to the larger reality, at peace within yourself, and expressing love. Go ego!

Gateway: Emotions

Emotions are the gateway into the Pillar of Connecting. Through feelings, you can experience resonance with other people and the whole. In the past, emotions have been condemned as untrustworthy by-products of the brain. Many religions label them troublesome temptations that test the spiritual will. Why would this be? As with ego, why would anything be created that doesn't have function?

Emotions are part of an internal guidance system. Every emotion carries a message from the heart, conveying the wisdom of the authentic core self. Emotions connect you with your environment, reveal what is important, warn of hidden motives, and give meaning and context to experience. Then they go a step beyond and provide energy to fuel action. Without emotions, you would not care about the dreams you pursue or have the drive to attain them. You would not find the path to expressing your authentic self or fulfill your purpose in being alive.

When discussing concepts such as holographic awareness with Tiokasin, he makes comments such as "big thoughts," perhaps meaning that trying to understand reality separates us from experiencing reality. He is right. What is important about overcoming the challenge of isolation or embracing ego is compassion. Compassion removes the barriers that form an "us and them" mentality.

Compassion leads to acceptance of others, which opens the Pillar of Connecting. When I wanted the attendant in the ER to let me be with my daughter, I first had to let go of my defenses, and own the fear and pain I was trying not to feel. Only when I was able to be in the truth of my feelings was I able to find the place in the attendant where we were both simply people doing our jobs. Compassion takes you to the essence in another and allows Connecting to occur. Connecting provides the pathway for the power of being to be expressed in Presence.

More important than offering guidance or revealing intent, emotions connect you to the world. Relationships are the foundation of life and relationships are formed on feelings. Giving and taking love are fundamental to happiness. To access the Pillar of Connecting, you must be willing to feel.

Gift: Authenticity

The gift of the Pillar of Connecting is authenticity. When the ego drops its defenses, you can experience your true feelings with no excuses or apologies. You can say, "This is who I am; this is what I feel; I am enough." At the same time, you give other people permission to be themselves.

How much energy do you spend struggling with yourself? Imagine what it would be like to be at peace and to equally accept your mistakes, successes, strengths, and weaknesses. The self-acceptance of authenticity reduces your inner struggle. The energy you spend in conflict is freed for creative pursuits and your self-acceptance reflects as clarity in your Presence.

The clarity that authenticity gives Presence creates a cohesive thought field. Most of the time, people walk around with clouds of conflicting thought surrounding their heads like Pig Pen's dust in the Charlie Brown comic strip. The sheer tumultuousness of such thought fields keeps Connecting from happening. The clarity attained when you lose the inner turmoil of trying to hide your true self is palpable and inviting. It is also free of projection, is accepting, and is welcoming of others.

Connecting gives your Presence the capacity to reflect for others who they truly are. Remember the scene in the movie *Avatar* when the Na'vi woman whom Jake Sully has fallen in love with sees past his avatar persona to the frail, broken human he believes himself to be? In complete love she says, "I see you." In that moment, Jake experiences himself as his true, whole self. Everyone wants to be seen, acknowledged, and appreciated. To facilitate this in another is a powerful gift.

In the words of the current Dalai Lama, "As human beings, we all have the potential to be happy and compassionate people, and we also have the capacity to be miserable and harmful to others. The potential for all these things exists within each of us."[1] In each moment, you make a choice: do I want to act with compassion or judgment? One feeds your spirit, the other an unbalanced ego.

The *Avatar* movie scene reflects the essence of Connecting. When we use the Pillar of Connecting, we not only let go of our own defenses, we stop projecting blame, anger, and judgment onto the people we are with, which allows them to drop their defenses and be more authentic. It is much more restful. Connecting creates the path for the exchange of love and provides the opportunity for happiness.

The Practice of Connecting

If Being provides Presence with power, Connecting provides the pathway for that power to be expressed. Connecting creates the opportunity for exchange. Feelings, materials, ideas, and activities flow along pathways of connection. It is much easier to share when the pathway is created beforehand. Try it. The next time you talk with someone, try creating a heart-to-heart energy link first. Then communicate from your authentic self. You may be surprised at how easy it is to express yourself and to understand the motivations and intent of the other person.

To use the Pillar of Connecting, it is helpful to fully embrace these key assumptions derived from holographic awareness:

◇ Your body-mind is aware of an underlying energy basis of reality.

◇ You are already part of everything that exists.

◇ Everything that exists out there exists within you: war and peace, cruelty and kindness, and judgment and compassion. All are within each of us; you decide which to align with and express.

◇ Essence is a vibration accessed through feelings.

The Pillar of Connecting makes conscious the link that already exists. You may be able to connect simply through the awareness that the link already exists, or you may want to use the steps described in the following paragraphs. Once the link is established, it can be used to share feelings and ideas or to send an intention. Intention is often confused with making a wish. A wish is passive; it is a desire that has no direction. An intention encompasses a goal, invests it with energy, and directs it to an outcome.

The steps to Connecting are the same whether you use them to link with another person, animal, or spiritual being involving a situation you want to assist, a circumstance you wish to attract, or a goal you are trying to achieve. The process is simple. Basically, you open to your authentic self, feel the essence of what you are connecting with, follow the feeling to your object, and respectfully use the link to transmit your request for information. The key elements are the mind, breath, and emotions. This means using your imagination and breath to direct your energy and your emotions to feel the essence.

If you need to see things broken down, here are direct steps to Connecting. If you already have the sense of this concept, don't confuse yourself with steps.

1. Create a coherent thought field.
    a. Focus your attention in present time using your breath as taught in the Pillar of Being.
    b. Gather free attention to use in Connecting.
    c. Clear your mind of conflict by dropping your defense attitudes. Accept and embrace who you are.
    d. Accept the person, situation, or circumstance you are addressing.

2. Establish an energy link.
    a. Energy follows attention. Respectfully focus your free attention on what you want to link with. In your mind, ask for permission for the link to be made.
    b. Find the vibration of the essence of what you want to link with inside yourself by finding the feeling of it.
    c. Magnify the feeling by breathing into it.

d. Focus on the person or situation you want to connect with and imagine the essence finding its vibration there. Remember: The link already exists—you are simply tuning in to it.

e. See-feel the vibration and create a linking pathway. Use your breath to send out and draw in vibration.

3. Use the pathway for exchange.

a. Now that your full attention is on the person or situation, imagine your words and feelings flowing along the pathway as communication.

b. Facilitate the exchange with your breath: send your intention on the exhale and receive on the inhale.

c. If you are forming an intention for a situation, direct your intent along this pathway.

4. Remember to say thank you.

So essentially, the steps are feel, follow, exchange, and give thanks. You create links naturally all the time. Breaking the process into steps is only for the purpose of being conscious of what is happening in order to use it more effectively and to be more respectful. These steps do not constitute esoteric information; they are natural and universal.

The first question you may ask is how to be respectful with your attention. This is really important because whatever or whoever you are connecting with may not want to connect! All you can do is open to the pathway and allow exchange. Don't force it; accept whatever comes. Asking for permission in your mind changes the nature of your energy from a potentially invasive force to an invitation. The key to being respectful is presenting and allowing, rather than directing and assuming.

The second question is how to identify the vibrational essence of what you are linking to. This is achieved through feelings. To find the energetic essence of something, find its feeling. In the example at the start of this chapter, what I needed to find was compassion in the attendant. So first I had to find compassion within me, which was easy as soon as

I realized the man was only trying to defend his job. The feeling of this realization was the essence I had to connect with. Creating the conditions to find the feeling required me to be fully present in the moment. The hardest part was dropping the defense attitudes that block perception.

If you are having difficulty finding the feeling of what you want to link with, simply focus your attention, imagine the link, and breathe into it. The link will happen. Attention, imagination, and breath are how your mind directs your energy. Notice how you feel, and then follow your inner emotion. Stay aware of your felt-perceptions and feelings, and over time you will begin to identify vibration.

The third frequently asked question is whether being open in a connection is safe. Boundaries are important and are addressed in the Pillar of Balancing. In this exercise, acceptance and compassion provide an environment of safety. If you have concerns beyond that, jump ahead to Chapter 6 and explore Balancing.

Finally, you may wonder: Are all these steps really necessary? No, they are not. The steps are just breaking down what is already happening. Being aware of what is occurring simply allows you to understand why your communication and intentions are working or why they are not.

Self-Reflection

How much energy do you spend struggling with yourself?

What parts of yourself do you judge as not being good enough?

How much of your time do you spend in self-criticism?

In what parts of your life do you feel isolated?

How much of yourself do you hide from others?

What do you gain from being isolated?

What are you protecting?

How much do you reach out to others who are isolated? What holds you back?

What parts of yourself do you believe are non-functional?

How much does your ego currently help your spiritual growth? How much does it hinder you?

What fears do you harbor about Connecting?

What situations cause you to lose your genuineness?

What situations cause you to lose connection?

In what situations do you remember holographic awareness?

How do you connect with the people you love?

How do you connect with your goals and ambitions?

What percentage of your energy goes to your relationship with work?

What percentage of your energy goes to your relationship with a significant other?

What percentage of your energy goes to your spiritual center?

What percentage of your energy do you spend with nature?

What percentage with your joy?

Do these percentages reflect what you think of as how connected you are?

Energy Exercises

Your breath and imagination are the keys to working with your energy field. These exercises are ways to become more aware of the process. Although eventually you will be able to maintain dual awareness of how you are processing and using energy while you are engaged in daily activities, for the purpose of these exercises, sit or lie down in a quiet place with no distractions. After you are comfortable with them, practice using the exercises during everyday activities.

Exercise 1: Connecting With Your Essential Self

Right now, before you begin and without changing a thing, create a picture in your mind's eye of your thought field. Draw it on paper. Feel what it's like to be within this thought field. Feel what it's like for another person to encounter you.

1. Take a deep breath and use the Breath of Opening exercise in Chapter 2.
2. Imagine you are sitting in a beautiful garden or a glade within the forest. Notice the light filtering through the trees. Hear the birds and other natural sounds. Feel yourself calm and peaceful.
3. Imagine you are sitting in a comfortable chair that was made just for you. Sink into the chair and allow yourself to be fully and completely supported. Let go of your resistance and feel your muscles melt into the chair.
4. Across from you in another chair is your essential self. Maybe this part of you has all your own features, maybe it is you as a young child, or perhaps this part of you is a wise sage, a beautiful animal, or simply a being of light.
5. However your essential self shows up accept him or her.
6. Create an energy pathway in your mind's eye between you and this image of your essential self.
7. Allow feelings of appreciation, self-love, and joy to flow along this pathway.
8. When the flow stops, allow your essential self to bathe you in appreciation.
9. Receive appreciation.
10. Make a nest in your heart and invite your essential self home.

Notice your thought field. Has it changed from before you started this exercise?

Exercise 2: Connecting With Nature

This exercise uses the steps of Connecting to link with a plant.

1. Sit next to a plant. It can be a house plant, an outside flower, a bush, or tree.

2. Use the Breath of Opening exercise in Chapter 2 to clear your thought field.

3. Use your breath to extend your awareness to the space around you.

4. Notice the feeling the plant creates inside you.

5. Feed that feeling by offering it your breath.

6. Extend your awareness to find and meet the plant's emanation.

7. Explore the boundary between you and the plant. What does it feel like? How do you know you are at the boundary? If you don't know you are at the boundary, guess. If you do know, where would it be?

8. Ask the plant for permission to interact. Do you feel anything in your body-mind that indicates permission or not? Permission might feel like a sense of flowing toward the plant; not having permission might feel like emptiness. If you don't feel either, proceed with respect.

9. Provided you did not get a definite no, give the plant your full attention. Extend your attention with the intention of love. Bathe the plant in love. Imagine your attention as golden stars filled with life-force and offer the stars to the plant. Be mindful that the plant may not want your offering and respect that. Be gentle in your attention.

10. Notice what you feel coming back from the plant.

11. You might want to exhale your attention toward the plant and inhale the plant's response.

12. When you sense that the plant has had enough focus, or when you have had enough, withdraw your attention.

13. Express gratitude to the plant.

Try this exercise with pets, lovers, plans, and dreams. Expect nothing; anticipate everything. Be open.

Exercise 3: Healthy Ego

The function of a healthy ego is to support your path and purpose. It is to keep you strong and balanced as you live your truth. An unbalanced ego is one that doesn't know its power.

1. Take a deep breath.
2. Use the Breath of Opening exercise from Chapter 2.
3. Come fully into your body in the present moment.
4. Where in your body does your ego live? If you don't know, use your head or solar plexus, the area under your ribcage and above your belly button.
5. Take your awareness into this area and invite your ego to join you. If your ego were a mask that you could put on or take off, what does this mask look like?
6. Create the mask in great detail. Imagine the facial muscles and expression; notice the expression in the eyes. Give the mask all the detail you can imagine.
7. Now, put it on. How does it feel to wear this mask? What is you muscle tension like? How connected do you feel to your essential self? How separated are you from the people in your life? Do you feel balanced or unbalanced? If unbalanced, what does your ego need to be balanced?
8. Now, take off the mask.
9. Look at your ego and sincerely thank it for helping you be strong enough to live your truth. Appreciate all the benefits your ego gives you. Give it whatever it needs to be balanced, appreciated, and part of your wholeness.
10. Bathe your ego in love.

The pillar of Grounding

PILLAR: Grounding
AWARENESS: Earth-Centered Awareness
CHALLENGE: Avoiding Pain
RELATIONSHIP: Mother Earth
GATEWAY: Physical Center of Body
GIFT: Alchemy
EMOTION/ATTITUDE: Gratitude
QUALITY BROUGHT TO PRESENCE: Assurance, Strength

Broken Bones

A nurse meets us at the elevator opening onto the ICU. She checks the identification band on my daughter's wrist.

"Erin?" she asks.

My daughter and I both nod. Today, it takes both of us to be Erin. The nurse gestures us forward.

The transport team wheels Erin's bed into a large room with mid-morning sunlight streaming through the window. I wonder fleetingly whether the previous occupant died or was transferred. I don't ask. I am just grateful the long hours of waiting for a room are over and internally claim this one as home.

I lean against the window ledge, keeping out of the way as the array of monitors are repositioned and the IV line reconnected. Pain killers drip into Erin's veins, and the intensity of her eyes softens. I relax my vigil and turn over the monitoring of her every breath and movement to the machines. Nurses introduce themselves. With extraordinary tact and kindness, they address the comforts of Erin's broken body.

I find it impossible to retain the names and jobs of people perpetually moving in and out of the room, but Erin remembers every one. She addresses each person by name as she answers questions and asks for what she needs. Unknown to me, although the room is bright, Erin's sight is dimmed. She is suspended in a murky haze, all of us indistinct shadows that form and recede out of the substance of dark. How does she know and remember and recognize everyone? Through voice, but also through feel.

There is a different doctor for each of Erin's injuries. The knee surgeon is the first to arrive. She is calm and kind as she relates Erin's MRI results, explaining that a chunk of cartilage is gouged from Erin's knee and the patellar tendon is completely severed; the quadriceps muscle has retracted up her thigh. The number of surgeries needed for repair is unknown. First, they must excavate the asphalt, gravel, and glass. Then they will decide how to move forward and better answer Erin's single question: "Will I ride horses again?"

Shortly after the orthopedic leaves, the neurosurgeon arrives to discuss the injuries of neck and spine. He is reserved as he describes broken ribs, a fractured lumbar vertebra, and other incidental injuries that, on their own, would be monumental. Erin cannot feel these singular pains; they are incorporated into the larger pain of knee and neck.

The doctor describes the impact of the accident and the resulting damage: Erin's head must have hit the roof of the car as the car flipped and hit the road. The force of it drove the first two vertebrae of her neck into her skull and exploded them outward into fragments. He explains her options: neck surgery to fuse the bones or a halo device, a cage around her body screwed into her skull to immobilize her neck and give the bones a chance to heal. The first will leave her unable to turn or bend her neck for the rest of her life; the second is not guaranteed to work. He explains the inherent danger of each and the possibilities of paralysis that accompany both.

The room quiets, filled only with sounds of breathing and the bleep of machines. I remember someone once telling me that the body is like the Earth and the bones like fossils, holding the history of our past. I imagine the force of all the pain stored in Erin's bones, the unhealed betrayals of childhood exploding outward; the accident an earthquake thrusting forth the fossilized hurt of her past.

I hover. Erin is not a medical person. She is drugged and traumatized. Can she maintain enough Grounding to make practical decisions? Does she understand the extent of her injuries, the important functions of the C1 and C2 vertebrae, and know what is at risk?

Astonishingly, Erin is both lucid and grounded. She takes in the information, then plies the doctor with questions, peeling back the niceties from essential truths. She grasps the significance of every detail and doesn't recoil from the hard reality. Where did she get this grit? When did she develop such fortitude? It takes her only moments to make a decision.

I am relieved that she chooses the halo. With all its uncertainties and discomforts, if it works, it offers the best outcome.

Later, looking at the CT-scan with my husband, he shakes his head in concern.

"How can this possibly work?" he asks. "How will immobilizing her neck bring all these pieces back to her spine? Surely she needs surgery to put them in the right place, doesn't she?"

I offer the only answer I can. "The body is designed to heal."

He snorts. "Of course, but this isn't a cut we're talking about. Surely the bones have to be touching each other to mend together. Look." He points to fragments seemingly floating free, at odd angles to their natural placement. "How can those pieces find their way back to where they're supposed to be?"

I shake my head. There is no logical answer. We have been taught to trust science over nature, but I know the body is like the Earth and the healing mechanisms in the body are not arbitrary. They are guided by intelligence within the design. In my mind's eye, I see the bone fragments retracing the trajectory of their expulsion as the body calls them home.

There is opportunity in this, if Erin chooses. As the vertebrae reform, she has the choice to leave out of the matrix the pain and hurt that has been released She won't need to relive old traumas; she needs only to unlearn the beliefs she created around them, to ground herself in beliefs that reflect a greater whole. It's a tall order.

I ache for my daughter's struggle, imagining my tears are nourishing the dry earth of her body.

Pillar: Grounding

Grounding is connecting through your body to Earth. It is identifying yourself in the physical world and understanding your relationship with nature. Typically, being grounded suggests being practical. To have your feet on the ground says you can get the job done, as opposed to having your head in the clouds, unable to bring your vast ideas into form. Grounding is reality based. It establishes your physical stability and ability to act.

Grounding is as natural and automatic as breathing. It is something your body understands on a cellular level. You "run to ground" for safety and security, "find your ground" when you discover your truth, and "stand your ground" when you act in strength. You are "down to Earth" when you are without pretense. Grounding, then, encompasses all of these and more: stability, action, safety, security, and strength. It reflects the courage to be yourself. When you practice Grounding, your Presence is instilled with assurance. You project calm strength.

Most importantly, Grounding recognizes that you, and everything else on the planet, belong to Earth. You become grounded when you are in harmony with the forces of Earth. More than a psychological state of mind, Grounding is an electromagnetic exchange. Natural settings clear the body's electromagnetic energy field and bring you into phase with the electromagnetic field of Earth. Energy fields that are in phase magnify each other. When you are grounded, you benefit from Earth, and Earth benefits from you.

In the past, humans lived closer to nature and there was little need to define or actively pursue Grounding. Today, there is a separation from nature that is difficult to bridge. The natural attunement to Earth has been replaced with the electromagnetics of computers and televisions. People spend less time outdoors, rarely looking into the sky to notice passing clouds or the brilliance of the moon at night.

Wanting to reconnect with nature often isn't enough. How does one do it? How is nature engaged? A walk in the woods seems a good first step, but once there, what do you do? How do you connect while swatting mosquitos and checking your cell phone? The difficulty is compounded when returning to nature is overly romanticized. Then expectations get in the way of experience. When the return to nature is not met with trumpets and confetti, the simple calm of Grounding is easily overlooked.

Being disconnected from Earth and nature cuts you off from Earth's abundance. This leaves you with only yourself to rely on, and Earth becomes a rather lonely place to be. Being cut off from Earth's abundance introduces scarcity thinking. The fear of being left out or left behind fosters greed so that you may take more than you need for fear of not having enough. Scarcity thinking distracts you from what's important. Focused on having, you lose connection with your spiritual center and the spiritual center of Earth. Grounding restores connection. It brings you home to yourself.

Awareness: Earth-Centered Awareness

Grounding is based in Earth-centered awareness, the awareness of the inherent design and intelligence of the natural world. Earth-centered awareness sees beyond the prevalent idea that the universe is an inert machine set in motion long ago and unfolding according to a set of laws. With Earth-centered awareness, you engage nature with open heart and mind to understand that the distinction between what is life and what is non-life is not as clear as science imagines. All matter is instilled with design, intelligence, and life-force. Grounding opens the awareness that everything you see, feel, and touch has consciousness; it is simply a type of consciousness not yet understood by humans.

Earth-centered awareness reveals that the design of your life is synchronized with the design of nature. One way to see this is through sacred geometry. Were you able to view the Cymatics demonstrations on the YouTube videos suggested in the last chapter? If so, you saw that sound vibrates physical matter into geometric patterns. Depending on their physical properties, different types of substances vibrate differently to the same sound. This creates intermeshing geometric designs.

All of known reality is organized within these geometric designs: from atoms to solar systems, from the helix spiral of DNA to the helix spiral of seeds in a sunflower and the helix spiral of galaxies. In sacred geometry, the same geometrical patterns are endlessly repeated from the most miniscule to the most vast, each part necessary to the creation of the whole, the whole governing the development of each part. Through sacred geometry, you are woven into this whole. The vibrational frequency of Earth, known as the Schumann resonance, is actually a range of frequencies based on 7.83 Hz. All life is entrained to this range of vibration. When you consciously tune to this vibration through Grounding, the design of your life is synchronized with Earth. Your intuition senses the unfolding patterns and helps you move within the flow.

Consciously incorporating sound and sacred geometry into your daily activity can be life changing, if this interests you, there is more in Chapter 13. My husband and I had a dramatic demonstration of the impact of vibration on synchronization when we installed a honey bee hive on our farm. We spend considerable time outside interacting with the birds and other wildlife on the property. After the hive was established, we noticed a profound change in the behavior of the animals. There was a subtle shift in choreography. It seemed that birds, squirrels, deer, and groundhogs moved in rhythm to a shared beat. It took us some time to realize the synchronization was due to the vibration of the bees. When the hive crashed, the absence of the bee's vibration was deafening. For quite a while, activity on the farm felt chaotic until other, more subtle vibrations established another rhythm.

Earth-centered awareness aligns you with Earth and brings your attention to your stability, movement, and relationship to your surroundings. It reveals how you direct your force. Earth-centered awareness encourages you pay attention to what you add to the vibration around you and how that impacts the design of life. It inspires you to ask permission from Earth before assuming you can take what you want.

Here are foundational understandings attained through Earth-centered awareness:

⬥ The universe is conscious (even though we can't truly understand what other types of consciousness might be like).

⬥ Earth is a living being.

⬥ You are in balance when you harmonize to and are in phase with the frequency of Earth.

⬥ Nature has inherent intelligence and design that can be accessed.

⬥ Gratitude is the emotional attitude that tunes you to Earth and nature.

⬥ The physical world, including your body, has inherent mechanisms to maintain balance and healing.

⬥ Asking permission from Earth dedicates your actions.

Through Earth-centered awareness, you are opened to the intrinsic design and intelligence in the physical world. Through Grounding, you are anchored into it. Grounding imparts strength, stability, balance, assurance, and calm to Presence.

Challenge: Avoiding Pain

When asked, most people say they don't have time for Grounding because they are under too much stress. "I have too much to think about, too many situations to stay on top of. I have to keep on moving to get every-thing done!" Does this sound like you? Do you have too many duties that create too much stress to take care of your essential self? Actually, the situation is probably the other way around. The stress, overwhelm, and overload may be the result of not practicing Grounding and Being out flow with the design of life.

Avoiding Grounding is a desire to avoid pain. Grounding requires that you connect with your physical body and connect your physical body with Earth. Inside your body is the history of your personal past; in the tissues of your body are the memories of every cruelty and every celebra-tion. The history of the planet lives inside the physical Earth; the layers of soil contain whispers of past civilizations, the form of extinct species, and the processes of creation.

The emotions you are afraid to feel remain inside. They drive your behavior and limit your experience. If you are willing to sit quietly with your painful emotions and not try to drive what you feel away or limit your experience of them, your emotions will impart their information, instigate action, and then discharge and recede. Emotions aren't meant to last forever. They do so only because they are held onto and buried inside. Chapter 8 provides insights into Clearing challenging emotions.

The desire to avoid pain places your attention on what you do, rather than on how you do it. Goals and outcomes are separated from the pro-cesses that achieve them. Pursuing goals can be achieved while living in your mind; experiencing the process requires that you live in your body, and this means you have to feel. The split between outcome and pro-cess, mind and body, reveals yet another, much deeper split that brings us round full circle. This is the split between spirit and matter, between what we call life and what we call inert substance.

In this split, humans are spiritual beings at odds with the material world. In reality, Earth-centered awareness shows us there is no separa-tion. Life-force is infused within matter at all levels. The force and intel-ligence within the bonding of atoms and the placement of planets in solar systems is as spirit-driven as the force within your body that we call life. Either everything is part of a conscious universe, or nothing is.

Science and spiritual traditions have both contributed to the spirit-matter rift. Both have ignored the sacredness of the physical to produce knowledge without heart, pitting humans against nature. The paradigm of this split has fueled unspeakable harm. The Earth-based spirituality of indigenous cultures such as Native Americans, Aborigines, Druids, and Taoists recognize that physical matter is more than inert playdough for the gods. In these traditions, spirit and matter are equal partners in the dance of creation.

Healing the spirit-matter rift requires integration. You are a spiritual being and a physical being, too. Grounding brings your attention out of your mind and into your body. It roots you in Earth and insists that you feel. The pain buried in your tissues must come into the light of feeling for the healing mechanisms of the body to work. Then the split between spirit and matter, mind and heart, and humans and Earth can be bridged.

Relationship: Mother Earth

Your body and everything you need to live comes from Earth: air, water, food, mystery, and companionship—everything. Every action undertaken, every idea brought into form, and every manifested dream is created out of the energy and substance of Earth. Too often, Earth is ignored in the making of plans and pursuit of goals. You may have been taught that all you have to do to get what you want is align with having it. This prescription rarely considers Earth's role in supplying your dreams and rarely considers the need to ask permission for what you take and give back after you've received.

Native Americans acknowledge the consciousness of Earth. They recognize her life-giving properties when they address her as Mother Earth. If Western culture acknowledged Earth as mother, would she be treated with the same disregard? Would we still treat her as a commodity? The inescapable truth is that we cannot poison the Earth without poisoning ourselves. We cannot destroy home without becoming homeless. As Chief Seattle is alleged to have said, "What you do to the Earth, you do the people of the Earth."

Establishing a relationship with Earth in all the complexity of our feelings is part of Grounding. Relationships are established on give and take. Consider how often you give back to Earth. Do you intellectualize the need to care for the planet? Do you feel helpless? Do you turn away from the ecological crisis because it's too painful?

Relationships are formed on more than happy celebrations and victory dances of success. Relationships are strengthened just as deeply through shared pain and adversity. While you can't form a relationship based on pain and expect it to thrive, avoiding pain does not make relationships stronger. What opens the door to a relationship with Earth is not guilt, obligation, or fear. Gratitude is the emotional attitude that connects you to Earth. Grounding brings you into a shared relationship.

As with the return to nature, how to express gratitude to Earth can be elusive. Start with the obvious: Participate in the health and well-being of Earth by taking care of your own backyard:

◇ Choose non-toxic cleaning agents.

◇ Compost food waste to create more soil.

◇ Care for the piece of Earth you live on and the animals that share it.

◇ Honor the rhythm of Earth cycles.

◇ Take care of your own body.

Does taking care of yourself seem strange in this list? Your body, mind, and spirit are part of Earth. Consciously caring for yourself by treating your body with respect—physically, emotionally, and mentally—is part of caring for and respecting Earth.

You can also give back through ceremony. Ceremony brings your attention to the sacred. Whether you light a fire or offer gifts, it's important to remember that even the items we gift came from Mother Earth. That awareness was shared in a conversation with Tiokasin Ghosthorse from the Lakota Nation. He says, "What's important is to say thank you to your momma. When is the last time you said thank you to Mother Earth?"

Why is it so hard for the Western mind to say thank you to Earth? One way to give thanks is to give your attention. Paying attention is thought of as taking in information. In reality, paying attention is giving your energy to what you put your attention on. Paying attention with appreciation converts your Presence into a force of transformation.

Here's a story about a man named Chris. His friend, Peter, described a beach outing his family went on with Chris and his family. The adults were sitting in the sun while the kids played in the water. The adult conversation was constantly being interrupted by calls of "Watch me, watch me!" as the children performed water acrobatics. Most of the adults watched with minimal attention or minor aggravation at the interruption. Chris, however, watched the children with rapt devotion. Afterward, when the kids had lost interest and gone to climb on the rocks, Chris turned to Peter and said, "So what do you think—attention is love."

Attention creates connection, and when that connection is one of appreciation, an exchange of love occurs. Through your attention, you create continuity between internal and external reality, the flow from one to the other. Within this flow there is no separation between the ecological crises of Earth and the spiritual crises of humanity. Healing one necessitates healing the other. The path to healing is the transformative power of Presence. Grounding connects your essence to the essence of Earth and fuels the strength and balance of your Presence.

In the documentary movie *Planetary,* available at www.weare planetary.com, Native American tradition reveals that while you may have stopped connecting to Earth, *Earth has never stopped connecting with you.* From the experience of my daughter's accident, I understand. A mother gives her last drop of blood for her children. When you are ready to give Earth attention, she is already there, waiting.

In giving your attention, you honor Earth. You acknowledge that Earth is worthy of reverence. When you recognize the Presence of the sacred in Earth, you connect with the spiritual part of your nature that resides within the home of your body. Your Presence grows as you are reminded of who you truly are and the split between spirit and matter disappears. You come home.

Gateway: Physical Center of Body

The gateway into Grounding is your body's physical center of gravity, located about three finger widths below your belly button. In martial arts, this area is called the Tan Dien or the Hara. The Tan Dien is the energy center that roots you to Earth and forms your foundation. The forces of your two primal needs—your need for stability and your need for movement— are balanced within the Tan Dien. When this dynamic tension is balanced, you are better poised to address the challenges of life. Your movements are graceful with a sense of effortless action.

Imagine you have to move a very heavy sofa. How do you approach the task? Do you drop your shoulder to the sofa and push? Do you press a hip into it and shove? Do you lie on the floor and push the couch with your feet? While men are naturally more muscled in the upper body than women and identify their strength with their shoulders, the approach you take indicates whether your energy is upwardly mobilized or downwardly mobilized. It pinpoints where you identify your center of gravity. When you identify your center of gravity above the Tan Dien, you are top heavy; when below, your feet are stuck in the mud, making movement difficult. When the Tan Dien meets the couch, pushing it across the floor is infinitely easier.

Though Grounding feels like sinking into Earth, it also has the element of a spring board. When you walk, the ability to take a step comes from having something solid to push off from. Earth lifts you up, sends you forward, and provides the platform for your liftoff. The force behind your rise is based on the strength and stability of Earth. Your ability to access the liftoff of Earth depends on having your center of gravity firmly established in your Tan Dien.

Physical, emotional, or spiritual trauma, stress, overwork, too much mental activity, and poor health can shift your perception of your physical center out of your Tan Dien into other areas in the body. Your sense of where your center of gravity is located can even be moved outside your body into your energy field. Now, your need to find stability surpasses your need to move because any movement will be out of balance. The stability required to maintain balance is achieved through excessive muscle tension, which inhibits movement because you must fight against the tension of your own muscles to move. Not surprisingly, the flow and harmony of your actions, decisions, relationships, and work are affected.

Very few people are rooted through their Tan Dien without consciously Grounding. Through the experiences of life, most people have shifted their perception of where their center of gravity is located. The practice of Grounding, also called rooting, or more recently, earthing, is achieved by shifting your attention into your Tan Dien, then dropping it down into Earth. The exercises later in this chapter will help you do this.

Wilhelm Reich, the father of body-centered psychotherapy, maintained that within the tension of a muscle is the history of its source. As you practice Grounding, your muscles may reveal the emotions held in the tension. You may feel the sadness, loneliness, or shame that made your body an uncomfortable place to be. You don't need to know what the events were that created these feelings. What you do need is the willingness to feel what is buried, accept it, create a new belief, and move on. Allow Earth to shift you to new ground.

When you ground, your consciousness is met by the consciousness of Earth. At first, you may not notice anything other than feeling more balanced. Over time you may notice the comforting Presence of Earth and nature. You don't need special training; you only need to practice Grounding and pay attention with an open heart and mind. Grounding brings calmness, stability, balance, and strength to your Presence.

Gift: Alchemy

Grounding is an alchemical process that transforms stress and chaos into a force of peace that is transmitted through your Presence. It takes enormous strength to remain peaceful in the center of a storm. If you look at the schism in politics, environmental problems, social injustice, and economic disparity, it is clear the center of the storm has arrived. This is a time when strength, assurance, peacefulness, and courage are needed. It is a time to look for answers in the wisdom of Earth.

This is the true gift of Grounding, the ability to use your body—the instrument of your awareness—to find answers and feel direction. Grounding and Earth-centered awareness keep you connected to the sensations, feelings, energy flows, and emotions in your body through which you connect to life. Using this connection, be willing to be guided. The ability to listen is the source of the quality of assurance.

We are reaching the end of where the current road of civilization can take us. Now is the time to create new paths. Listening to Earth is a way to engage the force of creation and dance new directions into reality. The paths are already unfolding. Listen with your body-mind for your step forward. Do you feel resistance, uncertainty, or lack of flow? Then wait. Ask for the right action. When you sense flow, opening, or welcoming, move forward even if you don't know where you're going or why. Soon enough, you will.

Accepting that Earth is sacred, every place on Earth must necessarily be sacred as well. Whereas natural settings like waterfalls and forests, Earth vortices, or sacred sites of past ceremony renew your energy field and bring you into phase with the energy field of Earth, even in the midst of a city, under the sidewalk, beneath the subway, and surrounding the sewer system, is Earth. Reach down and feel for Earth right now. Even in airplanes, you can reach with your felt-perceptions and find Earth.

When you pay attention, the underlying sacred nature of wherever you are is revealed. How amazing would it be to experience the sacred everywhere, in every moment? This is true alchemy. The best part is that every time you pay attention to the sacredness of Earth, you leave a sacredness imprint for others to step into. Every time you pay attention, you create a path.

The Practice of Grounding

The deeper you ground, the more you grow. Think of trees: the deeper the root system, the higher the tree, the stronger the roots, and the more the tree can bend. The same is true for you. The more grounded you are, the more stable, yet flexible, you are, and the more able you are to reach greater heights. Grounding enhances your ability to remain stable, calm, flexible, and energized, no matter what happens around you.

Even the most grounded person has moments of being ungrounded. Overwork, difficult decisions, shock, and emotionally charged situations can disconnect you from Earth and leave you feeling untethered. These are signs that you are ungrounded:

- ◊ Feeling spacey or having trouble concentrating.
- ◊ Feeling overwhelmed.
- ◊ Indecisiveness or having difficulty making even easy decisions.
- ◊ Not knowing when to say no.
- ◊ Feeling unbalanced, perhaps even bumping into things.
- ◊ Having trouble maintaining energy.
- ◊ Feeling unmotivated or unable to take action.
- ◊ Having difficulty accessing your feelings or knowing what you want.

Beyond the daily moments of being ungrounded are larger patterns of living separated from Earth. Here are some signs that your overall lifestyle needs to incorporate Grounding:

◇ Over-controlling situations.

◇ Obsessive thinking.

◇ Attachment to outcomes.

◇ Scarcity consciousness that focuses on what you lack.

◇ Engaging in repetitive patterns that don't take you where you want to go.

◇ Thinking more than feeling.

◇ Not being able to access emotions or living on an emotional flat line.

◇ Excessive muscle tension with no organic cause such as an injury.

◇ Focusing so much on goals you forget to enjoy the process.

◇ Not noticing your surroundings.

These patterns of disharmony represent beliefs about life that were picked up through teachings or painful experiences that haven't been integrated. You can choose to live by these beliefs or you can change them. Here are some suggestions for increasing Grounding through lifestyle changes:

◇ Be willing to reframe what defines life. You may not be able to pick up a handful of soil and believe it contains life-force and intelligence, but can you ask, *What if it did*? Can you approach everything with the question: What if this piece of reality I am engaging were conscious and alive?

◇ Consciously care for your body. This is more than eating well, exercising, and getting enough sleep. As you do all those things, add the awareness that all you receive comes from Earth and be thankful.

◇ Take the time to honor the cycles and rhythms of Earth. Celebrate, meditate, or do ceremony on the equinoxes and solstices. Look into the night sky and notice the phase of the moon and how that reflects on your activities. In the past, people planted on the new moon and harvested on the full moon. Try planting ideas on the new moon and being open to receive insight on the full. See what happens.

◇ Take positive action to reduce the impact of your lifestyle on nature. See Chapter 13 to learn simple yet profound daily steps to support nature.

◇ Honor the fact that you stand on the shoulders of your ancestors just as the generations to come will stand on yours. Appreciate your ancestors. Think about what you are creating for future generations.

◇ Listen. Just stop and listen to the birds, the wind, and the stream. Can you hear nature over the sounds of technology?

◇ Listen to the viewpoints of others. Instead of trying to change what they think or feel to match your own, just try and understand what they feel and why.

◇ Pay attention to the other species you share each minute with. You are surrounded by life! Be amazed.

◇ Use awareness-enhancing practices, such as meditation, Tai Chi, Yoga, and Qi Kung.

◇ Use the energy practices below on a regular basis.

Using the following energy exercises will also help you practice Grounding and develop Earth-centered awareness. Before you start, make sure you aren't suffering a physical condition such as dehydration or haven't gone all day without eating. The energy process is easy: Where you put your attention is where your energy flows. When you put attention on Earth, you connect with Earth, and Earth energy flows back to you. Put your attention on Earth with appreciation, and you will be amazed at what comes back.

These simple steps use your attention and breath to quickly reestablish Grounding:

1. Take three deep breaths and bring yourself into present time.
    *   Inhale calm.
    *   Exhale tension.

2. Breathe into your Tan Dien.
    *   With every inhale, imagine your Tan Dien filling with energy.
    *   With every exhale, imagine energy flowing from your Tan Dien into Earth.

3. Form an image of what the connection between your Tan Dien and Earth looks like. Common images are a waterfall and a light-filled root.

4. Notice how this connection changes your felt-perceptions in your overall body.
    *   Notice your muscle tension.
    *   Notice your emotions.
    *   You don't need to change a thing. As you notice, change happens just from your body-mind receiving attention.
    *   Be open to insight.

5. Once the connection between your Tan Dien and Earth is well established, allow the direction of flow to change.
    *   Inhale Earth into your body.
    *   Exhale your attention into the Earth.
    *   Maintain this circular breathing.
    *   Allow Earth to fill, support, and sustain you.

6. Say thank you.

The formula in a nutshell is breathe, drop your awareness into your Tan Dien, sink into Earth, and let Earth energy rise into your Tan Dien.

The first obstacle to Grounding is fear of Earth energy. Fear of the natural world has been used to control and direct people for so long it may be hard to let go and trust. If this is true for you, spend time in nature and reestablish a relationship with Earth as mother. Consider this: You are already filled with Earth energy. The food you eat is the life-force of Earth, as are air, water, and your body. You are Earth energy. What are you afraid of? Take the time to feel your fear, hear its message, and allow it to recede. Then choose the relationship you want to have.

The second obstacle people confront is guilt, another perfectly functional emotion that has been misused to control people. While guilt might be useful to bring you into awareness of the need to be responsible, after that, it is done. Its job is over. Let it go. Let love be your motivation. Love is the one currency accepted everywhere: by Earth, people, and the divine. Use it.

The third obstacle is derived from the second: concern of overburdening Earth with feelings of personal grief or other charged emotions you want to release. Consider the function of trees, taking in carbon dioxide and releasing oxygen. Think of the cycles of life, death, decay, and regeneration. What you release to Earth is transmuted and returned as energy to fuel new growth. There is nothing you can energetically feed Earth that will harm her. Rather, as you let go of what consumes you, you become Earth's ally instead of an errant child.

Self-Reflection

In what areas of your life and pursuits do you feel the most grounded?

What situations make you feel ungrounded? How do you self-correct? Start a journal to record what works for you.

What does being grounded give you?

How do you use Earth to catapult your life?

Have you asked Earth for permission to pursue your goals? What changes if you do?

In what situations would Earth as mother deny you what you need to thrive?

If you really believed that Earth is your mother, how would the way in which you treat her change?

What is your relationship like with your mother? How is that reflected in your ability to be grounded?

What if this piece of reality in which you are engaging is conscious and alive?

How much time do you spend watching the news or browsing the Internet versus being outside enjoying the world of nature?

How does your body feel when you're in nature?

Do you have any fear of connecting with Earth? Explore where this comes from. Can you remember events in your past or comments made by parents or teachers that influenced your fear?

How much do you trust your body?

In what ways do you honor your body?

In what ways do you honor and give back to Earth?

Imagine your energy is artificially divided into four categories: spiritual, physical, sexual, and emotional. Which area has the most energy? Which has the least? What can you do to promote better balance?

What does your vibration bring to the space around you?

Energy Exercises

These first two exercises can be explored standing or sitting. After you have done them the first few times and feel comfortable, you can initiate them simply through your awareness that the flow exists. Use them anytime you feel unstable, unfocused, or afraid.

Exercise 1: Earth Strength

1. Acknowledge Earth and give thanks.
2. Inhale and fill your body with energy.
3. Imagine you have three roots, one growing from the bottom of each foot and one from your sacrum.
4. Exhale and imagine your energy flowing down through these three roots into Earth.

5. Inhale, imagining the energy of Earth rising up through your roots, bringing strength, stability, and safety into your body. Let every cell receive the strength of Earth.

6. Exhale downward, sending energy through your roots into the soil, releasing tension, fear, and uncertainty. Thank Earth for receiving these and transforming them into light.

7. Continue breathing through your roots, inhaling strength, stability, and safety into every cell and exhaling limiting thoughts and beliefs.

8. When you feel stable, solid, strong, and free of self-doubt, acknowledge Earth through thankfulness.

9. Maintain awareness of your connection to Earth as you continue your daily activities. Let your awareness of Earth guide your actions

Exercise 2: Connecting Earth and Sky (From The Path of Energy)

1. Imagine yourself as a tree with your body as the trunk connecting to Earth through roots forming from your feet, and connecting to sky through branches emerging from the top of your head.

2. As you inhale, visualize the energy of Sky flowing through the branches into the top of your head.

3. Breathe this energy into your Tan Dien, then let it overflow to fill every cell with space, freedom, and openness.

4. Exhale through your Tan Dien into the roots, sending energy deep into Earth. Imagine giving Earth the gift of space, freedom, and openness.

5. Inhale and imagine bringing energy up through your roots into your Tan Dien, filling yourself with the safety, stability, and strength of Earth. Let this overflow into every cell in your body.

6. Exhale and imagine sending this energy flowing out the top of your head into sky.

7. At your own pace and rhythm, continue to be the bridge between Earth and sky.

8. When you feel balanced and complete, continue your day taking this connection with you.

Exercise 3: Walking on a Living Being

This exercise explores and connects with nature in moving meditation. Turn off your cell phone and use your senses to explore the natural world.

1. Imagine your energy as beams of light shining through your feet and extending three feet deeper into the ground, connecting with the consciousness of Earth.

2. Inhale, filling your body with light, and exhale through your feet to strengthen these beams of light. Let the light become an extension of your felt-perceptions.

3. As you walk, be mindful of lifting your feet, extracting the beam and then replanting it with your next step.

4. Listen to the natural sounds around you.

5. Notice the movement of birds, squirrels, wind in trees and grass, and sunlight through leaves.

6. Imagine all belong to an orchestra of light and sound.

7. See-feel the rhythm within and around you.

8. Notice how you feel.

5

the pillar of centering

Pillar: Centering
Awareness: Heart-Centered Awareness
Challenge: The Giveaway
Relationship: Essential Self
Gateway: Heart Center
Gift: Heart-Centered Path and Purpose
Emotion/Attitude: Unconditional Love
Quality Brought to Presence: Stillness

Pictures

The hospital lights are low, signifying the late hour. I recline in a sleeping chair off to the side to be out of the way of Erin's friends who claim her room. They gather to see how she is, eager to hear her story about how it happened and how she feels. Erin says little. Talking is an effort. Besides, she remembers nothing beyond getting in the car and leaving the parking lot of the 7-Eleven convenience store a few miles from her house. Her next memory is awakening in the ER.

Details of the accident are supplied by Erin's cousin who is an EMT and heard about the event from colleagues who were present. Listening, I learn that Erin was coded at the scene. She was dead, restored to life, and brought to the hospital with a heart rate of four beats per minute. She was not expected to live. I add this piece of information to my internal litany: alive, not dead, not paralyzed, not brain damaged.

Erin is newborn, raw and exposed, confined within the halo device surgically screwed into the bones of her skull. Four titanium pins secure the metal ring to her head; four bars descend to anchor it into a hard plastic vest. It settles around her like a cage, gifting her with distance from the people streaming in and out. Restricted to a bed in a room over which she has no control, the halo is her sanctuary. The device provides the only space she can claim as her own.

Inside the bubble, her fragmented self coalesces as she receives the kindness of friends, family, nurses, and doctors. And as the pieces of her vertebrae begin the journey back to her spine, Erin begins the process of review. What parts of her old self will be knitted back into her bones? She is making choices. Old beliefs, sheltered and nourished since childhood, present themselves: I'm not good enough, nobody loves me, I'm better off alone, I can't rely on anyone, I'm unlovable. These limiting beliefs can now be swept away as road debris.

Stripped of defenses, Erin reaches for deeper anchors. With new understanding, she realizes her life is interwoven with the lives of those around her. People show up in ways she could never have anticipated. She cries upon learning her boss, even though he runs a family business and extra money is hard to find, continues to pay her salary and medical insurance with no certainty she will return to work. New beliefs present themselves: I'm not alone, I'm loved, valued, and I belong.

I take photographs of Erin's journey. A picture in the ER of Erin's head on the blood-soaked sheet, her hand making a victory sign into the camera; one in the ICU after the surgery that installed the halo and another of the staples in her head holding closed the gap opened by the road. I take these pictures to help Erin come to terms with what has happened and to help her create continuity from before to after. She will look at them as she evaluates the path she was on before and where it was taking her with where she wants to go now. She will need the pictures to understand that the physical limitations ahead are not as restrictive as the beliefs she is releasing.

In this pressure cooker of events, I am meeting my adult daughter for the first time. Barriers of guilt and blame dissolve as we share this journey into her essence. She is glad for the company. Abandonment issues melt into phantoms, replaced by the truth of unconditional love. Through her accident I, too, am reborn and allowed to find healing around the many insufficiencies of motherhood.

This stripped-down version of Erin impresses me immensely. She never asks, "Why me?" or "What did I do to deserve this?" She doesn't make herself a victim. The questions she asks are formed in the heart. She searches for meaning and direction. She considers the issue of purpose and wonders if her soul called the accident into being as a course correction: a necessary change in direction. She wonders if there is something she is supposed to do with this second chance.

"What have you always wanted to do?" I ask.

If she could shake her head, or even shrug, she would. She makes a face at me instead. I stifle a laugh.

I do not worry about whether or not Erin will find her path; she never left it. Each foot has fallen on a road for the growth she is determined to achieve. Could she have avoided the accident? Yes, of course. There are a million different routes to the same destination. She could have arrived at this point of shifting beliefs without the interception. But she didn't, and here she is, still beautifully, magnificently on her path of self-discovery.

Pillar: Centering

Wholeness is the message in the Pillar of Centering. Through Centering, your scattered attention spread among various activities, people, and plans is brought back inside your body. As shards of attention coalesce, your fragmented self is returned. Through Centering, you are drawn inward to the core of your being where your essential self resides. Also called core self and authentic self, your essential self connects you to the deepest truth of who you are and what it is to be human. No one can define this for you. It is your personal truth that guides your particular walk through life.

Center is the balancing point between mind and body where thoughts are merged with body perceptions. The subsequent insights set your course, determine your choices, and establish the meaning of your experiences. Your center speaks through feelings and intuitions that align you with the design of your life. Living this design is your path and purpose.

Located in your heart, your center is the sacred space that hosts the partnership between your spirit and your path. Here, all of who you are, everything you bring to the table, and every part of the story of your life is honored. Mistakes and hardships are nothing more than opportunities to dig deeper and to find what directions do not fit. In learning the art of discernment, many different paths are tested to find the one your foot is comfortable walking. While your mind might judge your actions as right or wrong based on outcomes, your heart is interested in growth, compassion, acceptance, and forgiveness. It offers stillness in a chaotic world and honors the sacredness of self-reflection. Here in your heart, it is safe to look at the tender vulnerabilities of new growth.

Self-trust is needed to follow the heart. Discerning the messages from your core is challenging, made more so by the false opposition created between heart and mind. We think one is right and the other wrong when, in reality, the two are designed to work together. The mind is meant to offer ideas to the heart: the heart to examine them in relation to inner truth and wisdom. Your feelings let you know whether or not the ideas of the mind have value for you. Equally, the heart may be inspired with a direction, and the mind creates the path to make it happen.

Centering balances your mind and heart in their natural state of harmony. When there is discrepancy between the two, you are on alert that there is more to the situation than first appears. Wait. Don't do anything until your heart and mind are in agreement. Then, when you do act, you will be doing so in your wholeness. No part of you will be fighting another part. You will be acting in the power of your authentic self.

Centering, balancing heart and mind, and expressing your authentic self are lifelong pursuits. Just when you think you've arrived and that you've found your voice, your truth, and your purpose, you find that your core has moved deeper and you are encouraged into new territories of self-discovery. Centering is an endless journey where the only goal is to experience the path.

Awareness: Heart-Centered Awareness

The awareness of the Pillar of Centering is heart-centered. Heart-centered awareness syncs your actions to the design of the whole and to the all-that-is. All of creation intersects within your heart, your nodal point in the hologram. This is where your vision feeds the all-that-is and where the all informs your life.

Heart-centered awareness awakens the plan within your life. It lets you see yourself and others with acceptance. The way you are, with every fear-based mistake you've ever made, is you: whole, complete, and impeccable. Every quirk and imperfection that you judge and despise is accepted with an open heart. Accepting yourself allows you to accept others. When you connect to the world from the heart, you are enfolded inside something larger than your personal self-interest. You see beyond what appears to be broken to the light within.

Heart-centered awareness uses your senses and feelings to align with your deepest truth. More far reaching than human morals and ethics, this awareness takes you beyond judgments of right and wrong. You may not see the bigger picture, but using your heart as a compass, you navigate your direction by the feel of your path.

When you quiet enough to listen to the heart, intuition and energy awareness are opened. Decisions based in heart-centered awareness follow one basic criterion: What sits well in your heart and what doesn't? When you are true to this, whatever decisions you make, no matter the outcome, are exactly right.

Invariably, whenever something is done that is later regretted, it's due to not listening to the voice of your authentic heart-centered self. The question that arises is, how can I hear the voice of my authentic self and how do I know when I am out of my center?

Using the criterion of heart-centered awareness, ask yourself how the situation sits inside. Does it sink in, becoming a cradle for feelings of contentment, fulfilment, and aliveness, inspiring you to greater creativity? Or does it bounce around, refusing to settle, causing you to second guess yourself as it generates unease, suspicion, and fear?

Everything you do, every decision and action, is guided by instinct, intuition, learned behaviors, and beliefs. Heart-centered awareness strips habituated responses and outmoded beliefs and brings your instinct and intuition into center stage. Connected to your core, your consciousness expands. The continuity between internal and external reality is readily perceived as the design of your life flows into and through the design of the all.

These are the foundations of heart-centered awareness:

◇ Through your heart you are synced with the greater design of life.

◇ Inside, beneath ideas, behaviors, opinions, and cultural mores, people are essentially the same.

◇ No matter how broken you feel or other people appear to be, inside the tapestry of life is wholeness.

◇ The well-being of the all is critical to the well-being of the individual and vice versa.

◇ Cruelty to one is cruelty to everyone.

◇ Your heart is your internal compass; feelings and intuition are the cardinal points.

◇ Feeling-thoughts generated in the heart flow through your Presence to the world.

In your heart-space, you are enfolded into something larger than your personal self-interest.

Challenge: The Giveaway

The biggest challenge to the Pillar of Centering is the giveaway. This takes place whenever you step out of center and give away your heart-space. You know exactly what this means: Despite a truth felt deep inside, despite a pull to pursue a specific direction, and despite the whisper of your authentic self, a sideways step is taken that gives away your center. You move out of your heart and let someone else, or some other idea of what is right, step in.

Why does this happen? There are many reasons. Here are a few:

⬦ The need to protect yourself or another person.

⬦ Self-doubt.

⬦ The need for approval.

⬦ Wanting to be loved.

⬦ Fear of standing alone.

⬦ Fear of being wrong.

⬦ Fear of hurting someone else's feelings.

⬦ Believing the needs of others are more important than your own.

⬦ Needing to prove yourself in someone else's eyes.

⬦ Needing to feel important.

⬦ Putting an ideal or principle ahead of your gut feelings.

⬦ Succumbing to revenge, jealousy, and envy: emotions that express how much you undervalue your place in the design of the all.

Through such feelings, someone else's definition of who you are and how you ought to feel, see, believe, and behave is accepted over your own. The cost of the giveaway is more than your center; it is your identity.

Essentially, the giveaway abandons your authentic self. Abandonment seems to be a universal part of the human experience. If you are lucky, your start in life as a baby is celebrated; you are loved and cherished just for the fact of being alive. At some point, however, the unconditional love and acceptance you receive as a baby changes. For no reason other than growing up, you inexplicably fall from this time of grace. Conditions are placed on what you must do to maintain acceptance, and love is withheld to control your behavior. You no longer trust that you are enough and no longer trust that you are part of something bigger. This wounding becomes the central influence of your life, the focal point of growth and self-discovery.

The woundings that happen in childhood are rarely intentional. Parents don't have children in order to hurt them. Mostly, people act from their own training and fear as they work their way to their own healing. Some parents try so hard not to wound their children they go too far in the other direction. Unconditional love becomes an excuse for allowing any behavior, and parents offer no guidelines for respecting others and living peacefully. How can nations be expected to live in peace when parents don't teach how to their children?

No matter how deep the wound to your psyche, however, your core self is protected. It slumbers in the center of your heart like Sleeping Beauty, surrounded by layers of defense, awaiting awakening. In order to avoid the pain, your self-awareness lives on the surface of who you are. As your heart-voice gets softer and more distant, you may lose yourself in being good and living up to standards and making money until it's difficult to identify your center at all. All the while, your authentic self is guarded fiercely until one day you start the journey inward to recover it. What you learn about yourself on the way back to center creates unshakable self-assurance.

Relationship: Essential Self

What kind of a friend are you? Do you drop whatever you're doing when a friend is in trouble to help? Do you hear their pain and support their dreams? Do you accept them for who they are rather than make them into who you want them to be? What kind of friend are you to yourself?

Imagine being given responsibility for one person on this planet, one person you are charged with protecting and nurturing. Your job is not to indulge this person's self-importance and supply their every addiction; it is to help them live to their truest calling, to support their inner fulfillment, to share humor and enjoyment in being alive, and to illuminate meaning and service. What would you do to support this person? How would you befriend them?

To regain your center, you must befriend yourself. You are the only person you are given 100 percent charge over. Even your children are only in your care for a short while. Yet self-care is often neglected out of a fear of being selfish. When you see yourself as part of the larger tapestry, caring for the color and weave of your particular part of the design is no longer selfish. Nourishing yourself nourishes the all. How do you nourish yourself? In what ways do you support the inner journey to your core?

Unconditional love is the way back to your core. However, unconditional love needs defining. It is the act of holding yourself and others in a vision of wholeness. No matter what harmful actions have been committed, although rectification must occur, unconditional love allows you to see yourself and others with heart-centered awareness. Harmful or cruel behavior is not excused; responsibility is not avoided. Unconditional love simply refuses to erase all that you are and have to offer because of your one worst moment.

Here is the crux of being in unconditional love:

◇ Don't use love as a reward or withholding love as a punishment to yourself or others.

◇ Allow love to be constant.

◇ Love fully and completely while still maintaining boundaries.

◇ Lighten up.

◇ Use the mistakes you paid so dearly for to grow.

◇ Befriend and embrace yourself.

◇ Embrace life and open your heart.

Maybe you have withdrawn from the heart to avoid pain and suffering. As with everything, even pain and suffering offer opportunity. From the blog of Krista Tippet, "Violence is what happens when we don't know what else to do with our suffering. Show me a person who makes others suffer and I'll show you someone who's 'working out' his or her suffering by passing along the pain.

"But suffering, held in a supple heart, can break the heart open to compassion instead of breaking it down into cruelty. When we live with broken-open hearts, our suffering leads us to love life more, not less. Then we can become light-bearers and life-givers in a world of too much darkness and death. How to keep our hearts supple is one of the most important questions we can ask."[1]

A supple heart is the key to your relationship with self: Embrace your feelings, pain, and all, and allow them to "break open" your heart. A supple heart is open and discerning, flexible and adaptable, and maintains integrity. When you are brave enough to embrace your pain, the friendship with self begins. Unconditional love is your companion, providing the nourishment needed for growth and renewal.

Gateway: Heart Center

The gateway to Centering is the energy center of the heart, which is located in the chest. This is where attention meets intention. Attention opens the present moment; intention uses that present moment to transmit a specific focus. Attention and intention. The mind and the heart. Wherever your intention turns the focus of your attention, life-affirming, creative energy is set to work.

The heart center is enormously powerful. Nourishing the heart is like fertilizing and watering a plant. Held in the laser beam of attention and bathed in the intention of love, people, goals, visions, aspirations, abilities, animals, plants, the Earth, and even your perceptivity flourish. When you pay attention, you create a sacred imprint and you create a path.

Grounding and Centering are most powerful when practiced together. In fact, it is difficult to practice them separately, as one necessitates the other. Balancing the Tan Dien with the heart center affirms where you stand between Earth and sky. It establishes the trunk of the tree. When Grounding and Centering are balanced, your body, mind, and spirit are nourished.

Messages from the heart center arrive as felt-senses, intuition, and emotion. Emotions generated in the heart range from expansive emotions of joy, love, and connection to painful emotions of loss, grief, and sadness. Each conveys a message and each shifts a state of energy. Receiving the message from within the heart is achieved by not turning away and sitting with the emotion, letting it grow and take all the space, filling the chest to overflowing.

Sometimes, the messages in the heart reveal past pain that has not been cleared. When a painful emotion is suppressed, muscles tighten around the area where the emotion is felt. This is called muscle splinting. It creates a shield of muscle armor that protects your core. Muscles splinting is a subconscious process. It helps mute overwhelming emotions that are too raw to feel. Muscle splinting also disconnects you from feelings of happiness and joy that you believe you don't deserve. Those emotions are for others. You may help others achieve happiness but deny it to yourself.

The process of closing down the heart to hurtful emotions through muscle splinting is not selective. You can't close down feelings of grief without closing down feelings of joy. Consequently, enjoyable activities that open the heart can result in unexpected, overwhelming grief or sadness as the muscles of the chest relax and suppressed emotions surface. This organic surfacing provides an incredible opportunity for healing.

For three weeks before her car accident, my daughter experienced severe and debilitating anxiety. It started around the same time her horse, Emerson, developed his mysterious neck injury. Now she looks back and understands that she, too, was feeling the bow wave of the accident as it approached the horizon. Not understanding the message, she avoided the anxiety she felt by disconnecting from her body. Hindsight is always 20/20. If she had been in her body, would she have felt the warning not to get in the car?

The best any of us can do in such situations is to take the time to sit with anxiety or any overwhelming emotion in an attitude of acceptance and appraisal. Allow the emotion all the space it needs. Instead of pushing it away and trying to avoid it, flood the emotion with your attention. Let your creative energy flow and, as you do, pay attention to the images, feelings, and awareness that emerge. What increases anxiety? What decreases anxiety? What serves the inner knowing of the heart?

Gift: Heart-Centered Path and Purpose

Do you yearn to know your path? Are you waiting to be called to an important purpose? Do you long to be of service but don't know what you are supposed to do?

The need for purpose is innate. It helps propel you toward a meaningful, fulfilling life. Every person has purpose, even if it is undefined and amorphous. However, the desire to have a specific purpose can be so strong it actually gets in the way of living a purposeful life. Constantly looking for a big calling gives rise to overlooking the little acts of kindness and small opportunities to live on purpose. While not knowing your path may feed your self-doubt and feelings of unworthiness, an obsession with purpose can feed a need for self-importance. It can sweep you away from your core and unbalance your ego.

What if you are not called to a purpose, and instead, you call a purpose to you? *Choose the purpose you want to live and call it to you.* Align to it by making your choices in life based on that purpose. Calling your purpose is the gift of the Pillar of Centering.

There is partnership between spirit and the path living in your heart. Spirit brings the design; you decide how to live it. You don't need to know your purpose or even what the design is; each step you take is still part of the larger picture. The design of it unfolds slowly and is seen fully only when looking back. Looking forward, each step is a movement into mystery. Walking your path is about listening to your heart-voice in your decisions and directions. Let your heart be your guide.

In your longing for purpose, what are you really yearning for? The essence of purpose is belonging. Are you really longing to be enveloped, loved, and welcomed for who you are? Truthfully, you are woven into the tapestry of life with a specific pattern and colors of your own choosing. In this partnership with spirit, you bring to life something no one else can. You bring into awareness an aspect of reality no one else sees in exactly the same way, perfectly accenting the design of the whole. Purpose is a natural extension of who you are. *Your purpose is to be all of yourself as fully and completely and lovingly as you can.* Your place is established and you can allow yourself to flourish.

Developing Presence carries you awake and aware into mystery. You are aligned with your purpose even while you can't quite see it. Presence helps you be more of who you already are. Centered in your heart, your actions carry meaning. You create purpose.

The Practice of Centering

The energetic act of Centering is easy. All it takes is drawing your attention into the center of your heart. Where your attention goes, your energy follows. The difficult part is living a centered life. Living from your center means bringing decisions into your heart to evaluate how well they sit with your spirit, path, and purpose.

Sometimes it can be difficult to discern the difference between following your heart or letting your intuition be overridden by old patterns and even higher ideals that don't fit the situation. Here's an example.

I was invited to participate in the development of a product related to one of my passions: the function and energy of emotions. It was a great idea, the woman was sincere, and my mind came up with several good reasons to partner with her. The reasons I compiled fed my ideals: the project allowed me to communicate my passion and support another woman entrepreneur stepping forward and taking a risk. Being honest, there was also an element of seduction: I was attached to having the information presented in what I considered to be its highest truth and hoped the project would be a spring board for work I wanted to pursue.

While my mind was providing reasons to say yes, my heart was saying "This isn't for you." I performed the classic giveaway. Every step into the project left me unsettled, squirrely, and tired. Because I couldn't come up with any reason why the project wasn't right for me, I rationalized. I told myself I was succumbing to old fears and pushed myself forward. It didn't take long, however, before the differences in our approaches began to show.

Out of center, I was unable to access my heart. I wasn't aligned with the plan and had to change myself to fit. Rationalization was an attempt to bring my mind and heart together, but it wasn't truth; it was accommodation. I yo-yoed back and forth between engaging and withdrawing. The net result was that I undermined the very reasons I said yes—to support this woman's vision and communicate the information in its highest light. Had I listened to my heart, I would have found a better way to meet my ideals and, perhaps as an advisor rather than a participator.

The difference between being stopped by old fears and walking a path that doesn't fit is this: With the first, the opportunity is exciting; it provides a lift of energy and brings mind and heart into alignment. Then, when you are stopped by old fears, enjoyment and forward progress is sabotaged with self-doubt, self-judgment, or concern about the judgment of others. But underneath the fear, the original excitement is still present.

With the second, walking a path that doesn't fit, the opportunity is met with an initial loss of energy. Instead of inspiring and giving a lift, the project feels like a chore. You have to change something in yourself to fit. Almost immediately, self-preservation brings out less than ideal behaviors. When this happens, there is no judgment. You may meet parts of yourself you thought were long gone, but, as in my case, meeting those parts and bringing them to healing may be the purpose within the design. Then growth can be engaged as you leap ahead into a greater expression of your authentic self.

Practicing Centering and learning to walk the path that fits you is never ending. Be gentle with yourself when you are off course. Take responsibility for what you do when you are out of center. Everything is course correction.

The steps to Centering are incredibly simple:

1. Take three deep breaths and bring yourself into present time.
2. Place your attention on your heart center in the middle of your chest.
3. If you want to and are in a place where you can, place your left hand over your heart, then place your right hand over your left. Otherwise, omit this step.
4. Use your breath to draw your energy and attention into the heart center. Call all of yourself home.
5. Stay with this invitation and allow your heart to fill.
6. Be mindful of what you feel as you go through the day. Allow what you feel to be part of your decisions and connections with people.
7. Let what you feel be as important as what you think.

The first obstacle in Centering is being able to locate the center of your spiritual being in the heart area. Some people feel this center in their solar plexus, the area below the ribs and above the belly button. Truthfully, true center balances the heart space with the Tan Dien, so if you locate your center lower, you are probably balancing these two areas. Use whatever location is natural to you or use the Balancing exercise later in the chapter to fully integrate your physical and spiritual centers.

The next obstacle is trusting that what is felt is real. We're used to giving supremacy to the mind. In the beginning, you might have to pretend that what you see, feel, and sense as you go through your day using heart-centered awareness is real. Act as though you believe it. Start by extending your trust with small decisions. What do you want for breakfast? Ask this or any other relatively unimportant question while maintaining Centering. See if different sense of choices create a different ease or unease. Practice so that when big issues present themselves, it is easy and natural to stay centered and use your heart-wisdom along with mind-logic.

Probably the greatest obstacle to Centering is finding the balance between mind and heart. When this balance is found, instinct and intuition become finely tuned instruments. In the beginning, simply notice what logic dictates and how your feelings of comfort or discomfort respond. Feeling flow is your major indicator that your heart is in alignment. Keeping a journal is helpful. Notice the patterns that form and keep track of how often your logic would have benefited from listening to your center. Eventually, Centering will be second nature and you won't have to think about it. If you're not sure of what your center says, wait. Trust yourself; keep exploring with open mind and heart. When all the information is in place, the right choice will make itself known.

Be willing to be quiet. You don't need to run at life; life comes to you. Meet it with an open heart and mind. As you settle into the Pillar of Centering, you will establish stillness in your Presence.

Self-Reflection

How connected do you feel to your authentic self? What situations allow you to shine? What situations create a desire to hide?

How focused is your attention?

Remember a situation in which you used attention and intention together. How did it feel?

Remember a time when you ignored the discomfort in your heart and gave away your center. What was the underlying motivation?

When life brings pain or disappointment, what is your most immediate response?

Where is your growth-edge? What stops you from realizing your dreams and from standing up for yourself and your values?

How do you nourish yourself?

How much do you trust your authentic self?

What are the signals you look for when listening to the heart?

In what ways do you support the inner journey to your core?

In what ways do you experience your wholeness? Where do you judge yourself as not being whole?

What does it feel like to be visible in your authentic self?

What purpose are you calling to yourself?

Energy Exercises

In addition to the Centering exercise, use these heart-based exercises to bring greater awareness into your center and bring your heart into your daily choices.

Exercise 1: Creating a Heart Altar

1. Bring yourself into center with three deep breaths.
2. Place your left hand over the center of your chest and your right hand over your left.
3. Bring your attention out of your head and fully into your heart.
4. Feel the warmth and love in your hands spread into your heart-space as you appreciate all this center brings to you.
5. Inhale and use your imagination to invite a blessing into your heart. Visualize light streaming in through the top of your head and landing in the bowl of your heart.
6. Spend a moment bathing your heart with love. Nourish yourself, appreciate yourself, and enjoy connecting to your authenticity.
7. Now imagine your heart is an altar to your spirit. Visualize what the alter looks like. Perhaps it is a flat rock or a piece of polished wood. Maybe it is an altar cabinet with doors or a thicket in a meadow. Allow your altar to present itself in the form that feels most authentic.
8. What would you like to put on this altar? What objects remind you of your truest self? Place items on the altar until everything feels complete and whole.

9. This is your sacred space, your place to retreat for nourishment and sustenance. Bring your troubles here and place them at the foot of the altar. Let them be blessed by spirit and transformed with the wisdom of the heart. Listen to the insights that come to you.

10. Care for this sacred space by visiting it and bringing in energy. Allow yourself to be cherished. Visualize yourself as whole.

Exercise 2: Balancing Tan Dien and Heart Center

1. Begin with three deep, cleansing, and centering breaths that bring your attention into your body.
2. Put your right hand over your Tan Dien and your left hand over your heart.
3. Notice how balanced you immediately feel. Doing this any time you feel unbalanced will bring you into center and ground.
4. As you inhale:
   - Imagine light from your spiritual source entering the top of your head and collecting in your heart, filling it with brilliance.
   - Imagine energy flowing upward from Earth and collecting in your Tan Dien, filling it with strength.
5. With each inhale, let energy build in both your heart and Tan Dien.
6. With each exhale, invite the energy between the two centers to flow toward each other and merge.
7. After a few minutes, stop and notice how you feel.

Exercise 3: Cracking Open the Heart

1. Take three deep cleansing and centering breaths. Inhale peace; exhale tension.

2. Balance your Tan Dien and heart by placing your left hand over your heart and your right hand over your lower abdomen.

3. Consider a recent conflict where you did not feel centered.

   + In terms of your authenticity, how did you show up?

   + At the point you left your center, what were you confronted with that unbalanced you? What emotion were you feeling?

   + Is this an emotion you often experience that takes you out of your center?

4. Bring the emotion into your heart.

   + Notice the constraints you place around this emotion and give the feeling an image. Is it a winding chain, a locked cage, or a black box? Whatever the image, acknowledge it. Thank it for protecting you and then state it is no longer needed.

   + Give this emotion all the space it needs. Let it grow. Let it get as big as it deems necessary .

   + Give it a color, a shape, and a texture.

   + Let it grow and keep growing. Allow yourself to fully feel it.

5. Notice the beliefs that arise around this emotion. Notice them, acknowledge them, and let them go.

6. Let the emotion get so big it cracks open your heart-space and lets in the light.

7. Invite light to flow from all points.

   + Let light stream into you and to your heart through every pore.

   + Breathe in through your crown center and inundate your heart with light.

8. Embrace the emotion and see it as a young child, a younger version of you.

- With the intention of love, give this younger you all of your attention.
- Love your younger self unconditionally; support and nourish your younger self. Say thank you for holding this important place of growth.

9. Allow the emotion to get bigger, smaller, or disappear altogether.

10. When you feel complete, take three grounding breaths and release anything you want to let go of.

6

the pillar of balancing

PILLAR: Balancing
AWARENESS: Energy Awareness
CHALLENGE: Dependency
RELATIONSHIP: Responsibility
GATEWAY: Solar Plexus
GIFT: Personal Power
EMOTION/ATTITUDE: Respect
QUALITY BROUGHT TO PRESENCE: Integrity

Boundaries

My daughter bolts upright, straining against her metal cage, screaming in pain. She clutches at her left leg, frantic. I jump out of my chair and lift her leg, swinging gently back and forth in an attempt to override the spasm.

"Pressure," she pants, eyes wild and pain-filled.

Erin is just returned from the recovery room, the third, but not final, surgery on her knee completed. Wire threads through her knee cap and attaches to the top of her shin bone as the process of creating a new patellar tendon is begun. The severed muscle, happy in its relaxed, rolled up position, is being

pulled down. The pain is that of a thousand charley horses. We are not pre-
pared. The enormity is unexpected. We thought the worst already over.

"How?" I ask, pushing into her thigh muscle as much as I dare. She claws
my hands away and pushes down with all her might. I put my hands over
hers and press.

"More," she begs, pulling her hands out from under mine.

I press as hard as I can, putting all my weight into my hands and com-
pressing the attachment of her quadriceps muscle to ease the cramp. I alternate
back and forth: lifting and swinging, dropping and pressing. Each of Erin's
screams tears my heart. Until this, her stoic strength has been unbroken. Now
pain strips her of defense and protection. She is naked in her vulnerability. I
shield her as best I can.

Hours pass, filled with endless rounds of frantic pressing and back-break-
ing leg swings; I cannot sustain the physical and emotional rigor. I am flagging
as I press with what strength I have left. Erin looks at me, horrified with the
realization of her dependency.

"I couldn't do this without you," she gasps. She is brought to her knees in
the realization that alone, we are nothing.

I feel how terrifying this awareness is for the child who determined so
early that she would need no one, and I start to tumble down the rabbit hole
of taking responsibility for her. I pull myself back, reaching for the balance
between what is me and my path and what is Erin and her path. I cannot fix
her fears; I cannot fix any part of her path, nor is it broken to begin with. All
I can do is love without restraint, hold a vision of her wholeness, and let my
Presence be a healing force she can access. If I lose myself in her pain, physical
or emotional, we will both go down.

I ground, center, and establish my boundary. In my mind I define my
personal space. "This is me," I internally affirm, feeling and filling the space
around me. Then I focus on the space around my daughter. "This is you," I
internally assert. I confront my fear that by creating boundaries I am aban-
doning her. I acknowledge the fear and let it go. "This is me, this you, this is
me, this is you." I continue the exercise of shifting focus between the two of us
until our individual spaces are defined and clear.

With renewed strength, I lean into my daughter's leg. With renewed love, I support her on her path.

The need for balance shows itself in a variety of ways. Many days later, after the final surgery on her leg, we receive permission to take Erin out of her bed to the healing garden on the roof. This is the first time she is allowed out of her hospital room for something other than tests or surgery. She has asked daily for this privilege and is ecstatic. She bubbles with excitement.

We maneuver her into the wheel chair, use blankets and pillows for support around the halo device, hang the catheter and IV line to the overhead hooks, stabilize her leg, wrap her in blankets, and half an hour later, are off.

The sense of forbidden adventure is highlighted by the late hour. Lights are dimmed and visitors gone. Nurses smile as we pass. We take the elevator down to the first floor and cross the cafeteria plaza. Erin gazes with delight at items in the gift store window as we pass. She casts curious glances at the one or two people slumped over coffee in the plaza, perhaps wondering if they notice her head gear and what they think of it. We continue to the north tower, up the elevator to the seventh floor, and out onto the roof.

Here, in the middle of the concrete city, a small space of nature is suspended above the streets. A slatted wooden pathway winds between trees and bushes. I am struck by the juxtaposition. How strange that the healing power of nature is recognized while progress simultaneously destroys the Earth it comes from.

I sit on a bench and breathe deeply of the city air that passes for fresh. A light mist shrouds us in this hanging garden. We are in a world apart; the real world is out there, somewhere else. Here, we are protected.

I give my tiredness to the bench and let the metal structure support me as tension melts out of my body. Erin takes control of the wheelchair and twists away. Managing it is more difficult than she anticipates. She wheels down the small decline a little too quickly and spins around the corner.

Her movement away opens unexpected emotion. In little more than two weeks she is gone from infant to toddler. I am watching her first steps, watching her reclaim her independence. The moment is poignant, more so than any so far. I swallow the lump in my throat as I let her go.

She heads up the incline on the opposite side of the roof, putting the planting of bushes and small trees between us. She gets stuck as a wheel jams into an abutment and whips her chair sideways.

"Don't help me," she calls.

"Not planning to," I answer.

I see her headgear through the bushes, metal rods weaving back and forth as she manhandles the chair out of the trench.

"I can do it," she declares as she struggles.

"I know you can," I answer.

"Watch me, Momma, watch me" echoes from the past. From deep inside, I answer. Did I give you enough attention? Did I damage you when other needs took precedence? Am I doing a better job now?

Eventually, Erin succeeds. Minutes later she emerges victorious at the lookout point over the city.

I know the balance created by the boundaries I hold is as important for her as for me. I respect her too much to take over her path and honor myself by not getting lost in her challenge. I love from the heart, releasing attachments one thread at a time.

Our relationship is a balancing act. We are negotiating a tight wire over Niagara Falls.

Pillar: Balancing

Life is a balancing act. Pulled by emotions, assailed with demands on time and attention, and driven by inner impulses, it can be a struggle to walk a steady path. The Pillar of Balancing weighs the demands of the world with those of your heart and helps you live with integrity. Balancing fine tunes focus without overcompensating in one direction or another. This

Pillar maintains your personal space and establishes self-care and nourishment as essential priorities.

Balancing requires boundaries. Without boundaries, there are no distinctions between inside and outside, and no regulation of input and outflow. You can be swept away by strong currents or drowned in overflow. Boundaries allow the balancing of your emotions, thoughts, and feelings with external demands and physical requirements. They help you field and evaluate the multiple forces in life to create equilibrium. In addition, boundaries protect you from taking on harmful energy or projecting your imbalances onto others.

At first, the creation of boundaries seems to conflict with the concept of being one with a larger whole. Consider a cell. It is one with the body and separation from the body is certain death. On the other hand, without the boundary of a cell wall, a cell cannot fulfill its function and regulate its needs, which also means certain death. In the same way, individuals exist within the whole, fulfilling specific functions, adding particular viewpoints, and performing set tasks. Boundaries define your personal space so that you can function in physical reality.

Using the cell as a model can be useful in understanding what type of boundary you want to create. Cell walls are semipermeable. They have enough porousness to let in what is needed and keep out what is harmful. The degree of permeability changes depending on conditions. The ability to respond to conditions is a key feature for the type of boundary that will keep you balanced. Too rigid and your fears will be in charge, depriving you of a vital flow of energy; too weak and your lack of self-definition doesn't let you hold enough energy to function optimally. Balancing depends on boundaries that are flexible, strong, and discerning.

In the hospital, I would have gladly traded my health and well-being for Erin's pain. As this was not possible, in order to be any help at all, I needed to separate; I had to create boundaries. What did this feel like to her? Did she experience the separation of my energy as abandonment, or did she appreciate my help more when I was clearly and cleanly apart?

A clear, well-established boundary is clean. You don't give out of guilt, and your help doesn't trigger the need for guilt in others. You give out of love and receive in love. You don't transfer your unprocessed emotions and unfinished issues onto others. In managing the flow between inside and outside, boundaries ensure you are not toxic to others and are protected from energy that would be toxic to you.

Boundaries differentiate conflicting needs in work, relationships, spiritual practice, and other aspects of life. The problem is that the need for boundaries is amorphous and can be difficult to discern. Boundaries encompass behavior and attitudes whose effects are not easily measured. To make boundaries more concrete, you might make lists of what you will accept and where you draw the line. However, the parameters of such lists shift with different people. Behavior you would never accept with one person is perfectly comfortable with another. What differentiates the two may be the attitude each person carries, but often it is less definable. Consequently, Balancing requires present time attention. You can't establish a boundary and expect that it will never need to change.

Your body knows when your boundaries need adjusting and your life needs balancing. Here are some of the signs you might be familiar with:

- ◇ Diminished joy as life becomes all work and no play.
- ◇ Irritation anytime anyone asks anything of you.
- ◇ Disliking advice.
- ◇ An inability to say no, even when you want to.
- ◇ Being unable to prioritize self-care practices such as exercise, eating well, meditating, or going out with friends.
- ◇ Needing to make people like you.
- ◇ Feeling locked in the same routines, even though they don't satisfy you.
- ◇ Creating unhappy relationships.
- ◇ Thinking you know what's best for others.
- ◇ Feeling drained, exhausted, and burned out.

◇ Hiding who you are and what you need.

◇ Pretending you don't need anything.

◇ Spending your time on electronic devices and forgetting the upliftment of nature.

◇ Focusing so much on the negative you can't see the positive.

◇ Setting unrealistic goals that will require massive sacrifice to achieve.

Balancing is dynamic and fluid. It requires you to shift with changing conditions. Whether you feel the continuity and flow between inside and out, or the boundary that regulates this flow, depends on what is needed at the time and where you put your focus.

Awareness: Energy Awareness

Balancing depends on being able to define your personal space—the landscape of your thoughts, beliefs, and emotional projections in the physical space around you. Even though it cannot be seen, you are acutely aware of this space. When someone steps too close and moves inside the circle around you that is your personal space, you feel it through energy awareness.

Energy awareness assesses the ambiance and evaluates the level of charge and degree of safety. Energy awareness establishes boundaries and pays attention to how others affect you and how you impact them. This sixth-sense operates below your conscious awareness and feeds the information to your brain through gut feelings, intuition, and emotions. Though this degree of surveillance may sound arduous, it isn't. The feeling is like a spider in the center of her home, sensing vibrations in the web around her. You, like everyone else, are the center of a field of perception, reacting instinctively to the information you receive.

Your personal space is an area of heightened awareness filled with your non-physical self that has a measurable electromagnetic field. Aspects of this field are known by science and used in medicine. Currently, the superconducting quantum interference device (SQUID), a mechanism able to measure extremely weak signals, is the most sensitive measure of the human body's electromagnetic energy field.[1] Other devices that measure changes in the electromagnetic field to indicate levels of health may be more familiar to you, such as the electrocardiogram (EKG) and electroencephalogram (EEG) that measure the electromagnetic signals of the heart and brain.

Other aspects of the human electromagnetic field are as yet unrecognized by science, but equally real. Research published in 1999 by Russek and Schwartz confirms the human ability to feel the Presence of another and to know when someone else is looking at you, even when you can't see them.[2] The energy awareness that allows this is natural. You may mute your perceptions and repress your instincts, but they are still right there, just under the surface. When you open the door to energy awareness even the smallest crack, perception floods in like light.

Consider someone who invades your personal space. What does your body feel like when that person steps inside your circle, uninvited, even if they are someone you love and care about? What is your immediate reaction and how do you respond? How do others interact with your personal space? Does your Presence produce calm and comfort, or do people around you walk on eggshells? Does your energy take up all the space in the room or do you collapse in on yourself and try to be invisible?

Energy awareness observes the balance between connection and separation, the root of all boundaries. The crux of Balancing rests in knowing who you are and what you need. If you don't know what you need, or if your needs are so entwined with those of others, your boundaries no longer respect others or honor you. Then you can lose connection to your energy awareness and become unable to sense and respond to the world with deeper perception.

Boundaries that don't honor self give away your personal power. You become unable to produce meaningful action. Boundaries that don't honor other people's personal space disrespect them. Although your intention may be to give support, what you communicate when you overstep is that you think you know the other person's path better than they do.

Intentionally or not, what is communicated is a lack of trust in their decisions and respect for their direction.

Some essentials of Balancing learned through energy awareness are

- ◇ There is flow between internal and external reality.
- ◇ Deep connection and individual path can be simultaneously maintained.
- ◇ Balancing the outflow and inflow of energy increases personal power.
- ◇ Healthy boundaries allow you to welcome, grow, and thrive from differences.
- ◇ Boundaries unclutter internal space and ensure that your interactions with others are clean.
- ◇ No one knows another person's path and purpose better than they do; no one knows your path and purpose better than you do.
- ◇ Maintaining personal space is key to health, path, and relationship.
- ◇ Balancing allows your light to shine.

Challenge: Dependency

My biggest fear in establishing boundaries during my daughter's recovery was that she would feel abandoned. This appears to be common. Many people are afraid that establishing boundaries is somehow withholding love and telling another person they are not important. The fear is that being separate harms the connection.

If this is your fear, a connection that depends on giving yourself away is not a true connection. Actually, it is dependency and probably reflects how afraid you are of not being enough. Having boundaries does not mean you love less. It means you are clear on what is you and what is not. It means you can honor both. I didn't stop helping my daughter:

I just made sure, for both our sakes, that I did not get lost in her pain. Boundaries allowed me to balance my needs with hers.

Not holding boundaries actually makes you less accessible, not more. Without boundaries, it is easy to become drained, irritable, and disempowered. You have less to offer so what you give is tinged with resentment and received with guilt. The other person feels indebted, not loved. Consequently, self-care is a priority for balanced relationships. You cannot help anyone if you don't first take care of yourself. You cannot walk your path if you are consumed with helping someone else walk theirs.

Although it may look like boundaries cause separation, boundaries enable you to bring all of yourself to the table and accept all of the other person. You can be angry, lost, or afraid, and still be connected. You can take care of yourself without neglecting another.

Do you have a friend or relative who always wants to know the ins and outs of your life; who presses you with personal questions and seems to delight in uncovering your problems? You may think this person is simply nosey or trying to make their life look better in comparison with yours. While this might be true, it might also be that this person needs to be inside your boundaries in order to feel connected. This person might need to solve your problems in order to feel useful. Not a good feeling, is it?

I could easily have tried to take over and direct my daughter's recovery. It would have decreased my fears and helped me feel in control. But the truth is that I wasn't in control. Something much larger, the design of her life, was directing the picture. It is futile to pretend something that isn't true. Even in her desperation and need, Erin would not have let me take over; she would have held onto her self-reliance. For her to allow me to take control would have required that she abandon her center. If I had tried, I would have forced her to choose between me and her essential self. Old childhood patterns would have been reestablished. Boundaries allowed me to be present and help without taking over her path or losing myself in it.

Let's be very clear. The Pillar of Balancing and the construction of boundaries are not about selfishness. Having boundaries doesn't mean you won't sacrifice, push yourself, or do things you would rather not. Boundaries ensure you act with awareness of the need that drives you, respect other people's paths, and honor your limits. Maybe you are called to help another or your love is so great that all else vanishes in importance. Maybe your ideals drive you to perform difficult tasks. Maybe you have a big heart. Maybe you do what you do because you can. Whatever the need that drives your actions, awareness of it allows you to be clear and clean.

Knowing your needs is the key to Balancing with clear boundaries. Much of the time, you may not know what you need or take the time to find out. Then you can become burned out. Separation occurs because you have nothing more to give. How much easier it is to take the time to assess your needs and establish boundaries. Living in the Pillar of Balancing, you can give and receive and be connected and independent.

Relationship: Responsibility

Just the word *responsibility* tightens muscles. Immediately, your back straightens and your jaw locks as you brace yourself to step up and assume the mantle. This reaction is based in responsibility being linked to punishment and blame. You take responsibility for the things that go wrong and accept responsibility for the hard work that has to be done. Responsibility is a duty, a sacrifice, or an indictment. In addition, sometimes, responsibility is used as a foil for taking control of what isn't yours.

Understanding your relationship with responsibility is essential to Balancing. It is a given that you are accountable for your actions and their consequences. Beyond that, there are two key imbalances seen around responsibility. The first is avoiding responsibility and not giving something back to life for all you receive. The second is taking too much responsibility and assuming accountability for the consequences of other people's choices, leading to the belief that because you took responsibility, you have a right to control them.

In order to develop a better relationship with responsibility, it may be helpful to redefine the word. Put simply, responsibility is the ability to respond. What if, instead of being responsible *for* something, you are responsible *to* it? For example, instead of being responsible for my daughter's recovery, I was responsible to it: I had the ability to make a response that produced a meaningful contribution. Does that change the feeling of responsibility?

When responsibility means the ability to make a meaningful contribution, suddenly the desire to engage difficult challenges is greater. Instead of shirking the weight of obligation, you can embrace the joy of contribution. That is why it's important not to take over the responsibility for someone else. Doing so takes away their contribution and subconsciously communicates that their contribution isn't worthy.

Here is the core: Being responsible *for* something puts you in center stage. Unintentionally, the story line becomes about how well you take responsibility and what a good job you do. When you are responsible *to* something, the story line is about what is being accomplished. In my example, if I am responsible *for* my daughter's recovery, the story is about how well I do it. When I am responsible *to* her recovery, the story is about how well she recovers. That difference is crucial. It creates a relationship with responsibility that allows Balancing. It makes a clear distinction between stepping up and stepping over.

Being responsible *to* situations instead of *for* them allows you to let go of your attachment to outcomes and flow with the direction of the current, contributing as needed. You don't have to direct outcomes to avoid blame. You can't use the situation to make yourself important. Responsibility becomes restful instead of draining. It becomes your way of giving to life rather than having life demand from you.

Right now, wash away the debris of your old relationship with responsibility. Let go of needing to control outcomes and enjoy what's happening around you. Relax. Laugh. Tell a joke. Be part of the moment. Let your contribution to life shine.

In every situation, there are multiple items to be responsive to such as the demands of situations, the needs of the people involved, and the direction being aimed for. The better your relationship with responsibility, the better your boundaries and the more skillful you are at Balancing.

Gateway: Solar Plexus

The personal space around you is felt through the energy center of your solar plexus. This is the area under the rib cage and above the belly button. It is the balancing point between the spiritual center of the heart and the physical center of the Tan Dien. This is where gut feelings are generated. It is where instinct notifies you of information received through energy awareness.

For the next few days, pay attention to your solar plexus as you come into contact with different people. Notice the sensations you have and how they change with the person's proximity to your personal space. Do you adjust as they come closer, opening or hardening your energy to manage their impact on you? Notice changes in the sensations of your solar plexus with different circumstances and activities. This is just an exercise. In daily life you don't need to focus so intently. Your energy awareness is automatic. All you need is to trust your instincts.

For example, you may suddenly feel angry as your gut tightens (your boundaries have been overstepped by another) or overwhelmed, drained, and grumpy (you gave away your boundaries and took on something that wasn't yours). You may not have noticed boundaries were being negotiated, but your emotions gave you the information you needed. You just need to listen to your feelings. If you're angry, it means something. If you're overwhelmed, it has an origin. Step back and ask your gut. What do your instincts tell you? Assess your needs. What requires balancing?

Often, the difficulty in balancing is in knowing how to take appropriate responsibility. Should you step up or step back? It can be challenging to know when you are taking over someone else's space or making a contribution. This is when you may want to rely on a set of principles and values. Go back to the list of the essentials of energy awareness and pose them to yourself as questions.

◇ What action addresses both the demands of the situation and your own needs?

◇ What maintains connection and also holds your space and center?

◇ What action feels less cluttered, clear, and clean?

◇ What honors both your path and the other person's?

As you ask these questions, notice what your gut feelings tell you, not the thoughts in your head and not the adrenaline in your body. Listen to your gut feelings.

Gift: Personal Power

What was that? You don't want personal power? You think personal power will make you unlikable? Personal power has nothing to do with money, clout, persuasion, selfishness, or indulgence. It is not about control or domination. *Personal power fuels your ability to respond to life.*

The word *power* generates conflict. In a paradigm of domination, power has been a tool of self-importance used to control other people and amass physical wealth and property. Abuse of power is rampant. You expect power to corrupt, you expect people in power to be corrupt, and you suspect the character of people who seek power. On the other hand, most people like the idea of being empowered. You want the confidence to make a meaningful contribution. You want enough self-esteem to have a voice, to manifest your creative vision, and to live with purpose and ease.

Personal power is the ability to express your spiritual essence. The truth is, you don't need more power to be empowered. You already have enough power. You are already a powerful being with the ability to create and manifest in the physical world. You do it all the time. The ways in which you think, act, and treat others create, manifest, and direct much of what happens in your life. What you need is more awareness of the qualities you bring to power and how your attention directs power and creates outcomes.

If you want to live life differently, you need to change what you pay attention to. Do you spend more time watching TV than being outside interacting with nature? Do you pay attention to the artificial constructs of humans rather than the natural flow of energy through your life? You can claim your personal power by taking command of your attention.

Attention used with intention changes situations. Intention focuses the power of your attention into a laser beam of coherent thought that interacts with the energy around you. Intentional attention is the vehicle for your spiritual essence to express itself. When you pay attention with intention, your Presence becomes a transformative force.

If you doubt the power of your attention, consider this: Your attention can completely transform another person's life. You don't have to do anything. Without breaching another person's boundaries, simply by enhancing your attention with unconditional love and support, you can make the difference between someone feeling valued or not. Your attention can be the expression of divine love in the physical world. How powerful is that?

The positive feelings you transmit through your Presence are not conferred on you through power; they are the qualities you bring to power.

The Practice of Balancing

How well you achieve Balancing depends on how you feel about boundaries. It is difficult to maintain boundaries if you believe you don't deserve them. This is where knowing yourself and what you need comes in. Every situation gives you a chance to know yourself better, sometimes because you are proud of your contribution and sometimes because you are not. Either way, you have learned something. How do you value yourself? How do you value others? How strong is your self-worth?

To achieve Balancing, start with an internal inventory. Boundaries need attention. Here are signs indicating when your boundaries are too open:

◇ Losing energy when engaged with a particular person or involved in a particular activity.

◇ Needing the approval of certain people in order to act.

◇ Needing to be involved in specific activities in order to feel full, powerful, or important.

◇ Getting to the end of each day without accomplishing the creative activities that fill you.

◇ Feeling you should be part of all the decisions and life events of family members or friends and being hurt when you are not.

◇ Enjoying withholding important information about yourself from others or severing connection as a means of punishment.

Here are some signs that boundaries are rigidly closed:

◇ Being unable to hear another's opinion without feeling threatened.

◇ Being uninterested in the accomplishments, thoughts, and enjoyment of others.

◇ Working to a set routine regardless of circumstances.

◇ Being unwilling to take time off work for family events.

◇ Pushing your agenda irrespective of others.

◇ Not sharing your personal thoughts, feelings, and ambitions with those you love.

Make a list of the situations and circumstances in your life that are challenging for you. Assess your boundaries. Are they too open or too closed? Have you established them in the right places or do you protect small things and let the important things slide? Do this exercise in relation to the people in your life.

Energetic boundaries may seem insubstantial and imaginary, however, even if you aren't sure that energy is real; at minimum, visualizing your boundary will guide the actions necessary to maintain them. Developing an awareness of your energetic boundary can help you clarify where you are too entwined with others and/or over invested in outcomes. Holding an energetic boundary can help you achieve clear, connected relationships. Here are the steps for establishing an energy boundary:

1. Using your breath, bring your attention into your body and into present time.
2. Determine that an arm's-length space around your entire body is your personal space.
3. Imagine your arms outstretched with palms facing outward. Affirm that this is outside.
4. Imagine your arms outstretched with palms facing inward. Affirm that this is inside.
5. Continue to switch back and forth between inside and outside, each time distinguishing the feel of the space inside your arm span with that of the outside.
6. Link your breath with the direction your palms are facing: Exhale while your palms face away and inhale while your palms face you.

The major obstacle you encounter when establishing energetic boundaries is the disbelief that they can work. You understand holding boundaries with behaviors and decisions, but something as intangible as energy is hard to grasp. The best way to build your confidence is to do this exercise and notice how your body feels. Do you feel stronger, more substantial, more attuned to your environment, and more aware of your needs? Then the energetic boundary is working.

The next obstacle is expectation. What your mind expects and what the experience provides are most likely different. Try to let go of projecting what you expect to feel and notice what you do feel, no matter how insignificant it seems. Expectations want experiences to be bigger than life. Expectations are made of movies and fairy tales. Real life is subtler, more substantial, and, when attuned to, more fulfilling. It takes work, however, to let go of Hollywood and let real life be enough.

Finally, obstacles to boundaries are created through false beliefs such as "I am not enough, I don't deserve to have (fill in the blank), I must give everything to be enough, my job is to take care of others," and so on. Hold onto these beliefs or let them go; it's your choice. If you want to let them go, start everyday with the exercise above. Fill the space around you with affirmations that reflect a larger truth. "I am enough. I deserve to pursue my path. I have a contribution to make. I can make my contribution in a balanced way." Create and use statements that affirm your deepest truth.

Here is a litany to establish your personal space. It is part of the closing prayer from the Navajo Way blessing ceremony:[3]

In beauty I walk
With beauty before me I walk
With beauty behind me I walk
With beauty above me I walk
With beauty around me I walk

What better way to hold your space than with a surround of beauty?

Self-Reflection

How much are you influenced by the opinions of others?

What directions have you taken in life because it was expected of you?

If the personal space around you were a room, what would it look like? What would you like it to look like?

In what ways do you feel too separated from others? In what ways do you feel too enmeshed?

Do you fear that if you become too large, you will outshine or dominate others?

Who do you have strong boundaries with? Who do you have weak boundaries with?

Where is the biggest imbalance in your life expressed? What underlying beliefs support it? What beliefs will give you better boundaries? How will better boundaries change this imbalance?

Do you assume responsibility for other people's choices?

How do you feel when you consider responsibility? Do you feel drained or inspired? What is out of balance with responsibility?

Do you need to be in control? What will happen if you are not? Is that truly what will happen?

Energy Exercises

The energetic boundary around your body is naturally present all the time. It is part of you. It responds to your thoughts, feelings, and beliefs, becoming more or less permeable in different situations. You can trust your boundaries to function, especially as you become clear on your needs and responsibilities. However, there are times when consciously holding and working with your boundaries is helpful in maintaining your integrity and direction. Doing these energy exercises will help in very concrete and physical ways

Exercise 1: Creating Strong Boundaries

Boundaries are strengthened with Grounding and Centering.

1. Take three deep, cleansing breaths, bringing your focus inside your body and into present time.
2. Using your breath, bring your attention into Earth and bring the strength of Earth up into your body, gather it in your Tan Dien, the area under your belly button in the bowel of your pelvis (see Chapter 4), then send it to your solar plexus and hold it there.
3. Bring your attention to the crown of your head and use your breath to fill your body with air and sky. Gather it in your heart, then send it to your solar plexus and add it the energy from Earth.

4. Imagine an arm's length space around you in all directions.

5. Breathe energy from your solar plexus into this area. Fill this space with light. It may help to give your breath a color and breathe that color into your personal space.

6. If needed, define this space using the previous exercise, alternating palms facing out and in.

7. Now imagine that the boundary you've created is semipermeable. Program it to let in what is helpful and keep out what isn't to let you shine while still respecting others. You create a program simply by intending it. See, feel, and support this function of your boundary.

8. As you engage your day, periodically check into your space and fill it with your breath.

9. Construct this semipermeable boundary when you want to engage energy activities or share meditations with other people to ensure your energy safety.

Start each day with this exercise and, as you encounter difficult situations, take a few unobtrusive breaths to keep your personal space defined. This doesn't mean people can't stand next to you; it means that when they do, your energy field doesn't collapse. Notice how you feel over time.

Exercise 2: Making Sacred Personal Sacred

This is a deeper exercise for creating the feeling tone you want to live inside of. Do it as a meditation when you can sit quietly and not be disturbed by outside interruptions.

1. Take three deep, cleansing breaths, bringing your focus inside your body and into present time.

2. Ground and center. Connect to your support and path.

3. Imagine the arm's-length area around you as a room in a house or a garden hidden in a beautiful landscape.

4. Using your imagination and felt-senses, explore this space. Imagine what color it is, how much light is present, and how cluttered or spacious it is. Notice if it feels comfortable or uncomfortable. Ask yourself what you need to know about the condition of your personal space and then wait to hear an answer.

5. Now use your imagination and felt-senses to create a space around you that supports you. What color would you like to use? What would support, nourish, and inspire you? Allow the space to develop around you until it feels safe and sustaining.

6. Inside this space, everything is you. Fill your personal space with the thoughts and intentions you want to send out as emissaries into the world. Extend your Presence all the way to the edge of the boundary. Notice how you feel.

Take this feeling with you into your day. When stressed, challenged, or depleted, submerge yourself in your sacred space by immersing yourself in this feeling.

Exercise 3: Balancing Boundary and Connection

One of the greatest challenges for many people is maintaining boundaries and connection simultaneously, which is essential for Balancing. Here is a meditation exercise to do when you are able to sit quietly and not be disturbed.

1. Take three deep, cleansing breaths, bringing your focus inside your body and into present time.

2. Ground and center. Connect to your center and path.

3. Define the arm's-length space around you using any of the above exercises. Clearly state, "This is me."

4. Image a person you are having trouble maintaining boundaries with. This can be your friend, spouse, child, parent, or boss. Visualize this person inside their own circle that extends arm's length around them. Clearly state, "This is you."

5. Repeat steps three and four until you have a felt-perception of the distinction between This is me and This is you.

6. Now imagine a stream of energy extending from your heart to theirs that has a two-direction flow.

7. Observe this connection. Notice color, thickness, vitality, how much energy it carries, how much is flowing to you, and how much is flowing from you to the other person. Ask yourself if this connection is comfortable and how you would ideally want it.

8. If this is not comfortable, or the way you would like it, what energetic change can you make? Does this change respect your boundaries and the other person's? If yes, imagine creating the change you want. You may find the shift has already happened. Often, as soon as you become aware of the answer, the energy immediately shifts.

9. When you meet this person in the physical world, hold the image of being simultaneously separate yet connected during your interactions. Notice what has changed.

The pillar of Aligning

PILLAR: Aligning
AWARENESS: Cyclical
CHALLENGE: Forced Action
RELATIONSHIP: Time
GATEWAY: Third Eye
GIFT: Synchronicity
EMOTION/ATTITUDE: Surrender
QUALITY BROUGHT TO PRESENCE: Ease

Prayer

It is late evening as I head back to the hospital. It's been a long afternoon catching up with well-wishing friends and making inquiries about home hospital beds for Erin's future discharge. Nearly everyone I speak with either starts or ends the conversation with the same words: "I'm praying for Erin. I'm praying that she will be fully healed."

I know the pure intention of these prayers and am grateful and honored to receive them, but truthfully, I don't understand prayer. In the vastness of the universe, with all the tragedy and pain, how can we presume to ask God, or whatever our conception is of the divine, to do our bidding? It is a conundrum that stiffens my resistance.

I arrive at the hospital as Erin's friends are preparing to leave. Erin looks brighter. She has less pain as her quadriceps muscle has quieted and gotten used to being stretched. The final surgery is schedule for tomorrow. Her friends have soaked her fingers and dug the old dirt from under her nails. She holds up her hands. She is a nine-year-old today, proud to show off her shaped, polished, and painted nails. Her hands contrast the blood-dried dreadlocks of hair she is still unable to wash. When the halo device is removed, she will have to cut the snarls out. Surprisingly, she looks strikingly beautiful with her tangled mop and steel-wrapped head.

Erin sounds tired as she says goodnight. Her friends troop from the room, leaving a trail of food wrappers and soda cans. After they are gone, she picks up the back scratcher and slides it under the vest that holds the metal bars attached to her head, wiggling to get to the itch. After all this time, there is still dried blood that clings to skin imbedded with road grit and glass. It is incomprehensible to me that she wasn't washed before the surgery that locked her into this device. No wonder she itches. I put on a wet-wipe glove and slide my hand under the vest to swab her back. She is losing weight and there is plenty of room. Although this is a nightly routine, the glove comes out tinged pink with blood and dotted with grit.

The night dose of pain medications close Erin's eyes and her breathing slows. I pick up cans and wrappers, fold blankets, and put away Erin's toiletries, passing time until I am certain she is settled before I leave. I know she wakes in the night in terrible pain. I know she would like me to stay. She never asks me to and never complains that I am not there in the dark hours. I only learn about her nightly episodes when nurses incidentally pose questions.

I sit to rest and my eyes instantly close. The rhythmic beeping of machines and monitors lulls me into the exhausted trance of semi-sleep. Prayers from all the people I've talked with swim in my head. The prayers turn into knights in armor and form lines to march forth to the various saints and godheads where they have been aimed. They all carry the same banner: Erin is broken—please fix her.

I notice how often prayer aligns to what is broken rather than to what is whole. I am sensitive to the opinion that Erin's path is waylaid. I know there is a larger picture behind events. Erin is 32, and 16 years ago, when she was 16, she was the passenger in another near-fatal car accident. Coincidence? Not likely. There are forces at work within Erin's psyche, forces that align her on this path for reasons I can't pretend to know.

In my semi-trance, the group of prayer knights amass over Erin's bed. They brandish swords in the air and fight for dominion over the healing of her wounds. I have not prayed for my daughter, not in words, anyway. I honestly don't know how. Prayer for me is an approach to life. Words are weak vehicles. They get in the way of my heart and limit my connection to spirit and source. The only way I know how to pray for my daughter is to find the essence of her wholeness and align with it.

I surround my daughter with my love. The image of knights battling overhead dissipates and a beam of living light forms around her. People's loving prayers are transformed into individual filaments within this beam, each one magnified a thousand fold. My tiny, insignificant flame is added to the immensity of the whole, and my single light becomes powerful and substantial.

In this moment, I understand that prayer is not petitioning a higher source to meet our desires. Prayer lifts our fragment of light and magnifies it in the larger whole. Regardless of what divine essence is enlisted, regardless of whether words are used or not, prayer aligns us to higher forces and brings us into the flow of life. This living light celebrates Erin's path: the darkness she walks through and the light she carries into that dark.

I send all my love into this vision of wholeness. I see Erin embraced and upheld in light. I change my internal litany from alive, not dead, not paralyzed, and not brain damaged to alive, active, and aware. I send a wave of appreciation to the giver of every heartfelt prayer who has added to living light to this beam. I am beyond grateful.

Pillar: Aligning

The Pillar of Aligning celebrates you walking your path. No matter what challenge you face, Aligning acknowledges your success. Every effort to be fully yourself is embraced and magnified. You are far more successful than you realize.

Aligning provides synchronization between internal and external reality. Through Aligning, the path and purpose in your heart are brought into phase with the people and circumstances you move with through life. As with all the Pillars, Aligning is a natural tendency. You align with principles, goals, values, and standards of behavior that direct your choices. You choose activities to progress your ambitions that align with people, organizations, and educational institutions. However, if aligning to these takes you away from the intentions of your heart and path, you will have a hard time staying in flow. The movement of your life will take more effort.

The essence of the Pillar of Aligning is movement. Movement is the underlying unifying factor of the universe. Everything moves, and when you move in concert with the flow, life is a dance. Picture the harmonized movement of planets, solar systems, and galaxies or the accelerated film of a flower head tracking the sun. Then consider getting stuck in heavy traffic. Imagine tuning in to the openings in the traffic and flowing through these openings so you continue to travel gently and effortlessly down the road. What current can carry you through a traffic jam? Asking the question begins the process of feeling the answer.

The Pillar of Aligning harmonizes the forces at play in your life to create opportunity. When you are in sync, you flow into the openings. Opportunity is everywhere. It shifts and changes like the light through a prism as the sun moves. Doors open and others close, strengthening, weakening, and directing the flow. Sometimes, you choose the direction of life by the doors that are open. Other times, the direction is determined by the doors that are closed.

Erin's accident closed doors. Now she needs to shift her focus from what she can't do to find opportunity in what exists. Closed doors direct the current more strongly toward those that are open. If something in your life is frustrating you, doors might be closing to direct you into a current that better aligns with your heart. Which of your intentions opens your heart and allows you to be the most complete version of you? Which align you to the larger forces at work in your life?

Both lack of movement and movement that is out of synch creates resistance in your activities and ill health in your body. Such movement doesn't flow. To create flow, your heart needs to hold your path in harmony with the outside world. Your emotions reflect how aligned you are. Uplifting emotions let you know you are on course and disquieting emotions are directing you to make adjustments in what you are doing, who you are doing it with, or how you doing it. In every situation, there is at least one vision that is big enough to unite your inner truth with external events.

The vision you align with creates opportunity; your feelings produce motivation and your words open the door for your actions to step through.

Awareness: Cyclical

Aligning is achieved through awareness of cycles, phases, and patterns. In everyday awareness, events are sequential and described by Newtonian physics of cause and effect. In this mindset, events one or two steps in front of a situation are considered the cause. This linear cause and effect way of thinking gives rise to the idea there are only two choices: right or wrong. You can take the right path or the wrong one; you can say yes or no. Choice is linked to a hierarchy of power and achievement, a ladder of success.

The awareness of cycles, phases, and patterns sees beyond cause and effect to overriding forces. Like the phases of the moon, actions also have phases that precede and follow each other. Does the phase before a full moon cause the moon to become full, or is the revolution of the moon around the Earth and the Earth around the sun responsible? In the same way, there is a pattern in the movement in your life that is determined by a larger concept that you are living out. If you can step back to feel the pattern and align with the force that creates it, you can flow with the opportunity within each phase.

Cyclical awareness brings together fate with free will. Fate is the part of life determined by your birth. You are born in a specific time period that has specific challenges. Being born in 1920, growing up in the Great Depression, and serving in World War I brought a different fate to young people than being born in 1980 during a time of affluence and no imminent world war. What choices you make, how you carry out your dreams, and how you respond to fate is free will. Cyclical awareness helps you see the intersection between the two so that you know where to flow with fate and where you to exert free will. This awareness allows you to create a life map to align with.

Cyclical awareness frees you from hierarchies. There is no best part of a cycle. A cycle holds all the phases within a pattern from inception to completion. Sometimes, especially in long cycles, it can be difficult to identify the overall pattern and individual phases of a situation to know what to align with. A basic cycle that most situations fall within is a growth cycle. Think of a plant: A seed is planted in fertile soil and nourished. It grows into a plant, is harvested, and returns to Earth to become soil for the next planting. In every situation you encounter, try to determine the phase of the cycle the situation is in. Knowing the phase helps to know the direction of flow and what is needed in order to synch with the opportunities being generated.

When attention is paid to cycles, it's easier to anticipate what will be coming next and execute better judgment. If you discover a situation in its harvest phase, for example, rather than assume the good times will never end, you might prepare for winter. If you encounter a situation that is in its decline, rather than fight the forces of decay, you might remember that regrowth must be fertilized by the refuse of the past and find ways to use what is falling apart. If you engage a situation in the stage of seed, you might look for the conditions that nourish growth and invest in the situation rather than prepare too early for winter.

Cyclical awareness also focuses on the timing of movement. Your path may be perfectly aligned with the part of the cycle you are in, but timing requires you hold back or move forward more quickly. Timing is assessed through flow. Is everything lined up but not flowing? Are you feeling unready and watching events come together without you? Pay attention to the flow to decide your movement.

Aligning is a matter of feeling. If you are facing a choice or executing a task and encounter internal resistance, listen to it. Maybe you just can't settle or things just don't click. You can't figure out why, but things seem off. This is a clear indication that some part of the alignment is off. Wait, hold the task or choice in your mind's eye, and ask for insight. Don't try to create an answer, but also don't just let the situation go on as it has been. Hold the situation in your mind's eye as you evaluate different scenarios with how they make you feel. Does a scenario increase or decrease your disquiet? Does it create a sudden eureka feeling that blasts through the problem?

The foundations of cyclical awareness are the following:

◇   All aspects of life are part of greater cycles.

◇   Different cycles synchronize with each other and create moments of opportunity.

◇   Your path is balanced between fate and free will.

◇   The intersection between external events and your internal path happens in your body.

◇   Resistance, disquiet, and agitation communicate being out of phase with some aspect of what you are doing and require that you go within to find answers.

Cyclical awareness helps you follow the feeling that opens your vision and/ or actions to the greater cycle. Then your choices and actions are aligned with the opportunity within that phase.

Challenge: Forced Action

Do you know the feeling of working as hard as you can and getting nowhere? Conversely, have you felt the enjoyment of having your work fall into place to produce effortless result? The biggest challenge to Aligning is using so much force or will power to get where you want that you override the subtle timing and flow of events. Overcoming the use of force engages a concept called wei-wu-wei: the art of not doing, also known as wu-wei, the practice of non-action. To the Western mindset, this is a foreign concept.

In a world obsessed with action, wei-wu-wei offers the opportunity to simply be. Whereas movement is necessary and unavoidable, action frequently is neither. Action has the tendency to push opportunity prematurely and waste energy; non-action conserves energy by moving into opportunity through Aligning. Wei-wu-wei does not mean you are never to take action; it means the action you take is so perfectly placed that it uses the least amount of effort for the greatest result. It means moving away from engaging your will power to engaging your felt-perceptions of the current and timing of events.

Wei-wu-wei frees the need for endless activity. In fact, wei-wu-wei implies that the amount of activity you undertake may be getting in the way of accomplishing your goals or interfering with achieving your goals with ease. The idea that you can do less and achieve more, however, may stir up enormous doubt. How can things happen if you aren't busy doing what's necessary? What if you miss the next rung of the ladder, or worse, what if you fail and fall off the ladder altogether?

Well, if you want to, you can get back on. Or you might look around and find there is more to life than the ladder of success. You might find that the concept of achievement needs revisioning. Are you alive on this planet, at this time, to experience or to do? Wei-wu-wei helps you do what your heart compels, rather than getting lost in doing all that you feel obligated to, based on expectations, greed, and fear.

To find the flow of opportunity, observe events alongside what you feel. You may be saying, "Oh great, another thing to pay attention to" and are experiencing overwhelm. Actually, this is the same paying attention that is part of each one of the Pillars: Pay attention to events alongside what you feel and let your felt-perceptions guide you. This process is difficult only because of conditioning that suppresses the subtlety of feelings.

The Pillar of Aligning shifts you out of endless running after situations and objects that you think will make you happy, only to find that when you achieve them, you are no happier than you were before. Aligning awakens you to deeper senses. You don't have to learn a new skill or develop a new ability; you already have the senses you need, and you are already using them. Now become conscious of using them by paying attention to what you feel and using the information to guide your choices. And if you feel nothing, be willing to sit with nothing and what it means to you, rather than hiding from it through activity.

Though Aligning is about timing, to some degree, timing relies on the intention within your goals. Consider Vincent Van Gogh, an artist who created extraordinary works that are still greatly admired today. In his lifetime, however, he never sold a painting. Did Van Gogh miss out on the timing that would have brought him exceptional recognition and wealth, or was his vision so far ahead of the consciousness of the world that his role was that of pathfinder? Either way, he never stopped creating.

If things aren't happening as quickly and fruitfully as you hope, chances are that using more force and working longer hours won't help. Consider that a bigger cycle is underway and make an intention to align with it. Adjust your activity to synchronize with the bigger picture. Things may well be happening, but not in the time frame you're imagining. The deeper question is always this: Are you fulfilled by what you are doing simply from the joy of doing it, or is it only fulfilling if it brings the results you hope for?

Relationship: Time

Time, the ticking clock of the human dance, is the background noise that keeps you from trusting that you can move without undue action, that doing what you love will bring what you need, and that there is value in taking time to feel. For the most part, relationships with time are adversarial. Do you try to beat the clock to fit more into each minute than the previous minute held? Time is a constant reminder of aging and the reality that all shall eventually pass away.

Time is measured by how long it takes the Earth to revolve on its axis and travel the distance of its orbit around the sun. The number of revolutions and orbits are kept track of in calendars. Time relates to distance. It separates events and objects. Phrases like "that town is three days away" demonstrate the link between time and distance, and "I'm three days from finishing" create a link between time and work. As technology changes, the concept of distance and the idea of how much work can be accomplished in a day changes, also—hence, the perception that time is speeding up. In reality, the Earth moves around the sun at the same rate it always has; our activity is what is speeding up.

Time also tracks events and keeps them in sequential order to become history. Part of the adversarial relationship with time comes from this view that time is a linear sequencing of events. This perception creates a mindset of limitation. One of the first things noticed on entering the present time awareness of the Pillar of Being is the complete loss of time. The physical body is still governed by the movement of the sun across the sky, but awareness becomes infinite and timeless. In this state, Einstein's theory of special relativity seems proved—that time is not constant but changes with speed; as speed increases, length contracts and time expands.

There are other ways of perceiving time that create a different relationship. When I first studied the calendar of the Maya, my perception shifted so dramatically that my brain felt as though it had rotated inside my skull. The ancient Maya did not see time in a linear succession. They exceeded our short view of time based on the cycle of the Earth and sun, and based time on interlocking patterns among our Earth and sun, planets in our solar system, other solar systems, and star constellations. They watched sky patterns to know the precession of the equinoxes and understood qualities of the dark rift in the center of the galaxy that our scientists have only learned about in recent decades.[1]

Time for the Maya was an exquisite dance of alignments between interlocking spheres that created the qualities and experiences of life. Rather than a linear progression, time was a series of repeating patterns that determined relationships between celestial objects.

In today's worldview, time is nothing more than a measure. It has no inherent quality of its own as it is only a canvass on which we write history. To the ancient Maya, time was formative. Time had its own set of qualities that were reflected in events. So rather than events creating the quality of a time period, such as the hippie movement creating the quality of the 1960s, the quality of time in the 1960s, based on the alignments within celestial cycles, created the hippie movement. For the ancient Maya, time was the holy enactment of a cosmic plan.

Just for a minute, step back and perceive time in the light of the ancient Maya. Imagine all these celestial bodies moving in a complicated dance pattern in concert with each other. The points where one body aligns with another are points of contact in which pathways of interaction are created. Energy flows along these pathways. Can you see-feel what it would be like to link with these pathways and have your life propelled within this flow? The Maya based their entire cosmology on the pulsing of energy through the Earth as celestial bodies came into and out of alignment.

You are naturally aligned to these flows. The more connected you are to nature, the easier it is to feel them. Hooking your actions to these cycles anchors your intentions with nature and aligns you to larger patterns. You don't need to fund movement with your own energy. When you are in alignment, movement is powered with the energy of flow. Time changes from being a measure of activity to being a vehicle of movement. It changes from limiting your choices to creating the pathways for them to happen.

Coming from the present day and age, there is little chance any of us can fully emerge ourselves in this ancient concept of time. However, it is an interesting practice to feel the view of the Maya. It helps the step into wei-wu-wei by assuring that there is a larger rhythm and design at work. If you can align with this perception, life becomes infinitely easier.

Gateway: Third Eye

The gateway into Aligning is the combination of feeling and visioning called active imagination. This combination is not foreign; it is so innately a part of how you think and perceive that you may not even be aware of using it. However, everything you feel or think creates an image in the mind's eye. Consider an apple. Immediately you see it in your mind. The image evokes the perception of taste, the memory of past enjoyment, and possibly the belief that eating it is good for your health. All of these—the image, felt-perception, memory, and belief—come together to create your opinion of an apple. This impression is your natural, instinctive response to the lightning-fast subconscious process.

Imagery linked to feelings is a language that predates verbal communication. It is the language of the subconscious mind. Consequently, the use of active imagination used in Aligning activates the subconscious mind from which your inner knowing and body wisdom originate. The combination of images, feelings, perceptions, and beliefs that form your instinctive interaction with the world is consciously used to synchronize you with the flow of external events.

The process of Aligning is similar to that of visualization in that it consciously works with imagery to create your intention. In visualization, you construct an image in your mind's eye of what you wish to create in the world. The process of Aligning differs in that it is receptive, forming the image in your mind's eye from your subconscious perceptions. Consequently, Aligning accesses your essential self, not just the part of self that is based in desire.

It is draining and exhausting to live outside the flow of natural cycles, to live in action rather than in movement. Aligning keeps you in the flow of movement. Aligning acknowledges that you are part of something bigger and helps you flow within the current.

Gift: Synchronicity

The forces at work in everyday life are grand and large. You may not see them, but you certainly feel their effect. The stream of energy that orients people and events creates synchronicity, the meaningful coincidence that affirms your direction and timing. Synchronicity is the gift of Aligning.

Synchronistic events bring seemingly unrelated people and events into contact at significant moments. For example, you might be engaged in a project and need a particular piece of information, only to board an airplane and find your seat is next to the world's leading authority on that topic. Or you may not even know you need a particular person or piece of information until it shows up exactly when you realize its value. In the creative process, synchronicity keeps the project moving forward with vitality. You are puzzled by a problem only to open your inbox and find the solution provided in an unsolicited e-mail. The boost of energy from this event moves you forward with renewed vigor.

Most often, synchronicity is important not because of its content but because of its timing. The synchronic event validates your course. Sometimes, it can feel as though you're swimming against the tide, and no matter how hard you work, your goal gets further away. You wonder if you are on the right path and ask questions such as: Is this right for me, am I missing something important, or am I sabotaging myself? Synchronicity at this point might help you stay the course, reveal where you are out of balance, or show you what needs to change. Resistance to the direction you are taking may offer course correction. When synchronicity happens in the midst of chaos, pay attention to what you were thinking about, the direction you were considering, or the particular events that were occurring for clues to the direction of change that is calling.

Delays and disappointments don't necessarily mean you're moving in the wrong direction. Rather, subtle modifications may be underway to adjust your timing. A simple example would be driving over the limit because you're late to an appointment, being slowed by a squirrel running into the road only to discover that you are saved from a hidden police trap and speeding ticket. It's good to remember that sometimes setbacks and side tracks are operating within a plan beyond your awareness.

Synchronicity lets you know that you are aligned with the flow, traveling alongside other things in the flow, and all is well in the universe.

The Practice of Aligning

Aligning requires feeling as much as thinking. A jockey once told me of surging forward on her horse during a race into an opening in the field of galloping horses that hadn't been there when she began her move. The opportunity appeared as she arrived. She explained that she had felt the opening forming within the flow of movement. Did her intent to move forward create the hole, or did the alignment of events reveal themselves in her feeling? Sometimes, it is both.

The steps to Aligning are intending, perceiving, harmonizing, and allowing. While this process happens naturally, slowing down and paying attention to the unfolding of steps allows the process to be conscious. At first, take the time to sit in a receptive, meditative state. Later, you will be able to use the steps naturally and quickly in the midst of unfolding events.

Here's how:

1. Create an intention of something you want to create. This can be as modest as creating a happy family outing or as sweeping as designing the map of your business. If you are not sure how to make an intention, skip ahead to Chapter 12.

2. Open your mind and allow a vision of your intention to form in your mind's eye. What does your question or intention look like when it is lived? Ask for the highest good to be reflected. Allow the image to develop as an extension of the creative interaction between your imagination and felt-senses. Be willing to be surprised.

3. Harmonize to the vision through your emotions. As the vision develops in your mind's eye, you will feel different emotions. When the vision fully reflects you essential self, you may feel a rush of emotion and flow of energy that harmonizes your intention with your heart and path.

4. Allow this vision to guide your choices so that your movement is effortless. While you are sitting in contemplation,

consider some choices and feel for the action-steps that align with events to enact your vision. Allowing looks for ease of movement.

The first challenge in the process of Aligning is what to do if no vision presents itself. In this case, you will need to actively create a vision. Rather than creating exactly what you want, however, create one that feels right, even if it looks different from what you ideally want. Feeling right might be when your vision creates a sense of opening that relaxes or inspires you. Or it might be when your vision unites and uplifts a difficult situation or when your vision creates a rush of energy and you feel more alive. Finding your visioning is an important step in Aligning, so try not to rush through it. Once you've got the vision, stay open to changes.

The second issue is how to harmonize with the vision through emotions. Emotions that harmonize your heart and path with the various elements in life include compassion, gratitude, unconditional love, awe, and devotion. If you love your vision, you will harmonize with it. If you don't, it may not represent your essential self and path. Continue to work with it until you really love it and are devoted to manifesting it in the world.

The third challenge is letting go of action and allowing: the wei-wu-wei of Aligning. Although allowing seems passive, it is not. Rather, allowing is an activity that occurs within the flow. It is matching your ideal or goal to the natural world and greater good. Allowing holds the vision of an intention and feels for the course of action that takes you the furthest with the least effort. With allowing, you feel for the hole through the activity around you, hook into the current, and move.

You can use the process of Aligning to sync with the timing of events, establish a course of action, assist your creative process, receive spiritual direction, ease tension in interpersonal dynamics, and pretty much any other objective you can think of. The exercises below will get you started.

When you begin to use the Pillar of Aligning, the effort of striving eases. You bring a transmission of ease and surrender to your Presence.

With Aligning, wherever you are, whatever it looks like, you know there is purpose in being there. You know that everything you experience, however challenging, can be used in the process of self-discovery. You are able hold the question: What benefit can my Presence bring to this moment?

Self-Reflection

How is your life ruled by time?

Does your calendar control your life, or is it a tool to design the rhythm of your life? How do the two differ?

When do you trust your feelings? When do you override them? How has that worked for you?

Can you identify rhythm and design in your life? Can you envision larger forces at work?

Do your intentions open your heart and allow you to be the most complete of you?

What patterns have repeated in your relationships, business plans, and creative expression?

What parts of your life are aligned with your heart-based intention? What is out of alignment?

What people in your life are you in alignment with? Who are you out of alignment with? What, if anything, wants to change?

Are you fulfilled by the simple joys of what you do?

Are you fulfilled by the results of your effort?

Does the fear of missing out drive your activity?

Do other people drive your activity? How does that occur?

What do you feel when you miss an opportunity?

Imagine a time when your life flowed smoothly and easily. Can you identify what you were aligned with? Can you identify the emotions that harmonized you?

How are you different when you feel in alignment with a larger design? Can you use these differences to gage your alignment?

How has synchronicity shown up in your life?

Have you ever been fooled by synchronicity into believing you are acting with consciousness when you're actually projecting what you want onto the canvass of time?

What is a solid measure that synchronicity is confirming your path?

Energy Exercises

The exercise of intending, perceiving, harmonizing, and allowing can be used to align you with any goal, person, or elements. This process is used more fully in Chapter 12. These exercises to get you started are best done sitting quietly in a meditative state.

Before starting one of these exercises, create an intention for what you want to align with. What is the emotion or feeling of achieving this intention? Hold the intention in your mind while you generate the feeling in your heart. Allow the feeling to flow into the future where your intention resides. Open your mind.

Exercise 1: Aligning With Flow

This exercise achieves the deepest result when engaged in a natural setting.

1. Take three deep breaths and bring your mind into your body to occupy present time. Ground, center, and establish balance.
2. Immediately feel yourself sinking into Earth. Reach with your awareness and feel Earth welcome you.
3. Notice the sounds around you. Let go of identifying them and breathe into the sounds instead. Bring them inside your body, where you have access to everything.
4. Notice the pattern of the sounds. Feel the cadence of the birds, wind, and other elements. Notice how they resonate inside. What feelings do they generate? What patterns do they instigate?
5. Without directing or designing, feel yourself part of the symphony. If you feel to move in response to what you feel, then

move. Enjoy yourself. Understand yourself as part of this matrix, not outside of it, not directing it, and not above. You are part of it; even when you resist, you can't be anywhere other than where you are. You are here. You are a part of everything around you.

6.   Allow yourself to feel that you belong.

7.   If you want to go a step further, open your awareness to the celestial bodies that partner with Earth in a cosmic dance through time and space. Let your perspective expand and feel Earth and other celestial bodies as they travel together. What do you notice?

8.   Imagine the pulsing of celestial energy into Earth being guided by steps dancing in the patterns of sacred geometry that organize the physical world.

9.   Feel the dance. The dance is all there is. Join in.

10. When you are ready, return to everyday awareness, ground, center, and balance.

Exercise 2: Aligning With the Design of Your Life

1.   Take three deep breaths and bring your mind into your body to occupy present time. Ground, center, and establish balance.

2.   Imagine your mind's eye as a blank screen. Invite all the people, animals, activities, and events that you love to be revealed on this screen.

3.   Let your love and enjoyment grow as more images fill the screen.

4.   Accept that your love is the unifying force for everything you see. Notice in what unique way your love unifies all the images.

5.   Is there an overarching theme?

6.   Whether or not you see a pattern or theme doesn't really matter; what aligns you to the design of your life are your feelings of love.

7. Think of things every day that generate feelings of love. Create a fountain of love that flows into the world. Bathe the people around you in love. Offer the current of love to the plants and animals. Offer the current of love to Earth and the divine. Be lifted into divine love.

8. Love flows with the design of life. Keep love flowing, and you will be aligned to the design of your life.

Exercise 3: Decision-Making Through Aligning

1. Take three deep breaths and bring your mind into your body to occupy present time. Ground, center, and establish balance.

2. Give thanks to Earth and sky, your guides and beneficent forces, seen and unseen, for this opportunity to receive insight and help.

3. Hold the decision you are making in your mind's eye.

4. Imagine you are sitting in a council circle.

5. Place a chair in the circle for each choice you are considering. Add a chair for the choice you are unaware of.

6. Allow each choice, even the choice you are unaware of, to become a person. Notice what each choice looks like, what expression is on each face, what clothes are worn, and what Presence is projected.

7. Focus on each image individually. What do you notice? How do you feel sitting with this person as your partner? How much energy is flowing?

8. If you are drawn to the choice you are unaware of, ask that image for insight. Sit and allow whatever images, feelings, and thoughts to be present without judgment.

9. At the end of this exercise, you may have a good idea of the direction to take. If you don't, be willing to wait. Watch your dreams and revisit the council circle. Ask what information you are missing.

8

The pillar of clearing

PILLAR: Clearing
AWARENESS: Emotional Awareness
CHALLENGE: Processing in Present Time
RELATIONSHIP: Shadow
GATEWAY: The Voice
GIFT: Soul-Force
EMOTION/ATTITUDE: Humility
QUALITY BROUGHT TO PRESENCE: Vibrancy

Hitting Bottom

My chest hurts. It's difficult to breath. Erin sleeps soundly, yet I'm not ready to go home. It was a bad day. For the first time, beyond the managing of pain, there is fear in Erin's eyes. She is understanding that no matter how much she heals, she will never be the same. In all likelihood, she will never again be without pain. I know the debilitating effects of intractable, chronic pain. This is the primary challenge for the majority of people in my naturopathic practice. My heart breaks.

I am sinking into dark. Every conceivable fear wends roots into the depths of me. There are so many things to fear. What if Erin is never able to resume a normal life? What if her pain causes an addiction to painkillers? What if she is unable to work? What if she becomes depressed or suicidal?

The what-ifs are endless. They circle like vultures then land in the ever-present field of money. The driver in the accident was underinsured. I fear for Erin's out-of-pocket expenses for medical bills, co-pays, and physical therapy. She may have years of rehab ahead, never mind lost wages. I fear for her future. Even so, I am proud of the stance she takes. Clearing herself of fear, her choices are made from the heart. She withstands the pressure of lawyers to sue.

Erin and I are not alone in hitting bottom today. Earlier, my younger daughter, Adriel, calls in tears.

"Momma," she sobs. "I have to come home. I have to be there!"

Adriel recently moved to California. It is difficult for her to be away in this crisis. She is willing, without hesitation, to walk away from a new job she worked hard to land. She will do whatever is necessary for her sister.

"No, honey, don't come. We need you where you are," I insist. I would like nothing better than the company of my youngest. Her Presence is the family balm, the comfort that soothes troubled water. But I will not agree to sacrifice her.

"What do you mean?" Adriel cries. "She's my sister; I have to be there!"

"Adriel," I implore. "You are Erin's connection to normal. We need you where you are. We need you to remind us of the real world."

"I don't get it," she says, sniffling. "What does that mean?"

I take a breath and try to explain. "In the hospital, everything revolves around your sister's injuries and recovery. It's like a big bubble in an alternate universe. She is becoming acclimated to it. She is forgetting normal."

"Is that bad?" she asks.

"Well, it's what's needed now. But she also needs an anchor to the outside world. She needs to remember where she's heading. Just keep calling her every day. Be her touchstone to normal. I know you want to be here. But think about it."

It's difficult to describe the importance of something outside hospital walls for Erin to align with. Adriel's phone calls are her lifeline out of the labyrinth of her own concerns.

Adriel is quiet for a long time before she reluctantly concedes, adding, "But only if you promise to tell me the minute anything goes downhill. If things get worse, I want to be there."

"Of course," I readily agree.

I understand Adriel's feeling of being left out. I am feeling much the same. Before the accident, I was spearheading an event that held immense importance to me. Now plans continue without me. I don't hear from people to know what is or isn't happening. In my head, old records play. I am left out and left behind. Like Erin, I need a lifeline to my previous life. I need to know normal still exists.

With no diversion, there is nowhere to go except the dark, and I descend to another level of buried emotion, one I have been intent on avoiding: A second accident occurs the week after Erin's involving another resident of our town. The injuries to the passenger, a lovely young girl alive with promise, are nearly identical to Erin's injuries. This girl dies. The community is rocked by grief.

I am a mix of so many emotions that I cannot attend them all: grief and sorrow overlaid with guilty relief. I am so grateful my daughter is alive. I can barely spare a thought for this other mother. Her loss makes me feel apologetic for my own fortune, so I avoid thinking of her.

I pass the funeral on my way to the hospital and am drawn to go inside to offer my Presence in support and solidarity. But what can I say? That I am the mother whose daughter didn't die? I don't stop. For all the reasons my friends don't call, for all the reasons I have not showed up for others in the past: I am afraid I will cause more harm than good. I'm afraid I don't have anything of value to offer. Without the benefit of Clearing, I am ruled by fear and limiting beliefs.

Pillar: Clearing

Clearing is the Pillar that provides integration. Old patterns that distort reality are addressed to bring healing and welcome others into your Presence. With Clearing, preoccupation with fear, worry, and self-doubt is reduced so that you can accept and forgive yourself and those around you. Staying present through difficult emotions without projecting or deflecting what you feel gives your Presence safety. Through Clearing, your internal space stays alive and vibrant. You are able to show up in difficult situations and be present.

It is normal and natural to have fears, especially in the unknowns after a tragedy. Sometimes, however, fear is based in unprocessed feelings. Clearing shifts stuck emotional patterns and the beliefs they generate. As discussed in previous chapters, these patterns can be quite old and the memory of their origin buried within long standing muscle tension. Patterns are often developed in childhood. As a child, you may have learned that the expression of powerful emotions and the bad behavior those emotions can generate aren't acceptable. Perhaps you were scolded and shamed, as few parents are trained to help children process their feelings. Consequently, the feelings you were punished for expressing have been buried in your body. Over time, the suppression of unwanted feelings becomes an automatic, unconscious response.

It would be one thing if burying unwanted feelings meant that they simply disappeared, but buried emotions accumulate. They become hidden forces that direct your actions, decisions, and behaviors. The longer unwanted emotions are submerged, the more power they gather. Because they are unconscious, the behaviors they generate are assumed to be personality flaws. Sadly, suppressed feelings distort your self-image and unconsciously impact conditions and opportunities in your life, as well as short-circuiting your intuition.

Unprocessed emotions create limiting beliefs. A fear of rejection, for example, may cause you to believe that you are unlovable. With that as a foundation, you might imagine an innocent comment from another person means something it doesn't. Imagine someone has to reschedule a get-together that stimulates your feelings of rejection and causes you to conclude, "She probably has something better to do." The next time you see this person, without knowing if your thought was true or not, you might give her the cold shoulder to protect yourself from further hurt.

Isolation becomes what you expect the world to deliver, and so you interpret and attract such experiences.

Unprocessed emotions cause complicated behaviors others might not understand, especially because they contend with their own unconscious issues. The essence of Clearing frees old patterns, producing new ones to uphold a truer idea of what life is and what you have to offer.

Awareness: Emotional Awareness

The awareness of the Pillar of Clearing recognizes emotions as part of your sensory system and makes them available for guidance. All emotions have function. They provide direct and immediate information and generate the energy needed to act on the information given. Whereas you easily understand uplifting emotions, the use of uncomfortable emotions isn't always obvious. However, fear lets you know you are in danger and generates adrenaline to fight or flee; anger tells you your boundaries have been challenged and gives you the strength to defend them. A chart of the function and action of 25 common emotions, adapted from *The Path of Emotions*, is found in the Appendix.

The late Dr. Candace Pert, PhD, neuroscientist, and author of *Molecules of Emotions* (Scribner, 1997), discovered that emotions are generated in the body and carried on the chemical messengers of neuropeptides. She demonstrated the existence of a biochemical communication network between the brain and body, revealing that emotions are whole-body events that form the mind-body connection.[1] Her work significantly advanced the study of emotional intelligence.

As information providers, emotions are designed to be short lived. They rise to deliver a message and prompt change, then recede. Emotions that hang around haven't been listened to. Because emotions have a directive to complete their job; they remain until their message is received. The task of emotional awareness is to receive emotional messages, discern whether they are present time emotions or emotions from the past, use the information, and then discharge the energy that the emotion carried.

Suppressed emotions that surface in current situations tell you where you got stuck in the past, not necessarily what is happening today. If you expect rejection, the emotion of being rejected is no longer a reliable sensor; it is a patterned response. Rather than a signal of what is going on, the response is a faulty antenna that detects all input as the same. Emotional awareness identifies the pattern so you can use the process of Clearing and evaluate the truth in the beliefs that created your circumstances.

In their pure essence, emotions provide the basis of deeper perception. They synthesize what you see and hear with the undercurrents of energy in the environment around you to create your intuition. This type of perception listens to and utilizes emotional insights to discern deeper reality and improve the quality of your life.

Here are the essentials of emotional awareness:

◇ Emotions are part of your internal guidance system.

◇ Every emotion carries useful information along with the faculty to respond.

◇ Emotions are the language of subtle energy. They bring energy interactions into direct awareness and reveal the energetic subtext of life.

◇ Emotions are the communication link between the mind and the body.

◇ Emotions reveal information about the present or show you where you got stuck in the past.

◇ By paying attention, you can identify and neutralize old emotional patterns.

Throughout the Eight Pillars, feelings and emotions are used as guideposts for understanding the significance of events, the direction of your path, and the messages from your heart.

Emotional awareness provides the mindfulness to receive the information carried in your emotions and then use the energy they generate for positive change.

Challenge: Processing in Present Time

The challenge to Clearing is the ability to process emotions as they happen. In a natural state, emotions rise, you process the information they contain and respond in a manner that discharges the energy. Imagine being in the middle of the street you are crossing only to realize you have walked in front of an oncoming bus. Fear floods your body to inform you that, yes indeed, you are in danger. The rush of fear releases adrenaline, and you suddenly have the speed of an Olympic sprinter as you leap out the way. You received the information and used the energy the emotion provided. It may take a few minutes to recover from the herculean effort and flood of adrenaline, but the emotion has been processed and discharged.

Here's another scenario for the same situation. You realize you have walked in front of a bus and fear floods your system. Before you can act, however, you are pulled to safety by a helpful onlooker. In this situation, you received the information from your fear and your body was filled with energy to act, but you didn't release the energy in action. Fortunately, your body has a mechanism to deal with this. In his groundbreaking book, *Bioenergetics* (Penguin, 1976), Alexander Lowen explains that the body naturally discharges unused emotional energy through shaking, trembling, crying, laughing, sighing, yawning, and excessive sweating.[2] Saved, as you thank your rescuer, your legs shake and you alternate between uncontrollable laughter and crying.

Most people don't process their emotions in the present. To do so feels vulnerable and there is rarely time. Here's a real-life example of what present-time processing looks like from when my children were quite young. Two friends were visiting and they were all painting T-shirts. One of the girls, Chloe, made an amazing design of a large Earth complete with continents and oceans. To her dismay, one of the continents leaked into the ocean. Chloe was devastated and seemed overwhelmed with shame.

When the other kids ran out to play, Chloe stood in front of her T-shirt, visibly upset, clenching and unclenching her hands while gritting her teeth and frowning. Her forehead was wrinkled in concentration. After a few minutes, she began to shake, then gave a huge sigh before turning to smile at me and running outside to play. When her parents came to pick her up, she proudly displayed her T-shirt.

If Chloe had not processed her feelings around her perceived failure and discharged the energy through shaking and sighing, the emotion would have remained inside. Every time she looked at the T-shirt, she would have seen the damaged continent rather than the rest of her beautiful accomplishment. Through time, mixed with other unprocessed failures, it would become part of a limiting belief such as "I'm not good at art" or "I'm not creative."

Instead of processing as Chloe did, people diminish and dismiss what they feel, containing their emotional reactions through muscle tension. Then musculoskeletal pain develops along with trigger points that gets worse under stress. After a while, instead of feelings and emotions causing muscle tension, muscle tension begins to cause emotions. It's challenging to maintain an open, positive attitude when muscles are bound up, tight, and hurting.

Emotional awareness mindfully focuses attention on body clues to hidden feelings. Being aware of muscle tension, breathing patterns, and physical sensations leads to the emotional feelings stored in the tissue. The process of Clearing shifts the past out of the present.

Relationship: Shadow

Imagine there is a person inside of you who is everything you never want to be. Every unwanted feeling, suppressed emotion, and unacceptable thought that's ever plagued you has been sheered away and shoved inside this person. He or she has all the ugliness your parents warned you to avoid and all the traits you worked hard all your life to submerge. Now imagine the energy it takes to keep this person under control. This person is your shadow self, the feelings and thoughts that you haven't processed and integrated.

The more suppressed and less integrated your shadow self is, the more it pops out in self-destructive, vindictive, or unconscious behavior. The expression of such behaviors may be so shaming they are responded to with even deeper repression. Imagine the little child spitefully enjoying the cries of his sibling when pinched, only to feel immense remorse with promises of "I'll never do it again!" Most people will not experience the full expression of their shadow, and some will hardly believe it's there so well have the unwanted impulses been hidden. Every one of us, however, has a shadow self and are influenced by its unconscious drives. To see the shadow's full expression only requires being part of a righteous crowd. Then the unthinkable within is released.

In contrast, consider you also have a person inside who is the very best of the best of what you can envision. This person represents all the lofty aspirations of who you want to be: the very highest attributes, most altruistic motivations, and extraordinary gifts. You never really believe you can be this person, but you sure hope everyone else sees this image when they think of you! This person is your persona—the mask you put on for the world. The bigger your persona, the more afraid you are of not being quite good enough and the harder you work to be accepted.

The size of the persona is relative to the size of the shadow self. The two are opposite sides of the same coin. Neither the shadow self nor the persona are expressions of your essential self, yet both exert tremendous power. Created from the process of separating unwanted thoughts and feelings and submerging them, the shadow self's need for expression becomes a force the persona must always guard against.

There is no way to eliminate the shadow self. It must be integrated. The submerged parts of self have to be embraced and brought home. Integrating and owning all the hurts, judgments, rejections, and fears that create the shadow are the only ways to neutralize its hidden power and turn it into a constructive force. That means dropping the persona and facing hidden feelings. Acceptance brings the shadow self out of the dark. As the shadow integrates, the need for the persona disappears.

Do you have daily feelings and thoughts of not being good enough, not being lovable, or being unfit to offer your light? Do you hear yourself regularly saying such things as "I hate so-and-so; she makes me crazy!"? Because the shadow is the part of self that isn't accepted, it is typically

projected into the world. Listen to how often you use the words *I hate* or
I can't stand it when . . . Now imagine you are saying these things to yourself. Imagine what you hate about people is what you can't accept within
your shadow self. Imagine that the love and acceptance you feel other
people withhold from you is really the love and acceptance you withhold
from yourself.

Integrating the shadow self has immediate and tangible benefits.
First, you don't have to spend so much energy in defense. Your muscles
can relax, and you can engage in richer, more meaningful encounters with
people and express your truth rather than what you think people want to
hear. Life immediately becomes more meaningful.

Second, because the shadow works through the unconscious mind, it
is responsible for self-sabotage. Integrating the shadow opens the door to
greater, more fulfilling opportunity. You might find, however, that what
you previously thought you wanted doesn't really fulfill your true self. It
was fulfilling the persona: what you thought you needed to project into
the world to be accepted. Integrating the shadow frees your true path and
purpose. It allows you to be your authentic true self.

Third, and most exciting, the shadow is the seat of your creativity. Creativity is born in the subconscious mind through the bringing
together of dissimilar pieces of information into an unlikely whole. Your
shadow self is the petty tyrant who holds the door to your subconscious.
The better friend you are with your shadow self, the more access you have
to creative thought and expression. Your shadow self controls the grist for
the mill, the material for your creative work.

Have you evaluated your relationship with your shadow self? Are you
ready to begin the process of integration? The first step is to let go of
the belief in evil and good and move into radical acceptance. The more
you can move beyond judging everything as right and wrong, spiritual or
material, the more accepting you can be of the divine mystery unfolding
around and within you in each moment, and the more you will be able to
embrace your shadow. Stop judging. Witness the divine. Accept the larger
design of your life and embrace yourself, warts and all.

Gateway: The Voice

The gateway into Clearing is the voice. Clearing gives voice to your shadow self and brings it out of the dark. Giving voice means remembering that while the message of unwanted feelings is uncomfortable, it is nonetheless important. The message carries information that you need to be whole. When the shadow self is brought out of the dark, it ceases to be a terrifying monster and becomes a small child, alone and abandoned.

One way to give voice to the shadow self is through bearing witness. This is not the legal process of someone who has witnessed a crime giving testimony to what they saw, although in a sense, you are giving testimony. You are testifying to the events that gave rise to the suppressed information the shadow self holds.

When you bear witness to your unwanted feelings you are showing up for yourself. When another person witnesses your process with you, the perception within their Presence shines light where you are stuck. This is a gift your Presence gives to others as well. Presence is witness, not judge, analyst, or commentator, offered to give a little more energy and a little more clarity for the work underway. Suggestions and observations wait until the processing of the emotion is over.

Having a witness to your process is an amazingly powerful concept. I don't know about you, but I have cried alone for hours and resolved nothing. My thoughts continued in a loop around the same events, and the feelings that were generated never changed. However, after five minutes of crying with someone else present, the shift into a new perspective occurs. Why and how this works is a beautiful mystery. That it works is undeniable.

When you witness for another, you don't really need to say anything; your Presence offers another set of eyes and ears so the other person can hear him or herself more clearly. There is an energetic exchange, an unconditional acceptance that facilitates Clearing when you work with a witness.

If you are looking to be part of such an exchange to process your stuck patterns, you might want to find a co-counseling or re-evaluation counseling group to join at *www.cci-usa.org* or *www.rc.org*. In these organizations, people learn how to witness for each other and there is no cost for therapy.

Gift: Soul-Force

Bearing witness is also a spiritual concept. Your Presence has power. When you bring your Presence to bear on a situation, just by being present, you provide energy and awareness. No matter how hopeless the situation or how little influence you have, your Presence makes a difference. Consider what it is like to be alone and in pain. Being alone can be worse than the pain itself. Your witness surrounds those who suffer (Earth, animal, and human) with fellowship. When your soul touches another soul, suffering is shared, giving proof that the essence within is greater than the suffering.

Bearing witness is traditional for the Society of Friends (Quakers) and part of Gandhi's vision of non-violent social change. Living your inner truth and using your Presence in witness of injustice gives birth to what Gandhi called soul-force, a person's full spiritual strength. Soul-force suggests that awakening awareness doesn't stop with personal growth. Change starts within, but it doesn't end there. As you become the change you want to see, you awaken to social responsibility, the ability to respond to another's suffering.

Soul-force is central to Gandhi's vision of non-violence and living the truth of your inner light in everyday affairs. If you believe you are powerless, the only course for self-defense is violence. If you know you are powerful, you can achieve greater results with soul-force. If you believe you are powerless to change injustice in the world, you may turn your back on cruelty and suffering. If you know the power and mysterious action of soul-force, you might use your Presence to bear witness. While bearing witness feels passive, it unleashes a powerful force. Consciousness is elevated and the perpetrator, the target, and the witness are changed.

Developing soul-force requires integrating the shadow self. If you judge the unwanted parts of self, you are more likely to turn away from the need of others; not knowing what your Presence provides, you might feel you have nothing to offer. In the same way I didn't show up for the other mother in the loss of her child, you might turn away from witnessing what you feel powerless to change. Though it's important to honor your limits, it isn't true that your Presence does nothing.

In the energy exercises at the end of this chapter is one for giving respect to the light that shines within the darkest of the dark. Using this exercise will help you go within pain and heartbreak with something to offer.

The Practice of Clearing

Clearing does not happen magically. It doesn't work to simply release the unwanted feelings that are buried within. Equally, it doesn't work to relive and rehash every hurt that has ever occurred. The process of integration is one of awareness, of witnessing your feelings instead of burying them, and of choosing to deactivate the power they hold.

Katie Byron offers a process called "The Work" that consists of identifying and questioning thoughts entwined with anger, fear, depression, addiction, and violence. She believes these thoughts can be unwound to "allow your mind to return to its true, awakened, peaceful, creative nature" as stated on her Website *www.thework.com*. On her Website, she offers all the tools and techniques you need for "The Work," free of charge. The process uses four questions to work through old patterns.

Essentially, when an event occurs that triggers patterned thoughts and unwanted feelings, immediately question the thought. In the previous example of a friend rescheduling a get-together and stimulating your feelings of rejection, the minute the thought "she must have something better to do" arises, you begin the process of asking Byron's four questions:[3]

  ◇ Is this thought true?

  ◇ Can you absolutely know that it's true?

  ◇ How do you react when you believe this thought is true?

  ◇ Who would you be without this thought?

In the previous example of believing that you have been rejected by your friend, you don't know that the thought is true. There is no way to know that it's true without asking the other person. Understanding that you don't actually know the thought is true changes your reaction. Believing the thought is true causes you to withdraw from interactions and become isolated. By changing your reaction, you can consider another perspective. Contemplating who you would be without the thought allows you to visualize the life you would enjoy having as the person you truly are. Is this vision strong enough for you to give voice to your feelings and talk with the other person? As your soul-force develops, so does the inner will to be your authentic self.

Incorporating Byron's questions with the four-fold process of emotional healing from my book *The Path of Emotions* brings mind and body together in a healing moment. You can use this process as you are being triggered by an event or to explore long standing muscle tension that is suppressing emotion. Here are the basic steps:

1. State your decision to shift out of the pattern.
2. Become a witness to your body and feelings.
   a. To use long standing muscle tension and pain, feel the tension in your muscles and use your breath to follow the tension inward to the buried emotion.
   b. To use triggered emotions, use your breath to fully feel your emotions and follow them inwardly to tight muscles.
   c. To use old thought patterns, use your breath to engage the thought and follow it inward to triggered emotions and tight muscle patterns.
3. Dialogue with the tension, emotion, or thought, incorporating Byron's four questions.
4. Relax your muscles, discharge the energy of your suppressed emotion, and disarm your thought in the creation of a heart-centered action.

The first challenge in using this process is staying with your feelings in a state of surrender. Your instinct might be to resist discomfort as your muscles reflexively tighten and rationalize your emotions as your mind tells you that you don't need to do this, that your patterns are perfectly fine just as they are. If this happens, use your breath to stay in present time. Allow your thoughts to come in and go out. Stay with the awareness of your muscle tension and the feeling of your emotion. Reaffirm your choice to open, integrate, and shift this pattern.

The second challenge is the disbelief that the dialog with your emotions, muscle tension, or thought is real. In dialoging, you are fully engaging the power of your imagination. Your imagination is free of your rational mind and therefore capable of discerning a deeper truth. Treat the dialog part of the exercise as a game. It doesn't matter whether the essentials are true; it matters whether they reveal something you need to know. Letting it be a game disarms your rational mind so that you can explore.

The third challenge is in knowing how to create heart-centered action. When your dialog uncovers the information your emotion is trying to impart, the emotion will recede as it is designed to do, and your muscles will relax. The bound energy discharges as shaking, crying, and so forth. Heart-centered action is simply doing something with the energy the emotion held that expresses your true self.

Maybe heart-centered action will mean having a heart-to-heart with someone you care about, engaging in an activity you would normally be afraid of, or creating something like a painting or poem that expresses your true self. Taking action makes the shift out of the old pattern concrete. It establishes your new direction.

Using this process doesn't mean you will never have your limiting pattern ever again; it means each time you encounter the pattern, it has less authority.

Self-Reflection

What is your relationship with your shadow self?

How do you see the reflection of your shadow self in your response to life events?

In what way does your shadow self try to get your attention?

How well do you listen to your emotions? What messages are they trying to impart?

What situations trigger your self-negating thoughts?

In what ways does your shadow self charge your energy field?

Is feeling good a measure for whether you are living your truth? Why or why not? Is there ever an exception?

Who are you when you like yourself?

Is your strong emotion or persistent thought telling you about where you got stuck in the past, what is happening in the present, or what you are afraid of in future? Is the message true?

What does your body-mind want you to know in this moment?

What is hidden from you in your patterned response?

What have you forgotten or lost?

What do you need?

What feelings rise in regard to bearing witness and giving voice to your own pain and suffering: embarrassment, shame, or something else?

Is bearing witness to another's feelings easy and natural or difficult and uncomfortable? If uncomfortable, what thoughts and feelings get in the way?

What gets in the way of bearing witness to social injustice and suffering? Do you feel helpless?

What are your beliefs about the power of soul-force?

Energy Exercises

Exercise 1: Defusing Triggers

Use this process in the moment when something triggers an old pattern. Though it seems like this process is long and involved, it is really just about conscious breathing. Remember how this type of process was used the Pillar of Connecting to deal with the resistance of the hospital attendee. Although you may think it impossible to stay aware when you are being triggered, in fact, the hardest part is choosing to shift the pattern.

1. Take a deep breath and bring yourself into present time. State your decision to shift out of the pattern being triggered.

2. Take a second conscious breath and ground your energy into Earth. Feel the strength and support of Earth surround you. You are not alone.

3. On your third breath, breathe into your muscle tension and allow your breath to be a witness to your thoughts and feelings.

4. Ask yourself: Is the thought I'm having about myself or this situation real or not?

5. If the answer is yes, how do you know and how can you shift it?

6. Notice how the thought is affecting you. Notice your muscle tension, heart rate, and the cartwheeling of your thoughts and feelings. Offer your breath as a lifeline to normal.

7. If you release this thought, who are you? In this moment, as the situation unfolds, be the person who reflects your true self.

8. Breathe into your muscles and relax. How can you respond from your true self? Create a heart-centered action. Let go of needing the person you are with to respond the way you want. All you need is your own good opinion.

Exercise 2: Healing Your Shadow Self

Choose a recurring life pattern, a persistent unwelcome thought that limits your growth, or a pattern of muscle tension that you can't get rid of. Acknowledge that this pattern has been shoved into your shadow self and now limits your life in some way. Sit with pen and paper in a quiet, comfortable spot where you won't be disturbed.

1. Take three deep breaths and bring yourself into present time. State your decision to address your shadow self and to shift out of the chosen pattern.

2. Revisit the last time you experienced this pattern. Engage the feelings you had at the time, allowing yourself to fully and completely experience your emotions. Notice the primary

thought that expresses your emotions or belief about yourself, the world, and life. It can be a general thought, such as "Life sucks," or a personalized thought such as "I just can't win," "I'm such a loser," or "Why am I such an idiot?" Write the primary thought on your paper. Sit with it and allow your feelings to get as large and painful as they truly are.

3. Feel the tension in your muscles and use your breath to follow the tension inward to its center.

4. Surrender to your pain and discomfort. Feel the muscle ache and the heart ache. This is your pain complex: the muscle tension and pain, heartache, and limiting thoughts.

5. Offer your muscles the gift of your breath. Nothing to change, just offer.

6. Offer your heart the gift of your breath. Nothing to change, just breathe in light and be a witness to whatever is present.

7. Now engage your imagination. In your mind's eye, see yourself sitting in a chair. Opposite you is another chair and sitting in it is your shadow self complete with your pain complex. What does your shadow self look like? What are its weight, clothing, and body language? Does it smell? Write down what you notice.

8. Ask your shadow self for its name. If you don't hear one, name your shadow and write the name down.

9. Begin a dialog. Tell your shadow and the pain complex it carries exactly how you feel. Write down the details of all the ways the pain limits you. Don't hold back; write everything you feel no matter how long it takes.

10. When you are done, rest quietly for a minute and see if there is anything else that still needs to be expressed; if so, write.

11. When you are completely done, sit quietly and invite your shadow self to respond. Ask it to reveal the message it has for you. Write everything you think, feel, sense, hear, or see in your mind's eye. The message usually doesn't take long to be imparted.

12. Ask your shadow what it needs in order to be whole.

13. Once you receive and understand all the messages, you may cry, laugh, feel shaky, or not. Sit quietly, offering your body the gift of your breath. Witness the discharge of energy from your suppressed emotion and thank your shadow for the messages you received. You may want to get up and take a walk around the room, swinging your arms and shaking out your legs.

14. When you're ready, sit quietly and explore the new belief formed through your new awareness. Ask your shadow self for insight. Write what you learn.

15. Think of a way to immediately express this new belief in an action that involves another person. Congratulate yourself when you do. Have no expectations; how people perceive you or respond is not what's at issue. Your job is only to be true to your authentic self.

16. Thank your shadow for its insights and invite it to be part of your conscious awareness.

The muscle pain and tension carried by your shadow in the pain complex you are clearing may not completely disappear after this encounter, although it might. The pain complex should now respond to physical interventions that didn't work before such as massage, physical therapy, and exercise. Whenever you feel the pain, stop, affirm your new belief, massage the muscle, and offer the gift of your breath.

Exercise 3: Freeing Your Soul-Force

Not everyone is called to be a witness of social injustice, yet every one of us is confronted daily with some form of cruelty to people, animals, and Earth. Sometimes, the sheer volume of mutilated animal bodies on the highway takes an emotional toll. Here is an exercise to stay present, offer your Presence, and discharge the emotion so that it doesn't build up and cause internal imbalances.

1.   Take a conscious breath and exhale deep into Earth.

2.   Ask Earth for strength and support. Breathe Earth light, strength, and consciousness into your body.

3.   Ask the invisible realms for support.

4.   Breathe into your feelings and offer the breath of life, the breath of God to your feelings as they arise. Exhale the energy of your feelings into Earth and ask for her help in neutralizing them. Be thankful for support.

5.   Use this process to stay present without becoming over-whelmed with grief, anger, or despair.

6.   Affirm that you are a powerful being and that adding your soul-force to that of others matters.

7.   Create an image of lighting a candle in the dark and holding the candle before the scene you are witnessing.

8.   On your breath, send love, support, and compassion to all involved, including yourself.

9.   Affirm that your Presence ensures this person, animal, piece of land, or group of people is not alone and abandoned and their sacrifice not forgotten.

10. When you are finished, release your energy into Earth and give thanks.

Exercise 4: Clearing and Charging Your Energy Field

1.   Use your breath to come into present time. Ground and Center.

2.   Imagine the space an arm's-width around you in all directions: your personal space.

3.   Breathe into and through this space.

4.   Using your imagination and felt-perceptions, scan this space.

5.   Notice areas of too little or too much flow, of too empty or too full, or of too light or too dark.

6. Notice what needs to balance and offer that area the gift of your breath.

7. Notice areas that don't feel like you, that are attachments of other people's thoughts, emotions, or beliefs.

8. Fill your personal space with your light with your breath and push everything that is not you out.

9. Stand up. On an inhalation, stretch your arms over your head. Spread your fingers and exhale, bringing your arms down and sweeping the space around you with your spread fingers.

10. Do this several times, Clearing and charging your energy field.

9

the pillar of Honoring

PILLAR: Honoring
AWARENESS: Divinity Awareness
CHALLENGE: Carelessness
RELATIONSHIP: Life-Force
GATEWAY: The Crown and the Heart
GIFT: Nourishment
EMOTION/ATTITUDE: Reverence and Grace
QUALITY BROUGHT TO PRESENCE: Innocence

Grace and Grit

Erin grasps the bedrail, white-knuckled in pain. She is lying on a slight incline, her head garishly suspended inside the halo. I want to put pillows inside the device just so it looks like her head is supported by something other than four long screws penetrating her skull. I want to make myself more comfortable in seeing her.

She breathes with exaggerated control. Beads of sweat appear on her forehead and small shudders periodically shake the bed. Despite repeated calls to the floor's nursing station and promises someone will be there shortly, no one has come to refill the self-dispenser for pain medicine. It has been empty for more than an hour.

I am beside myself. I stride anxiously to the nurse's station to find it deserted. Helpless anxiety builds to a roiling anger. Too agitated to sit, I pace the hallway between our room and the station.

Erin's final surgery is behind her. There is nothing more to be done and the hospital is talking about discharge. Her progress is excellent and she will not go to a rehab facility. She will live at home supported by in-house physical therapy and a visiting nurse. Despite the nearly miraculous improvement, her pain remains. How will she manage it at home with so little help?

Standing vigil at the door, I catch sight of the nurse heading toward the station and charge forward, toenail claws digging for purchase to strengthen my stride. Gouge marks are left in the linoleum.

I reach the counter the same time as the nurse. My lip curls, bearing fangs. "Can Erin's nurse come and refill her pain med?" My question rolls out on a growl. "It's been over an hour that we've been asking."

"What was that room number, dear?"

"It's still 219." One more dear, honey, or sweetheart, and I will slap someone.

The woman ambles to the schedule and flips some pages in response to the number I've already given at least four times during the past hour.

"Hmm." She purses her lips. "Erin's nurse is still with an emergency. She'll be there as soon as she can."

"So no one else can refill the dispenser?" I snarl now, since the growl clearly didn't work.

"No, honey. They're registered drugs. Your care provider will be there as soon as she can." The station nurse is done with me and shuffles down the hall with an armload of sheets and blankets.

I am shaking on the return to Erin's room. The helpless witnessing of such pain is shattering. I stand at her side and reach out to stroke her hand to let her know she's not alone.

"Don't," she whispers on an exhale. "Can't take it."

A simple touch is too much stimulation. There is no energy to absorb it; every iota of attention is needed to maintain control. One nanometer away from constant vigilance and the pain will explode to shred the fibers of her being.

I sit in a chair at the foot of her bed and match my breathing to hers. Inhale into the pain and offer the breath of life, the breath of God; exhale away from pain, release, release, release.

After what seems like eternity, there is activity at the entry to our room. The computer tray that accompanies every medical provider is pushed through the doorway, followed by Erin's nurse who strides in purposefully, face furled in a frown and shoulders tight and square. She has seen the notes of our repeated requests. She is forewarned and ready for confrontation.

I am more than willing to comply. Recriminations form in my mind and descend to my mouth, but before I can hurl them across the room, I am preempted by Erin's voice wafting ethereally from the bed.

"Hi, Dorothy," Erin says weakly. Her eyes are closed and her clenched hands still clutch the bed rails.

Is that her nurse's name? Dorothy?

"I can't imagine what it's like to take care of a floor full of people like me," Erin continues. "You must be exhausted."

Dragon scales molt from my shoulders and clatter to the floor. Tears I have not allowed leak from the corner of my eyes. Where did my daughter acquire such grace?

Dorothy's shoulders relax. She abandons the defensive busyness of the computer and rushes to unlock Erin's dispenser. She scans the replacement bag to record drug, cost, quantity, and time, then secures the medication inside. She closes the lid, locks the unit, and pushes the dispenser pump several times. Within seconds, Erin's face relaxes and her hands fall from the rails onto her bed. Her breathing deepens.

"Thank you," she whispers before descending into semi-consciousness.

Dorothy straightens Erin's sheets, leaves some water on her tray, and turns to me. "I'm sorry," she says. "I know it took a long time for something that only takes a few minutes to do, but I really couldn't pull away."

"No," I say shakily. "I'm sorry. All this time and still I don't how to manage. But my daughter is teaching me."

Dorothy smiles and reaches toward my shoulder as she leaves the room.

Erin's eyes slit open a tiny fraction and she looks at me with the hint of a smile. "You know, Mom, I really am going to be okay."

When I move beyond her pain and suffering and reach her spirit, grace and grit is the essence of the daughter I discover.

Pillar: Honoring

The Pillar of Honoring is an awakening of the heart to the sacredness of life. The essence of Honoring is appreciation, the simple act of saying thank you. Stop for a minute, take a breath, and remember a time when you were truly touched by the sacredness of life. Did it happen at the birth of a child or the deathbed of a loved one? Birth and death, the two bookends of life, bring into clear focus the miracle of being alive and the mystery of not being alive. At the moment of birth and death, the worlds of the seen and unseen meet. Thankfulness is abundant.

Too often, awareness of the gift that is life is lost in the struggles of each day. "I will get to appreciation later when I have time, after I achieve this goal, after I put the kids to bed, or after this TV program, then I will give a few minutes of my attention in appreciation for life."

In the acquiring of goals and dreams, fulfilling of ambitions, avoidance of pain, and seeking of pleasure, it is forgotten that all are pursued for the experience of being alive. In and of themselves, at the moments of birth and death, they mean little. Ambitions for a child's future and accomplishments of a dying person are not the first or lasting thoughts. At birth, a child brings love. Parents delight in 10 fingers, 10 toes, a beating heart, and the softness of breath. Future hopes and dreams are for later. At death, the merit that touches people is the degree to which the dying person has loved and inspired love in others, not how much money was made or what success achieved.

The Pillar of Honoring restores the magic, love, and mystery of being alive. Honoring acknowledges that life is not an accident. The inherent design within life is not happenstance. The journey of your life is not based on a twist of fate. You, alive at this time, in this place, and with these challenges, are exactly where you're supposed to be. At times, finding the teachable moment within events and travails is difficult, so personal fate feels like chance. However, either there is design and meaning to life or there isn't. It can't be that there is design for some people and not all, for some parts of life and not others.

My daughter reminded me quite elegantly in the hospital that other people, and the rest of life itself, are not here as props for my script. Each being carries the sacred light of life. Each individual carries light forward in the experience of life to the best of his or her ability. That light must be honored in everyone or it isn't honored in anyone. No matter how another person's life looks, no one else knows what they're working out, what they're here to experience, or what viewpoint they give to the whole. You can put boundaries around what behaviors are tolerable, protect yourself and loved ones from the violent acts of another, and separate those who hurt people. However, to deny that the sacred light of life lives with everyone is to deny the divine.

The dictionary defines honoring as "regard with great respect."[1] Honoring another person recognizes their essential essence. Honoring life recognizes the profound privilege of being alive. Honoring, however, also means to keep an agreement. The Pillar of Honoring recognizes that life is a gift, that the sacred light of life lives within all beings, seen and unseen, and that each person is born into an agreement to further this light in the world by fully being their true self. Falling short doesn't negate the effort. Whatever you bring is enough.

The essence of Presence is to be all of who you are. Honoring helps you live your light, acknowledge other people's light, and decide for yourself who you are.

Awareness: Divinity Awareness

Divinity awareness sees the sacred within all: you, me, the chair, the tree. All are derived from one source. With this awakening, everything changes. Before, the idea sounded fanciful, even absurd. How can a chair be sacred? A better question is, what does it mean if it is?

Acknowledging the divine within all is more than tolerating other people's differences. It is recognizing that the spiritual essence sought in meditation and prayer exists in the person sitting next to you. It exists in the wind and trees and in the animal lying on the side of the road hurt by cars traveling too fast to make room for other life forms.

Divinity awareness shifts preconditioned perceptions. If you have been trained to believe that life is not essentially spiritual, you will not recognize the consciousness in other forms of life or value the development of Presence. You will not perceive the shift that is underway from the paradigm of domination into the paradigm of wholeness or have the impulse to participate. The desire to develop Presence comes from your essential self, your spiritual nature that aches to be witnessed. It is your spiritual nature that drives your awakening.

Sometimes the resistance to living in your greatest truth is so engrained that uncovering your essential self and shifting perspective requires a jolt to the system, an upset to the status quo. An accident as consuming as Erin's easily reveals itself as a transformative experience. However, transformation doesn't need to wait for such catastrophe, and catastrophe doesn't guarantee transformation. What Erin will do with her moment remains to be seen.

Transformation exists within every breath. What if, every time you inhale, you remember you are breathing in the gift of life? Right now, on this breath, accept the shift.

The consciousness of the divine holds the answers to the problems in the world today. Tune in to what is inside your heart and the value of the world becomes more than how much it can be bought and sold for. No need to run in a new direction, to learn another skill, or to change yourself. You already are who you need to be. You already know the answers you seek. Your best teacher is inside you. This is divinity awareness: listening to the teacher inside.

It is never too late to shift your perception. Here are some of the foundations within divinity awareness:

◇ Life is sacred.

◇ The sacred light of life exists within all.

◇ Life is formed out of unconditional love.

◇ Your spiritual essence shines through your hands and heart as you give of yourself to the world.

◇ Expectation of perfect is an illusion.

◇ You already are who you need to be.

◇ You already know the answers you seek.

◇ All that is comes from source.

The Pillar of Honoring highlights equality. Through Honoring, you understand your impact in the world and accept your power as a spiritual being with full awareness of the divine within all.

Challenge: Carelessness

The challenge within Honoring is to avoid being careless with life: to not take people, fortune, success, or the tree outside your window for granted.

Consider that the message of every mystic and sage of every age is that the energy from which the universe is derived from unconditional love. In the Pillar of Centering, unconditional love is defined as an ability: the ability to hold a vision of wholeness. Now we understand that unconditional love is also a substance and a force: the substance of matter and the force that binds matter into form, the particle and a wave of quantum physics.

For some, awareness of unconditional love as the essence of the universe feels like coming home to what they always knew. For others, thoughts of unconscionable, horrific acts that occur in the world deny the Presence of unconditional love. To them, the only way to believe in a force of love is to create an opposing force of evil to account for all the intentional cruelty and inflicted suffering. When bad things happen, evil has won.

The appearance of duality is not truth. In Honoring, we see that there is one force, that of source, divinity, and creative spirit. When the tap to source is turned on, unconditional love drives behavior; when the tap is turned off, confusion and self-hatred are acted out in the world. There are infinite degrees between on and off. Accepting this concept demands a breaking open of the heart. Judgment, emotional conditioning, and disbelief must be suspended. The challenge is tremendous.

A tap that is not fully opened decreases flow and creates a deficiency of the sacred. Opening the tap requires consciously Honoring the sacred. The starting place for change is always with the self: Before you will be able to see the divine in all, you must experience the divine within yourself. *Remember your essence* is the clarion call for opening the tap.

Our present technology-based culture is careless with essence. Self-awareness has been overshadowed by desire. What is desired becomes more important than the awareness of the sacred. When the material world is honored above the spiritual reality within, you give your essence away. Essence is invested in cars, houses, nice furniture, lawn mowers, the good opinion of others, clothes, jewelry, and everything on the bucket list that must be achieved before death. More importantly, when your essence is given away, connection to the sacred is reduced. Can you steal the pension plans of seniors while experiencing connection to the sacred? Can you have a clandestine affair and witness the sacred in your spouse? Can you destroy the environment and maintain an awareness of the sacred in nature?

The belief that there are two separate forces—a good force and a bad force—that are in battle with each other over your soul and the soul-force of the planet has done immense harm. This framework allows unspeakable things to be done in the name of God. The illusion of duality creates a vision of dueling forces that maintains judgments of right and wrong, spiritual and material. This belief may cause you to be afraid of your shadow self, so you exert more effort hiding parts you judge as less than perfect. How can you remember your essence when you're in hiding?

If you are careless of the beauty around you and lack contentment with what is in your life, you may be longing for perfect. Perfect, in the sense of meeting all the demands and expectations you create, doesn't exist. You can stop measuring yourself against an imaginary ideal and stop expecting that each new experience, purchase, or love object will make you happy.

Contentment comes from the awareness of beauty that is born inside your heart and given to your experiences. Accept what is as perfect. Embrace your shadow. Align with the deeper design with nature. Be part of the divine mystery unfolding around and within you in each and every moment. Be a witness to the divine.

In his book *Remember your Essence*, Paul Williams says "You can change and transform your entire universe. You cannot change your essence."[2]

Relationship: Life-Force

The relationship of Honoring is with your life-force. You probably pay attention to the physical needs of your body for healthy food and exercise, get your hair cut, keep your nails trimmed and clean, and dress with an eye to attractiveness. How much attention do you pay to the flow of life-force energy through your body?

Flowing into, through, and around you, life-force energy sustains your body. It nourishes and vitalizes you at a cellular level, promoting health and well-being. It animates and motivates your activity. Life-force forms the matrix for your physical body, including your personal space that interfaces between you and the external environment.

Your life-force is interactive. It carries your dreams and desires into the world and responds to your fears and limitations. Through your life-force, your consciousness is reflected in the circumstances and events you draw to yourself. A conscious relationship with subtle energy increases your connection to the sacred, so the transmission of your personal intent becomes a healing force. Consequently, your life-force is the vehicle of your self-empowerment.

Vital life-force helps you see and respond to life-enhancing opportunity. When life-force is low, connection to the world is diminished. Seeing the gift offered in each day is elusive. It becomes more difficult for your body to heal and for you to motivate your dreams. On the other hand, when life-force is vibrant and alive, you resonate at a higher level with events and possibilities. You can enact the design that overlays your life. Vibrancy is a function of movement and vibration. Free flow creates vitality; wherever there is blocked flow, health and vibrancy are diminished. However, don't imagine that you cannot heal because your life-force is low. You can.

Relationships are based on communication and care. Developing a relationship with your life-force energy requires that you start listening and keeping the channels in your body open. Listening is done through paying attention to the felt-perceptions discussed in Chapter 1. The best indicators of the health of your life-force are flow and vitality. Flow is measured in your level of relaxed openness. It is not dependent on having a perfect body in perfect health; it is dependent on how open you are to receiving and how willing you are to give. Vitality is assessed by how engaged you are. It is not dependent on your age or health; it is dependent on your willingness to be present in the moment as yourself and connect with others.

On a scale of one to 10, what is your degree of flow and your level of vitality right now? Where do you feel flow in your body and where do you feel blocked? Inhale and relax your muscles and your mind. Offer the gift of your breath to any muscle tension and mental resistance you find. Ground, center, and still your thoughts. Imagine a stream of light flowing into your body on your breath. Notice the sounds, textures, and feelings in the ambiance. Now what is your degree of flow and level of vitality?

Tai Chi, Qi Gung, and yoga are practices you can engage to clear and open your energy channels. Self-acupressure, self-reflexology, and Tapping are also solid choices to maintain flow and vitality. In addition, conscious breathing and the practices in this book also clear and open your energy.

As you improve the relationship with your life-force and increase the flow of energy in your body, you are enlivening the sacred within.

Gateway: The Crown and the Heart

Have you ever noticed in paintings of saints and gurus that the images are often depicted with a halo around the head and a fire in the heart? The Pillar of Honoring links the traditional placement of spirituality in the crown center with that in the heart center. Linking the crown and heart changes your encounter with the sacred from an ideal into a body experience. This linkage is the sacred union, the alchemical merging of mind and heart, spirit and matter through which the awareness of spirit within makes everything concrete.

The gateway into the crown and heart is opened through transcendent emotions. The term transcendent can be misleading as the word implies being raised out of the everyday world. Actually, however, transcendent emotions lift you out of preoccupation with self-interest. They inspire and change your state of being, and allow you to live more fully engaged with life. Transcendent emotions ground, elevate, and uplift simultaneously. While sinking into Earth, you are raised and connected to the sacred flow of life-force. The Presence of source becomes immediate, all pervasive, and personal.

Transcendent emotions do not rise and fall to communicate information as do other emotions. Therefore, they are able to sustain your Presence even in the onslaught of challenge. The reason for the stability of transcendent emotions is because they're not generated in response to what happens to you; they're not telling you about your immediate environment or situations. Rather, they're generated through your relationship with life-force and spirit. They rise and fall in relation to your internal process.

Transcendent emotions do not interfere with the function of everyday emotions. The delivery of information in response to events provided from everyday emotions continues. What changes because of the

Presence of transcendent emotions is your response to the information. Life becomes much less stressful as priorities become clear and beauty is easier to perceive.

Jonathan Haidt, professor of social psychology at Virginia University who specializes in self-transcendent emotions, explains their ability to lift you out of self-interest.[3] He specifically identifies elevation, admiration, and compassion as self-transcendent emotions, while I might add unconditional love, gratitude, devotion, and reverence. These emotions are inspired through witnessing qualities and acts that you admire, aligning with teachings that uplift you, meditation on saints or gurus, practicing gratitude, looking for the light in self and others, spending time in nature, and meditating on your heart and crown. All means of connecting with source inspire transcendent emotions. At some point in your life, you have experienced such an emotion and been uplifted. Find that feeling now and magnify it. Embrace the feeling.

The current Dalai Lama is an excellent example of someone who utilizes the power within transcendent emotions. He connects to the world through compassion and demonstrates that dignity resides in you, not in other people's impression of you or in what they try to do to you.

Transcendent emotions allow you to seek wholeness rather than separation. They create the internal condition from which Honoring flows.

The Gift: Nourishment

Honoring nourishes your essential nature, that of unconditional love. Have you ever met a baby born hateful, vengeful, or malicious? Babies are born loving unconditionally. They are taught to be hateful, to seek revenge, and to spread their suffering to others through acts of cruelty. Honoring is a return to the innocence of the child. When you look with eyes expecting to meet unconditional love, you inspire it in yourself and others. You draw it forth from under the layers of hurt it hides within.

Take a breath. Let go of everything that is nonessential, everything that is not unconditional love. Listen to your heartbeat. It is the rhythm of life. The Earth has a heartbeat, too. It is measured as an extremely low electromagnetic frequency (ELF) of 7.83 Hz, with additional resonance modes of 14.3, 27.3, and 33.8 Hz.[4] This frequency set is called the Schumann resonances (SR) as discussed in Chapter 4. All the natural world is entrained to the rhythm of this frequency set, which organizes the design and synchronization of life.

Step outside, take a walk in the woods, sit on a beach, and feel the heartbeat of Mother Earth. Feel your own heartbeat. Let them become one. Feel the flow of life-force on a wave of unconditional love.

There is an idea that the heartbeat of Earth is speeding up, and as it does, life will be elevated to a higher level of consciousness. This is a funny thought because the Shumann resonance wasn't discovered until 1954. Scientists have only been measuring it consistently since the 1970s. With less than 50 years of observation, how can we possibly know the parameters of Earth's heartbeat? What we know from 50 years is that there is a lot of frequency shifting between 6 and 50 Hz among the resonance modes of 7.83 Hz.

The idea of the Earth speeding up and changing consciousness reflects a desire to escape from pain and suffering. Who wouldn't want to escape this? Out there, up there, or over there, it is thought, something is better. What if the only thing wrong with this reality is our limited perception? The belief in a better reality that Earth is taking us into is a wonderful escape from actually having to grow.

Here is a thought to consider: The commonly held belief is that humans are the pinnacle of evolution. But what if we are simply the most nascent species? Still in our infancy, the human species is not yet grown up. This is the view of Mellen-Thomas Benedict after information revealed in a near death experience. You can read about it at *www.mellen-thomas.com*. According to what he experienced, all of nature is working toward our growth. All of nature is supporting us in growing up.[5]

Instead of being judged for being children, imagine being loved and supported in growth.

When you can open to the realization that your essential nature is unconditional love, you will be able to embrace and nourish your wholeness, and the heartbeat of Mother Earth will be enough, just as it is. The Pillar of Honoring nourishes your body, mind, and soul. It rains sweetness on your dreams. As Meredith Sowers-Young says in her *Inner Circle* video series, "Nourish what you have already given birth to."[6] Nourish your essence.

Google "heartbeat of Earth" to hear an audible sound translation of the frequency of Earth on YouTube while viewing the rhythm of this heartbeat operating throughout nature. It is exquisite.

The Practice of Honoring

Honoring is practiced from the altar of your heart. It originates from an agreement to live in wholeness and requires that you turn your attention away from your suffering and place it on your love. Where your attention goes, your energy follows. Let your energy flow into the feeling of love and magnify it.

Here are signs that you need to bring Honoring into your life:

- ◊ Criticism is your first instinctive response.
- ◊ Consistently giving priority to plans and projects ahead of family and friends.
- ◊ Treating Earth as a commodity that you can buy and sell.
- ◊ Reckless endangerment of yourself or others.
- ◊ Killing for enjoyment and sport.
- ◊ An inability to see and feel beauty.
- ◊ Being purposefully unkind.
- ◊ Lack of joy.
- ◊ Self-loathing and self-criticism.
- ◊ Anger at divinity, God, source, or creative spirit.
- ◊ Disrespect for and carelessness of what is precious.

Honoring is practiced by saying thank you for all that life gives. Just for a minute, leave the awareness of what you want and yearn for, and enjoy everything you have. Honoring merges the Pillars of Centering and Connecting to bring awareness of the sacred light of life into all of your connections. Meaningful connection occurs when you acknowledge the divine essence in another person. It is a powerful affirmation of life to remember that the person before you, no matter what pain is layered on top, is also created of unconditional love. Try to go through an entire day holding this awareness. You might be surprised at the result. Spending a day remembering your essence is unconditional love.

Nicolas Roerich, a famous 19th-century Russian artist, philosopher, archeologist, and visionary, believed the human soul is nourished through beauty. Beauty brings people into balance, soothes the emotions, and calms the mind. Roerich thought this concept so important that he placed beauty as the foundation of the changing paradigm. He said, "The evolution of the New Era rests on the cornerstone of Knowledge and Beauty."[7] Like transcendent emotions, beauty has the power to elevate your awareness. Surround yourself with beauty. Remember the Navajo Way blessing ceremony (from Chapter 6) and walk in beauty, saying thank you to Earth and spirit.

The energy steps to practicing Honoring are simple. Take your awareness into your heart and crown. Open your crown to receive the blessing of spirit and open your heart to express this blessing in your connections with others. Here is a basic exercise:

1. Ground and center. Take three deep, clearing breaths connecting Earth and sky through your body (as in Chapter 4).

2. Place your left hand over your heart; place your right hand over your left.

3. Breathe in through the crown of your head into your heart. Let your heart grow.

4. Imagine the light in your heart as the most beautiful light you've ever seen. Perhaps it is made of thousands of stars with prismatic rainbows and shafts of shimmering silver.

5. Imagine all the people you see in a day having this light shining from their heart.
6. Visualize yourself going through the day and meeting people with the light in your heart reaching forward to touch the light in their hearts.
7. You might say to yourself, "The divine in me greets the divine in you."
8. Put on your beauty glasses. Look for what is beautiful. Grass grows in the cracks of the sidewalk.

The first resistance you might experience is the inability to forgive yourself and others. Lack of forgiveness is demonstrated when you focus on what bothers you in others and so run them down in your mind. If you can forgive yourself, you won't need to elevate yourself by bringing others down. If you can forgive others, you will see them in their wholeness instead of their expression of broken. You are not alone in this resistance. It is universal. Confronting the need to forgive is the first true step in awakening to your essence.

The second resistance is the inability to see past pain and suffering to find beauty. Pain and suffering are powerful forces. There has never been a time and never will be a time when they don't exist. That fact can break open your heart and motivate compassion or close you down and interfere with Connecting. If you accept that pain and suffering are part of life, that they are teachers on the path of awakening, you can feel into the people (animal and human, seen and unseen) who suffer and find the sacred light of life that lives within them. Reach for the sacred light of life within yourself when suffering surrounds you, as it surely will. No one escapes life without suffering. Bringing the sacred light into the forefront turns your Presence into a healing force. In short, pain and suffering can be your stumbling block or your stepping stone.

The third resistance is really an extension of the first. It is lack of love. If you experienced a lack of love in your childhood, it is very difficult to believe that love exists within you and in the world at large and, if it does, that you deserve to experience it. But here is a truth: If love did not exist in you and in the world, you would not long for it. Rather than feeling its lack, you would feel nothing. You would have no relationship with the idea of love at all. Your longing tells you it exists. What keeps you from experiencing it is judgment. You judge yourself as unworthy to receive love, and judge your parents and probably your partner for not loving you better. Can you accept that your parents and partner are imperfect beings working out their own pain? Can you accept yourself for doing the same? This doesn't excuse behavior; it looks beyond broken to whole. Really, you have two choices: hold on to your grievances and live in misery, or let go and be free to experience beauty and love.

As Honoring increases in your life, the flow and vitality you experience does too. Your ability to connect with transcendent emotions becomes easier, and your life develops meaning and purpose.

Self-Reflection

What gets in the way of seeing the sacred in all life?

Where can you easily see the sacredness of all and where is it difficult to extend this awareness?

Does your life feel accidental or purposeful?

How do your ambitions reflect a belief in the sacredness of life?

How much time do you spend thinking about what you don't have and how to get it? How much time do you spend enjoying what you have?

How are you Honoring the people and experiences in your life?

What agreements have you made in life? Do you honor them?

What does it mean to you that everything is sacred? How does this awareness change how you behave?

How do you give of yourself to life?

Do you notice beauty?

What is easy to honor in others? What is difficult? Why?

Where are your challenges to experiencing unconditional love or seeing it reflected in the world?

What have you given your essence away to?

How conscious are you of the flow of subtle energy in and around you?

What feels blocked in your life? Is it a matter of timing, low vitality, or something else? What else might it be?

How do you listen to your life-force?

On a scale of one to 10, what is your vitality right now? What is the degree of flow? Take a breath; what changes?

On a scale of one to 10, how engaged are you with life?

What transcendent emotion is easiest for you to generate? Which is hardest? Can you make time each day to feel the easiest and the hardest?

Remember a time you felt a transcendent emotion. What was happening? what inspired you? How can you bring this inspiration more fully into life?

What if unconditional love is your true nature?

How does nature support your growth?

Energy Exercises

Increase the flow of energy in the space you live in by decreasing clutter and increasing beauty. Inspire transcendent emotions with pictures of people, saints, and gurus you admire. Look for the qualities you admire in self and others. Align with teachings that uplift and meditate on saints or gurus. Most importantly, practice gratitude and see the light in others. Spend time outside meditating on your heart and crown.

Exercise 1: Opening to Your Essence

1. Sit quietly where you won't be disturbed by cell phones or external distractions.
2. Ground and center. Take three deep, clearing breaths connecting Earth and sky through your body (as in Chapter 4).
3. Place your attention on your heart.
4. Breathe in through the crown of your head into your heart. Let your heart grow.

5. Find your heartbeat. Relax into the rhythm of your heart, letting your body rock gently to the beat.

6. Feel your heartbeat as the heartbeat of Earth and let yourself flow into Earth and merge. Feel the flow of energy meeting on the beat of your heart.

7. Continue to breathe in the most beautiful light you've ever seen through the crown and fill your heart. Offer this light from your heart to Earth, to the trees, the birds, the stream, the wind, your partner, child, parent, or friend.

8. Open your heart to receive love and support in return.

9. Receive the love of nature. Imagine all of nature supporting your journey into the fullness of your being. Imagine nature wanting you to succeed.

10. Allow love to flow unreservedly. Inhale love and feed your essence; exhale love and feed the essence of life.

11. You might say, "The divine in me meets the divine in the world."

12. Bring to mind a guru, saint, animal, or beloved teacher in your life and love them.

13. Sit with beauty glasses on. Look for what it beautiful.

14. Take a breath. Let go of everything that is nonessential, everything that is not unconditional love. Listen to your heartbeat.

Exercise 2: Appreciating Earth

This meditation is inspired by the teachings of Llewellyn Vaughan-Lee. After doing this exercise, practice putting whatever you are focused on inside your heart. Put people you love, visions, friendships, goals, and so forth into your heart space and bathe it in light. Love it, welcome it into your life, then let it go.

1. Take three deep breaths and bring yourself into the preset moment. Inhale peace and exhale tension.

2. Take three more breaths, breathing through your body and connecting Earth and sky.

3. Bring your attention to your heart. You can place your hands over your heart if you feel drawn.

4. Breathe into your heart and allow it to expand. Inhale love and exhale tension.

5. Feel your heart filled with love and appreciation.

6. Place Earth inside your heart.

7. Bathe Earth in the gift of your breath: the breath of life, the breath of God.

8. Love and appreciate Earth.

9. When the energy flow to Earth slows, relax.

10. Let your thoughts go. Feel.

PART II

stepping into presence

Whether you want to live a more fulfilling life, manifest a creative dream, be successful, protect the environment, or relieve suffering in the world, the quality of your Presence is significant in achieving your goals.

Your Presence is the emissary you send ahead of your actions to negotiate in the world on your behalf. Before you consciously participate in the choices of each day, your Presence is already engaged. It interacts with the environment and prepares the ground for your actions. It calls forth the circumstances you encounter.

Even while you are at rest, your Presence interacts with the creative force of life. You don't have to do a thing; your essence is broadcast complete with your intentions and awareness. It is woven together with those of other people on the warp-and-woof of Earth and spirit to create a tapestry that holds the circumstances and substance of life. The more developed your Presence, the more you contribute to the strength and beauty of this tapestry.

Having journeyed through the Eight Pillars, your Presence is altered. Without doing anything, you have shifted the interchange and renegotiated what you call forth.

Part II: Stepping into Presence demonstrates the usefulness of the Eight Pillars in bringing your Presence to bear in life situations. People have asked how the Pillars can be accessed for guidance and Chapter 10 provides the Eight Pillar Process which is demonstrated in several different ways in subsequent chapters. The Eight Pillars are practices to open your spirit; they are not meant as rigid instructions to confine your soul. Modify, use, or abolish as feels right!

The Eight pillar process

Check in with yourself right now. Are you in the same body-mind you were in before you started your journey through the Eight Pillars? What fundamentally changed as you explored deeper aspects of yourself and your relationships with life?

The journey through the Eight Pillars is a passage into and through deeper aspects of self. The changes within you are reflected through your Presence, and perhaps for you, that is enough. You received what you were looking for when you picked up this book. On the other hand, maybe you desire to use the Pillars more consciously as a guide for decisions and directions. Perhaps you have a desire to live life with a deeper engagement than everyday awareness provides. Then the Pillars of Presence become a path for living fully awake, aware, and alive.

In the same way that the wisdom of the Pillars presented themselves through the challenges of my daughter's accident, providing Erin and me support in consciously using our feelings and perceptions, awareness and support are present in your life. When you trust your felt-senses to guide you into and through tasks and challenges, you utilize the most creative and authentic aspects of self. The awareness held within the Pillars aids you in uncovering and developing this facet of who you are. The Pillars are here to support your path, not direct it.

How to consciously activate this support is not always obvious. You may be overwhelmed or drawn back to sleep by the apparent ordinariness of daily tasks. For this reason, this chapter offers a process for putting the Pillars to work. Called the Eight Pillar Process, the practice accesses the basic awareness within each Pillar through clarifying questions.

The Eight Pillar Process is explained in this chapter and demonstrated different situations in the chapters ahead. The process provides a path but is not etched in stone. Let your felt-senses guide and use the process only for validation.

Whether you realize it or not, you have changed from your exploration into the Eight Pillars. Your Presence now radiates more of who you truly are. Even if you've learned nothing new, even if you've attended to this type of awareness your entire life, you have brought more of who you are forward. Inner work never ends. Each additional encounter with such practices deepens in you. Take a minute to appreciate what you've done and what you bring to the world. Ground, center, and honor yourself.

Taking Stock

In your journey through the Pillars, your Presence has grown to reflect the different perspectives and the varied feelings you've encountered. Here's what has been offered to your Presence:

- ◇ Force, through the feeling of awe in the experience of Being.
- ◇ Clarity, through the compassion of Connecting.
- ◇ Strength and assurance, through the gratitude in Grounding.
- ◇ Stillness, through the unconditional love of Centering.
- ◇ Integrity, through the respect within Balancing.
- ◇ Ease, through the surrender of Aligning.

◇ Vibrancy, through the humility of Clearing.

◇ Innocence, through the grace of Honoring.

The attributes you carry in your Presence impact the people you interact with and situations you navigate. You may feel you've not grown at all yet for some reason, your response to life and the effects of your Presence are different. Doing all the same things, but with a different feel, you experience different outcomes. Pause and notice the change in your well-being and the flow in your life and connect to its cause. Inner changes can have subtle effects. Consider if any of the following situations are occurring:

◇ Without trying, you have more free attention for people, animals, and projects so others feel enveloped in the acceptance and appreciation of your undivided attention. More people are drawn to you, not only because they desire your attention, but because they want to enjoy and appreciate you.

◇ Awareness of interconnections, other intelligence, and the flow of life is heightened so that you feel part of what is happening around you. You struggle less with timing, and you sense direction and flow more easily. Synchronicity is becoming part of your way of moving through life and is no longer a chance encounter. There is a greater sense of ease.

◇ Projects unfold with less effort. When things don't flow smoothly, you know to wait, hold the elements you are resolving loosely in your mind, and go about other activities until the answers you need emerge. You find it easy to trust in a larger design and follow it based on your felt-perception, even if you can't quite see the path.

The single biggest change you might notice is a deep relaxation and feeling of trust. You know you are on course and enveloped in a universe whose substance is unconditional love.

If you don't notice any changes in your life from your journey through the Eight Pillars, did you reflect on the questions and take the time to explore the exercises or did you skim through? If so, you probably skipped through because you thought they wouldn't work or that the process was old hat, more stuff you've done before. Certainly, there is nothing new in the principles themselves; they have been around for eons. It might be interesting, however, to bring your life experience and awareness into the exercises. You have nothing to lose. Even if you've done this type of thing a hundred times before, with fresh eyes and heart new things can be discovered. No matter how often you are exposed to such material, there is always a new way to see.

At this point, four foundational precepts should be abundantly clear.

◇   Your purpose is to be all of yourself as fully, completely, and lovingly as you can.

◇   Your Presence has power. Without doing anything, your Presence is a force of transformation.

◇   Felt-perceptions and conscious breathing are essential for living awake, aware, and alive.

◇   Where you are, and what you're doing, is exactly right.

Take these foundations into the Eight Pillar Process to consciously engage Presence in your life.

The Eight Pillars Process: The Awareness Guides and Clarifying Questions

Developing Presence allows you to be present in the moment, using your attention as both a tool of perception and a creative force. You can relax. You don't need to run at life; you realize that life comes to you. You are aligned with your path.

The Eight Pillar Process is a method to use your attention with mastery. The process focuses your attention with eight awareness guides and sets of clarifying questions. Whereas the awareness guides are reminders of where to place your attention, the clarifying questions establish where you need fine tuning. The process is simply taking the guides and questions into whatever situation needs greater advancement. It is an easy three step process:

1. Contact the challenge: This simply means to put your attention on the situation you want to advance or understand.
2. Listen to your inner wisdom: Establish your Presence through addressing the awareness guides and clarifying questions.
3. Allow: Follow the understandings gained through the steps of listening to guide your choices.

Contact, listen, and allow. That's really all you need to remember. Then as you use the process, pay attention to your felt-perceptions; they are an essential component. If you need to review, return to the section in Chapter 1. If you find you're having trouble assessing a situation, it's a good time to find someone to witness for you as you consider your way forward.

The process is simple but not necessarily easy. In each of the chapters in Part II, different circumstances and objectives are addressed, using some arrangement of the guides and questions.

Awareness Guides

The awareness guides are distillations of the essential awarenesses listed for each Pillar in its corresponding chapter. They encapsulate the message of the Pillar and remind you where to place your attention. If you don't relate to these, go to the awareness section in each Pillar and create a distillation that reflects what's most important to you. Here are the awareness guides:

◇ Being: Here is where reality is perceived; now is when action occurs.

◇ Connecting: You are interwoven into the fabric of life; what you do affects everything and everyone else.

◇ Grounding: This is a conscious universe; you are made of the consciousness and substance of Earth.

◇ Centering: Your spiritual well-being and connection to the all-that-is resides in the heart where your essential self lives.

◇ Balancing: Internal and external reality are expressions of each other and require the use of boundaries to stay in equilibrium.

◇ Aligning: Being in phase brings you into flow and magnifies your energy field.

◇ Honoring: The sacred light of life exists in everyone and everything.

Most of the time, all you need do is remember the guides; your attention will focus on what's essential in the moment. Other times, you may not see how they apply. That's when the clarifying questions come in.

Clarifying Questions

Some of the clarifying questions are self-evident; others may create more of a challenge to answer. In different situations, not all will be relevant. When a question is difficult for you, go to the exercises in that Pillar for support and clarity. The purpose of the questions is to focus your intention, reveal where you are challenged, and discern which Pillar can offer support.

Modify these basic questions for use in a variety of situations and make them specific to the circumstance. You can use them in any order, and the order will change depending on the situation. Each chapter demonstrates a slightly different approach to their employment. Chapter 11 demonstrates using them at their most straightforward and therefore provides a basic model.

The questions are the following:

Pillar of Being

◇ What part of your past are you bringing into the situation and how much influence does it have?

◇ What desire for future outcomes or fear of future lack are you bringing and how much influence does it have?

◇ Is there something hidden, something you need to perceive or an ability you need to use?

Pillar of Connecting

◇ What is the essence of what you desire to connect with in this situation or person?

◇ What is the essence within you that is connecting, or needs to connect, within this situation or person?

◇ Is there anything getting in the way of connecting; is your ego supporting your essential self?

Pillar of Grounding

◇ How fully are you in your body in this situation?

◇ Have you given thanks for the physical things you need from Earth?

◇ Are you taking care of yourself and working within the design of your life?

Pillar of Centering

◇ How fully are you in your center in this situation?

◇ How much weight does the voice of your authentic self carry compared to the voices of others?

◇ What is the predominate emotion you feel in relation to this situation?

Pillar of Balancing

◇ Are your needs in this situation balanced with the needs of others?

◇ Is your attention to inner work balanced with your attention to outer effort?

◇ What inner needs motivate you?

Pillar of Aligning

◇ What part of the cycle of growth is this situation in?

◇ Where are you exerting excess force?

◇ Is there an unseen factor, cycle, or element you need to align with in order to synch with divine timing?

Pillar of Clearing

◇ Are unhealed parts of self that need to be cleared influencing you in this situation?

◇ What or who needs to be witnessed?

◇ Is your soul-force being used?

Pillar of Honoring

◇ Are you bringing the sacred light of your life to the situation?

◇ Are you Honoring the sacred light of life in others?

◇ Is the tap of unconditional love on or off?

These general questions are specialized to fit the situation you are applying them to. As you answer them, the wisdom of each Pillar is accessed. Remember: You can adjust what doesn't fit for you. At first, you may feel confused on how to do that, but as you absorb the application in the next few chapters, your ease with the process will grow.

Practicing Presence: The Power of the Feel

Contact, listen, and allow is all that is required. When you get stuck, use the awareness guides and clarifying question. If all is going well for you, life is flowing, and projects are unfolding with ease, you may never use the process. However, if you feel life is not working as smoothly as you would like, that your efforts are not bringing the return you want, or what you create isn't expressing the ideals you had imagined, the Eight Pillar Process can help. It is a process for developing feel.

Imagine you are starting a new project and want it to be the highest expression it can be. Once you release it to the world, you want it to fly on strong wings and bring value to people. You know what you want the project to achieve, but for some reason you are feeling stuck. Your energy has dropped; you start forward and then can't continue. Something isn't right, but you don't know what it is.

Stop. Contact what you want to achieve and listen to how that goal wants to be expressed. Are you addressing all the components that want to be present? Do you know how they want to be put together, not necessarily how you want them to fit, but how they actually do?

Now listen. Put forward what you want to achieve and find its feeling. Then provide as many scenarios for expressing it as possible, or provide the single expression you've been going forward with, and pay attention to your felt-perceptions. Which direction is aligned with the feeling of what you want to achieve? Which one sits comfortably and brings a sense of flow? If you feel nothing, wait. Apply the Eight Pillars Process. If nothing happens continue to wait.

Waiting is not giving up; it is giving the disparate pieces of the puzzle a chance to sort themselves out in your subconscious. This is where a good relationship with the shadow self is handy. Because the shadow self holds the door to the subconscious, it can help you find your creative spark. Shine the sacred light of life on your shadow self and continue to wait.

At some point, you will have an idea or understanding in which all the pieces come together. The expression comes effortlessly and you surge with renewed energy. All you have to do is give your body over to allowing the pieces to express themselves through you. The joy of such surrender is immense.

Contact, listen, and allow. That is all there is to the Eight Pillar Process.

11

Being Me

In every Pillar, you are encouraged to let your authentic, core, and essential self shine. Not surprisingly, one of the first questions to arise doing self-work is how do you know your authentic self? How is it possible for the essential self to shine when it has yet to be identified? A sense of concern or even anxiety can develop about what needs to be changed in order to be more authentic.

Being your authentic self is not meant to be another item on your to-do list, another thing you must change to be perfect. It's not about making perfect humans; it's about allowing real humans to feel good about who they are. There is nothing authentic about being at war with yourself. The concept of being authentic is really nothing more than living in a way that fulfills you. Not knowing what fulfills you or what your core values are keeps you from knowing your authentic self.

Being authentic means being yourself: expressing your creativity and spirit without fear of judgment. Why is this so difficult? First, it's the possibility of isolation discussed in the Pillar of Connecting. You might stifle your authentic self in a desire to fit in. When you do, even though it may be essential for your survival, you lose a little of your own self-regard. Second, the training you received within your family and school system most likely conditioned you to disregard your emotions and intuition, the basis of felt-perceptions, and the guideposts that tell you whether something is authentic or not. Before you can access your authentic self, you have to uncover your felt-perceptions.

Defining the Authentic Self

It may be difficult to find your authentic self if you're looking for a distinct entity who lives inside as a separate being. Sometimes, it's useful to separate parts of the self into distinct beings in order to probe the feelings and information buried within. The ego, the shadow self, the persona, and the authentic, essential, and core self all gather substance from your psyche to allow exploration of hidden depths with a fresh view. Though creating separate parts is a valuable tool, the ultimate goal is integration. When held too tightly, forming distinct parts of the inner self changes from being a useful tool of self-discovery to a limitation. Certainly, this can happen when trying to define the authentic self.

There is no separate, distinct part of you that is authentic while everything else is somehow not. Everything inside you is you. But sometimes you make choices that don't reflect what you truly want or believe or say things you don't really mean only to please another. Sometimes you act in order to hide thoughts or feelings that you have been taught to be ashamed of. These choices can be self-denying and separate you from your inner truth. Your authentic self is who you are after stripping away other people's expectations, cultural and family dictates, and the list you carry of who you should be.

Authentic literally means "not false or copied; genuine; real."[1] It also means to be true and accurate,[2] and in philosophy, it is an "emotionally appropriate, significant, purposive, and responsible" way of living.[3] The term *authentic self* is often meant to indicate that you take responsibility for your life. You are said to be the author of your life, free of the opinions and judgments of others.

The problem is you live with other people and are constantly giving and receiving, negotiating boundaries, and reforming your ideas of self as you grow. Maybe the best definition of the authentic self is the place inside that is capable of self-love: the part of you that can accept who you are, the choices you make, and the reasons why you make them.

Being authentic is easily confused with living without filters. However, expressing your opinion in all situations and controlling the people around you with the force of your convictions isn't being authentic: It's being dominating. If authenticity becomes an excuse for behavior that hurts others, it is merely an expression of self-importance.

Sometimes, accommodation in what you do and say is necessary yet still expresses your authentic self. For example, you act differently with different people depending on the role you play. Relationships with parents, friends, clients, and partners involve different levels of respect, intimacy, and shared values. All this determines how much of yourself you share. Are you less authentic because you use different words and expressions to tell the same story with one group versus another? Or are you respecting different relationships?

Authenticity recognizes that you are part of a larger whole and all aspects of that whole deserve respect. Authenticity is based on values: What is important to you? Authenticity is based on satisfaction: What fulfills and what inspires you? The truth is most people find who they are by first finding out who they are not. You must try on many different garments to find the best fit.

Being your authentic self isn't really about what you do or even how much you enjoy doing it. What defines the authentic self is the awareness you have about what is motivating you and what core values are at work. For example, imagine you disdain certain social functions, believing they are pretentious and hypocritical. It goes against your core beliefs to participate, except you love your grandmother. Such functions are important to her. Which is more authentic: boycotting the gathering she has organized or honoring her place in your heart? There are no easy answers, and whatever you decide will be true to some part of your authentic self, so knowing what motivates you is more important to being authentic than what you actually decide to do.

When your core values are overridden by the dictates of others and you submerge your needs and values, you can develop feelings of poor self-esteem, loss of confidence, and even self-loathing. Here are a few signs to suggest you are out of alignment with your core:

- Continually apologizing for your beliefs, choices, actions, and feelings.
- Not saying what you think when asked for an opinion, but saying what you think the other person wants to hear.
- Beating yourself up every time you make a mistake, even small, inconsequential ones.
- Rehashing conversations and agonizing over stupid things you said.
- Imagining what other people are saying and thinking about you.
- Needing the good opinion of other people to feel good about yourself.
- Living in fear the people you are with will leave you.
- Putting aside your needs as being selfish.
- Engaging in self-destructive behavior.
- Using food, alcohol, drugs, sex, or other addictive behaviors to avoid your feelings.

If you notice these signs, take a good look at what is motivating your choices and what you fear might happen if you become more of who you truly are.

Becoming Authentic

What is authentic for you is unique. No one but you can define it. Being your authentic self is not static or obvious; it is a dialog you have with life. Although you may think of authenticity as something you are and must struggle to express, usually it's something you discover and slowly become. Although there are some people who are born knowing, for most, authenticity is a process of finding what expressions, activities, and relationships fit you and which ones do not.

Consequently, much of your life may be spent trying on different roles, expressions, and ideals. Values and authentic expressions change over time. If you were a radical protester in the 1960s and became a legislator in the 1990s, it doesn't mean one expression is authentic and the other isn't. It means your ideas changed about how to be you.

The process of becoming authentic doesn't take you from fake to original; it takes you from uncertain to certain, from incongruous to congruent. When your values, beliefs, feelings, and actions are aligned, your life becomes a harmonious whole and your attention becomes focused. Your Presence is magnified and your inner light glows.

I'm sure you don't need to be convinced, but here are some benefits to becoming more authentic:

◇ People actually like you more, not less.

◇ You are happier and more fulfilled.

◇ You are able to express your creativity.

◇ Your life flows; what you think and feel is reflected in how you act and what you do.

◇ It's easier to make decisions.

◇ You become more truthful as you lose your self-judgment and fear of the judgment of others.

◇ It's easier to live according to your own terms, in your jobs, relationships, and life.

◇ It's easier to follow your dreams.

◇ It's easier to love.

Determining Authentic Action

The real challenge in knowing your authentic self is recognizing when something fits. You may be easily swayed by the opinions of others or conditioned so thoroughly that you lost the ability to know your own mind. You might think that doing what is fulfilling is selfish.

Reconnecting to your authentic self is dependent on restoring the felt-perceptions you were trained away from as a child. Your felt-perceptions lead you into knowing what is in alignment with your core values, reveal your creative path, and confirm what is meaningful and true. In fact, your authentic self is so related to your felt-perceptions they may well be one and the same. Remembering how to use your felt-perceptions is remembering the language of the heart. It is finding your way back to self.

Every day, you are confronted with choices. They range from simple issues of what to wear to difficult decisions that question what you believe. If you have difficulty knowing what direction aligns with your essential self, modify the eight sets of questions from Chapter 10 and apply them to your situation. Some questions will fit better than others, but all will reveal some aspect of the given situation and show you which Pillar you need to focus on.

To clear the obstruction that keeps you from knowing your authentic self, as you run through the questions, consider the suggested modifications. If you have more relevant variations, use them. Some question are not applicable and others need no clarification. Don't take too much time to do this exercise; 10 to 15 minutes should be plenty, although if this is your first use of the questions, it may take longer. Use your first response and validate it using felt-perceptions. Running through the questions will show you which Pillars can offer you the most support.

Pillar of Being

◇ **What part of your past are you bringing into the situation and how much influence does it have?** In this case, what influences from your past stifle your authenticity: a parent, teacher, partner, or shameful act? Acknowledge the person (or situation), forgive, and state your intention to be your authentic self. Use the Clearing and charging your energy exercise in Chapter 8. Consider an event from your past that supports your authentic expression and magnify it.

◇ **What desire for future outcomes or fear of future lack are you bringing in, and how much influence does it have?** If you are afraid that being authentic will cause you to be rejected, lose your job, or have some other negative outcome, the fear will inhibit your willingness to be authentic. Acknowledge the fear and look to your values for strength to overcome your fear. Think of a guru, saint, or leader to inspire your strength. Imagine a positive response to your authentic expression.

◇ **Is there something hidden, something you need to perceive, or an ability you need to use?** If there is, acknowledge it and determine to use it. If you don't immediately know the answer, answer yes, then no, and pay attention to your felt-perceptions for the answer.

Pillar of Connecting

◇ **What is the essence of what you desire to connect with in this situation or person?** Make a list of all the qualities and benefits of being authentic.

◇ **What is the essence within you that is connecting or needs to connect with this situation or person?** Using the list you made in the previous question, find the emotion that best expresses being authentic for you. Magnify the feeling. If this is difficult for you, imagine yourself being authentic in difficult situations. Support yourself on a daily basis with what you read and watch on television. Read books and watch programs that inspire this emotion.

◇ **Is there anything in the way of connecting? Is your ego supporting your essential self?** The desire to be authentic deserves to be supported by a balanced ego. If yours feels puffed up and self-important, recheck your motives. If you feel deflated and defeated, you may not have accessed the needs of your authentic self. This may be what was hidden in the previous set of questions.

Pillar of Grounding

- ◇ **How fully are you in your body in this situation?** Maybe all you need do to connect with your essential self is reconnect with Earth. Ground into your Tan Dien using the exercises in Chapter 4.

- ◇ **Have you given thanks for the physical things you need from Earth?** Give thanks to Earth and use the Earth strength exercise in Chapter 4, if needed.

- ◇ **Are you taking care of yourself and working within the design of your life?** What self-care actions will support you in being authentic? Do you need a yoga class, a life coach, or a healthy-eating regime? Be kind to you and trust that you are where you're supposed to be and doing what you're supposed to be doing.

Pillar of Centering

- ◇ **How fully are you in your center in this situation?** Your center—your heart—is your core, home of your authentic self. How well are you sitting in your heart right now?

- ◇ **How much weight does the voice of your authentic self carry compared to the voices of others?** Is your desire to be authentic coming from your mind telling you that you should be authentic or is it your heart's desire?

- ◇ **What is the predominate emotion you feel in relation to this situation?** Reaffirm the emotions of Connecting.

Pillar of Balancing

◇ **Are your needs in this situation balanced with the needs of others?** Check your personal space and make sure the area around you is clear and charged. Use the exercises in Chapter 6 if you need.

◇ **Is your attention to inner work balanced with your attention to outer effort?** Does being authentic impact your relationship with responsibility? Taking responsibility for something, instead of preferably being responsible to it, may keep you in obligation rather than contribution and may inhibit authenticity.

◇ **What inner needs motivate you?** Take a minute to assess your motivations.

Pillar of Aligning

◇ **In what part of the cycle of growth does this situation reside?** This may or may not be applicable, but it might help to consider what forces are helping or hindering your shine.

◇ **Where are you exerting excess force?** Sometimes, desire exerts so much force it gets in the way of the experience. Try to maintain neutrality. Be curious, not desperate.

◇ **Is there an unseen factor, cycle, or element you need to align with in achieving divine timing?** Find a saint, guru, or leader that exudes authentic expression and align with his or her Presence.

Pillar of Clearing

◇ **Are unhealed parts of self that need to be cleared influencing you in this situation?** You may have already identified this is the first question in the Pillar of Being.

◇ **What or who needs to be witnessed?** Whatever you have done that make you feel less than your full self needs to be healed. Acknowledge the action, forgive, and clear. You might use the healing your shadow exercise from Chapter 8.

◇ **Is your soul-force being used?** Call on your soul-force to heal the situation. Use the soul-force exercise in Chapter 8.

Pillar of Honoring

◇ **Are you bringing the sacred light of your life to the situation?** If not, now is the time to let the light of heart shine. You can use the Honoring life-force exercise found in Chapter 9.

◇ **Are you Honoring the sacred light of life in others?** Acknowledge that as you are more authentic, you give others the safety and inspiration to be authentic as well.

◇ **Is the tap of unconditional love on or off?** Use a transcendent emotion to inspire commitment to expressing your authentic self.

This exercise is just an example of how the Pillars can help you feel beneath the conditioning that separates you from your deepest self to experience a greater sense of meaning in life.

foundations of creating your vision

You, along with everyone else, have a vision, something you want to create in the world. To create is one of the strongest of human urges, right up there with survival and reproduction. In addition to feelings of unconditional love, creating is the closest you come to experiencing your divine essence.

Creating is the process that brings your vision into material form. The first step requires a foundation: creating a vision and magnetizing what you create. This is often called manifesting. The usual procedure of manifesting takes your vision and turns it into a force of attraction by investing in it with emotion. The formula is natural and automatic. As a child, if you wanted something, you made a wish and focused on it with desire. A wish, however, is passive, and desire does not contain the wisdom of your highest good or take into consideration the cost of your vision to Earth. Success is hit or miss. Even when your wish materializes, because it doesn't reflect the larger picture, it rarely brings the anticipated fulfillment.

Manifesting using the Eight Pillars brings a new element of responsiveness to the process. Your vision is invited out of the unseen into the seen and matures through the different states of awareness represented within the Pillars. As your vision passes through the lenses of the eight

Pillars, it evolves to reflect your relationship with the greater good. Your Presence guides the process through felt-perceptions.

Making your vision real begins with your attention and your intention: tools of the mind and the heart. Attention, used with intention, is a powerful force. Wherever your intention guides the focus of your attention, life-affirming, creative energy is set to work. Intention focuses the power of your attention into a laser beam of coherent thought that interacts with the energy around you.

Intentional attention is the vehicle for your spiritual essence to express itself in the material world. When you give the attention of your mind, infused with the intention of your heart, your Presence becomes a transformative force.

The Essentials

Manifesting is a process that unifies the force of spiritual energy, Earth energy, and human energy. Using this triad as your foundation brings what you want to experience into form. Your job is to address the basics revealed through the Eight Pillars:

◇ Knowing what you really want.

◇ Identifying your true beliefs about it.

◇ Finding the essence of what you want and connecting to it.

◇ Aligning what you want with your path and purpose.

Forgetting to include these underlying factors sabotages your ability to create what you want to experience. Personally, I'm challenged to manifest money. In the past, no matter how many prosperity-thinking and abundance techniques I employed, money remained in limited supply. The problem was in my beliefs about money—a paper construct that is given value to create equal exchange in commerce. Except, from my perspective, money doesn't create equal exchange; it is too infused with manipulation, control, and indulgence. Because I obviously don't relate to money, prosperity exercises built on attracting it simply don't work. However, I do identify with flow. When I focus on what I need or want and stay in flow, money arrives rather effortlessly. As long as I don't require a big bank account to feel safe, as long as I stay in the flow, everything arrives exactly as needed.

The concept of focusing on what you want to attract, rather than on the money that will buy it, is a key principle. It's often described this way: you are on the island of pain; where you want to be is on the island of pleasure. In between the two is the vehicle that will get you there. The tendency is to focus on the vehicle, in this case money, rather than on where it is taking you. When creating your intention, focus on the outcome you want and, in the meantime, do what you love, just for the sake of loving.

Using the Eight Pillars Process

To start, choose something you would like to create in the world or a condition in your life you would like to improve and use the process described below. Change the steps to best fit you. The goal for this demonstration is prosperity, simply because so many people are financially stressed. Going through the process for yourself, obviously choose an objective that meets the condition you want to address.

There are three steps to the process: forming the intention, creating a link, and broadcasting the intention. The Pillars are reorganized to fit these steps like so:

- ◇ Forming an intention starts in the heart in the Pillar of Centering, includes Grounding in Earth, and uses the present time awareness of Being.

- ◇ Creating a link starts in the Pillar of Connecting, advances through Aligning, and meets the criteria of Balancing.

- ◇ Broadcasting begins with Clearing and is released through Honoring.

Forming the Intention

Forming your intention is aiming your creative energy. This is an important step, so be sure take your time fully developing your intention in the three Pillars below. Unlike an action plan, the intention does not include the steps to create your goal; it sets up the ambiance to receive your request and provides the energetic material from which it is formed.

An intention is similar to an affirmation in that your final destination is declared in positive, present tense terms. Your intention also includes your starting point and your motivation. The goal is to take your focus away from the island of pain to the island of pleasure.

In this example, perhaps you want to create more prosperity by finding work that pays well and provides you with more free time.

Pillar of Centering

In the Pillar of Centering, two important events occur: You clarify your motivation, and ask for the support and direction of spirit. To do this, bring your intention into the heart and determine what your authentic self really wants. What is the larger goal, the island of pleasure, that you are trying to reach? Are you looking for security, freedom, or the ability to feed your children?

Identify the motive driving you to reach the island of pleasure. To find the motive, consider the condition you want to leave and the condition you want to attain. For this exercise, you want to leave the situation of living paycheck to paycheck and never having enough money to pay all the bills, and move into a state of having more than enough to care for your family and still have time to enjoy life. Perhaps your motive is to be able to take care of your family and make sure essential needs are met, such as having a house to live in, clothes to wear, and putting food on the table, with enough free time to enjoy your spouse and children. Now take these motives through the questions.

⬦ **How fully are you in your center in this situation?**
   Your center is home to your spirit. It is where you receive

guidance from source. When you are aligned with your center, you are aligned with your spirit, which is connected to source. Ask for guidance and help from your unseen spiritual source. Be sure your intention allows you to be more of who you truly are and doesn't need you to change your essential self to succeed. For example, if you love nature, you won't want a job clear-cutting forests, no matter how well it pays. If you love people, you won't want to work in a job that denies people insurance benefits. A job that doesn't align with your core beliefs will destroy your soul.

Check your motivation in the heart-center by assessing how well it sits there. If this motive enlarges your heart, lifts your energy, and calms your spirit, it is congruent. If you feel agitated or unsettled, or experience a drop in energy, you may need to refocus to uncover your deeper needs and fears by answering the next question.

◇ **How much weight does the voice of your authentic self carry compared to the voices of others?** If your answer to the first question is congruent, this question isn't necessary. But if your answer didn't sit well, dig deeper to find your motivation. Maybe part of your motivation is wanting your children to be proud of you. Acknowledge this in your intention. If you find a hidden motivation and you still feel unsettled in your intention, don't worry. It will all come clear by the end of the process. You can use the altar of your heart exercise in Chapter 5 or continue with the questions.

◇ **What is the predominate emotion you feel in relation to this situation?** This question addresses the feeling of your motivation as well as the emotion of your anticipated outcome. Are you motivated by fear that your children will be harmed, despair that they are hungry, shamed you haven't done a good enough job, or anger that the system is

unfair? Are you motivated by excitement that you can make
a difference?

There is probably a mix of emotions. Don't judge what you feel; just
acknowledge your emotions and address them by providing for them in
your intention. If you are motivated by fear, your intention must provide
safety. If you are motivated by despair, your intention must make you feel
encouraged: Shame is transformed into conviction and anger into boundaries. If you are motivated by excitement, be sure to ground it. Your emotions are the fuel that power your intention. Rather than avoid them, use
their energy to fuel action in the way your emotional system is designed.

Pillar of Grounding

For your intention to have legs in the world, it must be grounded and take
Earth into consideration. Grounding asks that your goal and intention be
believable. If you don't believe the outcome is possible, you will sabotage it.
You don't need to know exactly how it will happen; you just have to believe
that it can happen. What you believe is what your Presence will broadcast
and what your subconscious mind will enact. You don't have to be 100 percent confident all the time; however, you do need conviction. Chances are
this is where you stumbled in past attempts to manifest. By not acknowledging your doubts, you may collapse into disbelief at the first challenge.

◇ **How fully are you in your body in this situation?** Assess
how grounded you are as you envision your goal. If this process is taking place in your head and does not include your
feelings, or you are so excited your energy is jumping out of
your body, do the Grounding exercise in Chapter 4. Staying
out of the body keeps you from feeling what your body
holds, what you need to be in touch with. As you come into
your body, the doubt and pain you are trying to avoid will
most likely present themselves. Acknowledge your doubts
and take them into the next question.

⬧ **Have you given thanks for the physical things you need from Earth?** Be grateful for what you have now and will receive. They come from the body and soul of Earth. Be respectful of Earth in the creative process. Ask for Earth's permission to use her body to fulfill your objectives or ask that you be shown where you are out of alignment with her needs. Then use the exercise in Chapter 4, Earth strength, to address your doubts and allow the strength of Earth to support you.

When you are aligned to the spirt within yourself, source, and Earth, there is nothing you can't achieve.

⬧ **Are you taking care of yourself and working within the design of your life?** Be sure your intention respects the needs of your body, mind, and spirit. All three are vital to give life to your vision. What if you get your new job only to be too sick to perform? If you can believe there is design in your life, you can relax and include self-care in your plan.

Pillar of Being

Once you understand your motivations are in your body and in alignment with source and Earth, use present-time awareness to make your goal as effective as possible.

⬧ **What part of your past are you bringing into the situation and how much influence does it have?** Assess whether your past is holding you back or inspiring your future. If you discovered a hidden motivation but don't know what it is, it is probably a past experience that haunts you. Use the breath of life in Chapter 2 and offer your breath to your resistance. Make sure you honor your past while affirming your future.

⬧ **What desire for future outcomes or fear of future lack
   are you bringing in, and how much influence does it
   have?** Sometimes you can be so focused on leaving the
   island of pain and having the enjoyments of the island of
   pleasure that you miss opportunity to feel the pleasure of
   your intention in the moment. If your intention is to have
   more time to enjoy your kids, for example, use the time you
   have now to enjoy them. If the intention is to provide for
   more necessities, have gratitude for what you presently have.

An important part of forming an intention includes creating it in
present time. Reword your intention to reflect the present. In this example, the wording might change from find work to have work, enjoy work,
engage work, or some other action word that puts the result you're after
in present time.

⬧ **Is there something hidden, something you need to perceive or an ability you need to use?** Sit with this question
   for a few moments and see what comes up.

Now reform your intention. Perhaps it becomes to have and enjoy
meaningful work that uses all of your skills, pays more than your needs,
and gives you free time to spend with your family and pursue your hob-
bies. Set up a series of affirmations that support this goal and address your
fears and doubts. These affirmations come to your aid when old program-
ming fills your mind with self-negating thoughts. Affirmations are positive statements said in present tense. Here are some suggestions:

⬧ If you have never been able to make good money, your
   affirmation might be "I am a money magnet, attracting all I
   need and more."

⬧ If you are afraid you can't do the job, you might say, "I have
   everything I need inside to meet every challenge" or "I am
   supported in all I need."

◇ If you feel selfish for wanting something, "I am grateful to Earth and source for every opportunity."

◇ If you don't believe you are worth being paid good money, "What I bring is valuable" or "What I offer brings value to my employer and the world."

Create as many affirmations as you have fears, write them on little cards, and put them in your wallet or purse. Use them as needed.

Having formed a clear and heartfelt intention, you will breeze through the rest of Pillars. If anything is still out of alignment, it will be revealed before the end.

Creating a Link

Creating a link to what you want is every bit as important as identifying what it is and setting your intention. To be able to manifest what you need or want requires that you feel it. Without feeling it, not only is it difficult to create, you also might not recognize it when what you intend arrives. The mind is meant to be used alongside the heart and felt-perceptions. Knowing the feeling of what you are attracting keeps your heart and mind working together.

Pillar of Connecting

Once you have an intention, the ground is prepared to receive your actions. Now you need to link with what you want and create a solid connection. Your emotions create the link that forms the pathway for your heart and mind to travel into the world.

◇ **What is the essence of what you desire to connect with in this situation or person?** This is essentially what you found as motivation in the Pillar of Centering. It is the essence of the island of pleasure. In this example, it might be safety for your family, meaningful work that uses your talents and pays well, or a job that expresses your path and purpose. The core feeling might be belonging or fulfillment.

◇ **What is the essence within you that is connecting or needs to connect within this situation or person?** Find the essence of what you want within yourself. If you want to feel valuable, find your feelings of self-worth. If you want to use your talents, feel your creative ability. If you want safety, feel safe. If you want work that is part of your path, feel fulfilled. If you have trouble with this, you may want to go to the Pillar of Clearing and engage in some healing of your shadow self.

◇ **Is there anything in the way of connection?** Now create your connection. Link the essence of what you want with what you feel. Imagine a pathway. When this connection is made, you may feel a tingle of excitement as your felt-perceptions let you know you have succeeded. If you don't have confirmation, however, it doesn't mean the link isn't made. It probably means you don't have enough practice hearing your felt-perceptions.

Pillar of Aligning

Aligning is essentially visualization in reverse. You have created an intention and know the feeling of achieving it. Now hold the intention in your mind's eye while you generate the feeling in your heart. Allow the feeling to flow along the line of connection you have made and take it into the future. Open your mind and allow yourself to see the future you intend. Rather than trying to create a vision of exactly what you want, receive a vision of what your spirit, source, and Earth can create together.

◇ **What part of the cycle of growth is this situation in?** You may be just starting out in your life, building on training you've already finished, ready to harvest the fruits of your hard work, or ready to let go of what you've always done to create something new. Identify where you are in the process and consider what opportunities exist in the cycle.

◇ **Where are you exerting excessive force?** Identify where you are pushing too hard and look for flow. How can you achieve more by doing less? Maybe you are spending a lot of effort interviewing for every job whether it is a fit or not instead of targeting the jobs that you are better suited for. Maybe you try too hard to please in interviews instead of being your authentic self.

◇ **Is there an unseen factor, cycle, or element you need to align with to establish divine timing?** Just sit with this question. Make sure you are aligned with your path and purpose, whatever you define that to be. If you don't know, simply state that each footstep you take is guided by path and purpose and happening in right-timing. Chances are if you've identified the phase of the cycle and are not exerting excessive force, you are in right-timing. However, if things don't happen as quickly as you want, relax into the timing of the greater cycle.

Pillar of Balancing

In order to find balance, you need to know what your boundaries are. What if you get the perfect job, but your boss starts asking you to go on trips that pull you away from your family? Know ahead of time how much you're willing to give and how much you need to receive for the relationship to have equality. Assess your needs. Know where you draw the line. Not being balanced is a prime reason for not being happy once your vision is achieved. When your goal seems more important than holding your own space, you may not find until after you succeed that you traded an essential part of yourself to achieve your vision. Take the time to identify where your boundaries are and double check by asking these self-explanatory questions:

- ◇ **Are your needs in this situation balanced with the needs of others?**
- ◇ **Is your attention to inner work balanced with your attention to outer effort?**
- ◇ **What inner needs motivate you?**

Broadcasting

Your Presence has been broadcasting everything you've been working on into the ambiance. From the moment you identified the need for something different, a force was created in your Presence. At first, what you projected was chaotic and filled with longing that had no direction. As you clarified your intention, the vibration it carried has become focused and amplified. Now it can create the conditions for what you really want. The last two Pillars refine this process further.

You can support the process of broadcasting by talking about your vision. Be selective about what you share and with whom; however, be sure to let people know who you are truly are and what you are seeking to do. Today's world relies on word of mouth over all else. As you stand in your truth and broadcast your essence, you will draw a response that may come from unexpected places.

Pillar of Clearing

As you went through defining your needs and identifying your doubts, you cleared your intention. However, double-check and ask the following questions. As you ask, take the questions deep inside and listen to your felt-perceptions. There's no need to get hung up on this part. If you feel clear, you are. As you begin to take action steps, if there are places that reveal themselves for Clearing, just come back to this step and clear them.

⬥ **Are unhealed parts of self that need to be cleared influencing you in this situation?** This is a recheck that what you've identified as what you want truly represents your essential self. If asking this question reveals that you are still trying to live up to your parents' expectations, or some other trigger issue is discovered, use the exercises in Chapter 8 to clear them.

⬥ **What or who needs to be witnessed?** This clarifies the author of your trigger issue. Maybe opinions of others are holding you back. Do those opinions have merit? Are they something you should to listen to or are you being influenced by other people's fear and jealousy?

⬥ **Is your soul-force being used?** Use your awareness over force to achieve the results you want.

Pillar of Honoring

As you consciously broadcast your intention into the world and take steps to grow what you have planted in the fertile soil of the ambiance, be sure to invite awareness of the sacred. Honor the sacred within all: you, the divine, the Earth, your path, the path of others, and the sacred light in everyone. As you meet each person, look for their divine self. Send your light into the world. If things seem off course, check with the following questions:

⬥ **Are you bringing the sacred light of your life to the situation?**

⬥ **Are you Honoring the sacred light of life in others?**

⬥ **Is the tap of unconditional love on or off?**

Taking Action

You have created the foundation to carry your vision into the world. Everything you do now is consciously guided and directed by your vision. This is an awesome accomplishment. Now step into action. There are many great resources on the Internet, so research how to create action plans. Chances are you already have good ideas for moving forward, and with your current clarity, you're now aimed and ready to fly.

opening to nature's design

Opening to the idea that all matter is instilled with design, intelligence, and life-force changes your interaction with nature. If everything has some type of consciousness, even far removed from human consciousness, how does that alter the manner in which you treat the world around you? With a little more care, a little more attention, and considerably more respect is the probable answer. Simply being in the environment with greater awareness of the creatures with whom you share the space opens the door for different types of interaction.

Although all aspects of nature share consciousness, animals are more understandable for most people. At first, you might project onto animals and other creatures, seen and unseen, the same perception and internal thought processes that you possess. While the same building blocks are used in making the genes of our DNA and the rest of nature, the differences in how these building blocks are combined into genes, transcribed into proteins, and used in the body create extraordinary variation. For example, in terms of senses, animals see in a greater range of light frequency, hear a larger range of sound frequency, and have greater smell detection. Clearly, different organisms perceive the same environment differently.

The fact that animals respond to the environment with a greater array of senses than our own is seen in the way they respond to natural disasters. According to a report in *National Geographic News*, approximately one hour before the tsunami hit Sri Lanka and India on December 26, 2004, people reported "bizarre" animal activity. Elephants started wailing and some broke free of chains and headed to higher ground. Dogs refused to go out for their daily beach walk, and snakes, rodents, nesting flamingos, and even bats were reportedly seen fleeing the coastal area. Although 150,000 people perished in the ensuing disaster, relatively few animal carcasses were found.[1] What exactly did they perceive? Vibration in the ground from the approaching wave? A change in the smell of the breeze? Or did they perceive another type of energetic shift?

To overlay human perceptions and thinking processes on other creatures minimizes the unique perspective they offer. To paraphrase 20th-century philosopher Henry Beston, other creatures are not the underlings of humans; they are other nations, in some ways more finished and complete. Rather than treat animals as little mini-mes, learning what they offer can be more meaningful.

What biology does show is that regardless of brain size, all animals, humans, and others use the innate sensory system of emotions. Research by neuroscientist Candace Pert into the biochemical basis of emotion reveals, "The same, simple physiology of emotions has been preserved and used again and again over evolutionary eons and across species."[2] Emotions, it appears, are ancient and functional. That emotions are not unique to humans should come as no surprise. It is not difficult to read the emotional language of bared fangs of warning or wagging tails of delight. Animals exhibit a large range of emotional expression recognizable in its resemblance to your own. Though this does not mean animals experience the world the way humans do, emotions do provide a method of communication. Emotions are an energetic link. Here's an example that happened to me several years ago.

I walked into the corn crib on our farm and startled a squirrel that was raiding the rabbit food. If you've ever encountered a squirrel in an enclosed area, you can imagine the frenzy that ensued. I was between him and his exit hole, and he scrambled frantically up the walls and all around the space in terror. Naturally, I was a little scared, too. Although my instinct was to duck and run, instead I stood very still as he dashed about. I generated an intense feeling of love and appreciation and, with the excess energy available from my fear, sent a wave of love to the squirrel, all the time saying, "You're safe. It's okay. You're safe." Almost immediately the squirrel stopped its frantic activity, then calmly descended the wall, passed within inches of my feet, and exited through the hole.

I have witnessed similar events with wasps and am convinced that emotions are the key to communication with nature. Emotions may not be experienced exactly the same way; however, they represent a language all life reads and understands.

Here is my favorite passage from Beston's best-selling naturalist philosophy book *The Outermost House.*

> Touch the earth, love the earth, her plains, her valleys, her hills, and her seas; rest your spirit in her solitary places. For the gifts of life are the earth's and they are given to all, and they are the songs of birds at daybreak, Orion and the Bear, and the dawn seen over the ocean from the beach.
>
> When the Pleiades and the wind in the grass are no longer a part of the human spirit, a part of very flesh and bone, man becomes, as it were a kind of cosmic outlaw, having neither the completeness and integrity of the animal nor the birthright of a true humanity.
>
> We need another and a wiser and perhaps a more mystical concept of animals. . . . We patronize them for their incompleteness, for their tragic fate of having taken form so far below ourselves. And therein we err, and greatly err. For the animal shall not be measured by man. In a world older and more complete than ours they move finished and complete, gifted with extensions of the senses we have lost or never attained, living by voices we shall never hear. They are not brethren, they are not underlings; they are other nations, caught with ourselves in the net of life and time, fellow prisoners of the splendour and travail of the earth.[3]

The Shift

What if Mellen-Thomas Benedict is correct and all of nature supports the growing-up of humans?

Engaging nature with intentional attention may deepen the collaboration that is already underway. In truth, a change in interaction seems to be unfolding. More people than ever before are interacting consciously with nature, and nature appears to be responding. My husband and I notice this phenomenon with the wildlife on our farm, and people we speak with are having similar experiences. I am reminded of the small sparrow that landed on presidential candidate Bernie Sanders's podium during a campaign speech in Portland, Oregon, in March 2016. Despite a crowd of 30,000, the bird flew onto the stage and, amidst the roar of the people, flew to the podium and observed Sanders for several minutes. What would prompt a bird to perform such an action? You can view numerous videos of this event on YouTube. It is quite remarkable.

In many traditions, from Native American to ancient Egyptian, birds are considered the messengers between the realms. On our farm, my husband, Colin, and I notice the greatest changes in interaction with varied species of bird. Rather than scattering as we approach, some birds seem to be behaving differently. They are engaging us in unusual encounters. We wonder if this is the result of a paradigm shift that has been underway for quite some time. It seems the scales may finally be tipping.

Here's an example. I was pushing a full wheelbarrow to the manure pile when I looked down to see an adult, red-winged blackbird sitting in the grass with his wings outspread, sunning. Because I was so close and he hadn't moved, I assumed he was hurt and sank slowly to my knees, trying not to startle him. I waited for him to try to fly away, but he didn't. Without my glasses, what looked like a wire seemed to be resting against his wing. I suspected he was tangled in the wire and marveled my proximity wasn't causing him to struggle to get free. However, because it's not unusual for hurt animals to accept human help, I slowly reached toward him and slid my finger along his wing. It turned out what I thought was wire was merely a blade of grass he was resting next to. The bird didn't move as I stroked his wing. Bringing my hand back to my lap, I spoke and asked him what he needed. He rose up, demonstrated he could fly by circling, then landed a few feet away and resumed his sunning. I determined he needed nothing and went on to dump the wheelbarrow. He was gone upon my return.

Colin has equally close encounters on a daily basis. Lately, he is being surprised with visits from an Oriole. The bird repeatedly hovers at the screened window next to Colin's chair, looking into the room where Colin watches TV. Twice, that Colin has seen, the bird has met our King Charles Spaniel nose-to-nose through the screen. The dog and bird seem to be greeting each other, as the meetings last for several minutes. Remarkably, this dog, bred for birding, wags her tail and appears to enjoy the exchange. See Colin Andrews on Facebook for more of his animal stories.

The feeling of these encounters is one of being welcomed into a larger community. No longer on the outside, we are accepted as part of nature. As such events continue, Colin and I wonder: Could the nascent human species be waking up and nature welcoming us home? That is how it feels, as though these small encounters are a shadow of what awaits and will soon become commonplace. Our friends who run a raptor rehabilitation center report such interactions daily. Check out their website at *www.aplacecalledhoperaptors.com* to see some amazing photographs.

The way to access communication with nature is to be aware of the sacred light of life in everything. Acknowledge the sacred and be open to the possibility that everything is conscious, and your perception will deepen. Ask permission, and the door to exchange opens. To change what you experience, change how you experience: Send your heart energy in front of you to greet the world from your essence.

Nothing opens the heart more than experiencing connection with other forms of life. Here is a truly wonderful exercise that uses the Pillars of Being, Connecting, Grounding, Centering, Balancing, Aligning, and Honoring. Create your own experiences bringing all Pillars into use.

Flowing With the Essence of Tree

1. Take a deep breath and bring yourself fully into the present moment. There is no better place to be than here, no better time to be in than now.
2. Ground, center, and give thanks.
3. Sit or stand with your back against the trunk of a tree.
4. Acknowledge the consciousness of the tree, even if you can't grasp the type of consciousness it has. Ask permission to engage.
5. Generate feeling of love and appreciation and offer it to the tree.
6. Feel the energetic flow of connection and honor the sacred light of life.
7. Sink your back into the tree. Let your back be completely supported; maintain boundaries and awareness of your separateness even as you merge into the consciousness of tree.
8. Slow your mind to the speed of tree.
9. Sense-feel the flow of sap. Sap rises and falls in pulses.
10. Align your breath with this pulse. Inhale with the active pulse and exhale with the rest phase.
11. If you don't feel the flow, breathe with the awareness of Earth and sky as in the exercise in Chapter 4.
12. Follow your breath.
13. Find silence and just be.
14. Notice what you feel.

Aligning With the Designs of Nature

The structure and forms of nature are based on building blocks of geometrical patterns that are referred to as sacred geometry. Because the basic structure of everything we see, feel, and know originates in the mathematical designs of sacred geometry, these patterns are tools to understand the underpinnings of nature and reality.

Essentially, sacred geometry is revealed through relationships. The same proportions that are found in the cosmos are found in the human body and are also proportions reflected in the musical scale as discovered by Pythagoras in the sixth century BCE. In addition, the intervals of the musical scale are related to the frequencies of light in the rainbow. The more you study these relationships, the deeper the interconnections discovered. One of the most important is that interconnected frequencies influence brain wave patterns and consequently impact states of awareness.

Sacred geometry is described through mathematical equations. The opening spiral of a galaxy and that of a nautilus shell, for example, proceed proportionally along a growth ratio called the golden mean ratio described mathematically by the Fibonacci sequence. The growth sequence starts with the number 1, and proceeds by adding the two previous numbers. So the second number in the sequence is also 1, then 2, 3, 5, 8, 13, 21, 34, 55, 89, 144, and so on. A graph of this sequence replicates the natural spirals in galaxies, bracts in pinecones, scales in pineapples, and more.

Some examples of sacred geometry include the five Platonic solids. Discovered by Plato, the Platonic solids are three-dimensional polygrams with all sides equal to each other. Each Platonic solid is thought to represent one of the five elements as follows:

◇ Tetrahedron—thee-sided pyramid—fire.

◇ Cube—four-sided square—Earth.

◇ Octahedron—eight-sided pyramidal structure (two four-sided pyramids base to base)—air.

◇ Dodecahedron—twelve-sided sphere—ether.

◇ Icosahedron—twenty-sided sphere—water.

In addition to the golden mean spiral, other two-dimensional representations of sacred geometry include the flower of life, Metatron's cube, the toroid (donut shape), and many more.

To be honest, the mathematics of sacred geometry makes my head spin. The importance for me is that the inherent geometry reveals the energetic vibration contained within. Geometries entrain and direct energy.

I am reminded of organic chemistry in which the shape and function of molecules is related to the amount of energy contained in the bonds that join the atoms together.

Beyond the fascination and enjoyment of sacred geometry, you can use these patterns to create environments that generate energy in Earth and are more conducive to higher states of awareness. This is not a new thought by any means. Sacred geometry is incorporated into the oldest cathedrals, temples, and mosques. The use of sacred geometry is intercontinental. It is encoded in ancient sacred sites such as Stonehenge in England, the pyramids of Egypt, and the Mayan temples of Central America, and seen in the Yantric paintings of Tibet and the sand paintings of the Navajo and Zuni nations.

Employing sacred geometry in the landscape is also a well-known utilization. Bill Witherspoon is an artist who creates land art with the healing intention of reintroducing people and society to nature. His most famous work is undoubtedly the huge Tibetan Sri Yantra he drew in the desert in Oregon in 1990, a story you will want to read at the provided link.[4] Witherspoon won the Arts and Healing Network Award in 1998 for his work creating healing and Earth friendly housing. The award seeks to "honor and thank Bill for his unique contribution to the field of healing arts and for his leadership in inspiring so many people in all walks of life, to awaken to the understanding that creative acts of reverence and gratitude to the earth are effective in increasing earth productivity and decreasing earth toxicity."[5] This amazing statement appreciates the power of sacred geometry and the need for gratitude to Earth.

Those who have experienced crop circles know of the inherent power within landscape art. Colin, my husband, was among the first to research crop circles in the 1980s. In fact, he is responsible for coining the term. His research documents the magic that happens when the energy of spirit, Earth, and humans unite in sacred geometry. The increased energy within crop circles creates unusual experiences for those who make them, visit them, and live in proximity to them. The circles are known to induce deep emotions and create experiences of spontaneous healing, increased psychic ability and telepathy, and states of altered consciousness. Even electromagnetic equipment is impacted, causing the malfunction of compasses and cameras. Whatever you believe about crop circles and how they are made, the energy released through their Presence ignites the imagination of the world. If you choose, you can carry the magic forward.

Using sacred geometry in your home and environment feeds Earth, nature, and self-awareness. Here are some ideas you can use:

◇ Instead of planting your garden in rectangular beds, design it as a spiral using the Fibonacci sequence of growth.

◇ Draw and color mandalas, and include common sacred geometrical patterns such as the flower of life and Metatron's cube.

◇ Activate the sacred geometry in your body by using sacred chants, healing tones, or specialized music such as Solfeggio harmonics.

◇ Visualize geometric patterns, perhaps while listening to specific tones.

◇ Create a simple labyrinth in your yard and walk sacred geometry into the energy of Earth and into your cells.

Your knowledge is the only limit to your constructive, healing use of sacred geometry. Fortunately, there is abundant information in books and on the Internet. There are even architectural institutes dedicated to teaching design using sacred geometry.[6] If you are interested, one of my favorite books is a gem titled *Explore the Sacred Through Geometry,* self-published in 2012 by Paul Stang. It's available on Amazon and printed by Create Space. I like the book because it provides the geometry of nature through architecture in mathematics with abundant visual aids, and Stang, who clearly loves the information, provides exercises for feeling the geometries in your body. It is an enlightening, experiential book that offers everything you need without boggling your mind!

In Support of Wildlife

The desire to connect more fully with other forms of consciousness on this planet comes with a responsibility. Nearly everything humans do impacts wildlife. Common products you may not even think about cause immense pain and suffering to wildlife. Avoiding some and paying attention to how you dispose of others can help. What is thrown away ends up in landfills, so taking a few precautions before putting something in the trash can make a big difference. In addition, every dollar you spend is a vote. Buy cruelty-free beauty products, eat humanely grown foods, and support research into edible or biodegradable plastics that will help wildlife and humans in the future.

◇ Deflated balloons look like attractive little morsels and, when eaten, can lodge inside an animal's throat or stomach, leading to suffocation, starvation, and death. Be sure to dispose of all balloons in the trash and don't just let them fly away on the breeze into natural habitats.

◇ Balloon strings and fishing wire can get tangled around an animal's mouth, feet, and legs, causing a long, painful death. Be sure to dispose of your trash appropriately.

◇ The netting wrapped around Christmas trees or placed over trees to protect them from being eaten by deer can entrap birds and other animals. The best choice is not to use them, but if you do, cut them into little pieces before discarding.

◇ The handles of plastic bags are often seen caught around the necks of seagulls and other birds. When the bag gets caught in trees, the birds are hung. Cut the handles on your plastic bags when you discard them or, better yet, use cloth bags.

◇ Fishhooks become lodged in beaks, wings, and feet, causing injury and death. Keep track of your fishing gear and take it with you when you leave.

◇ Pieces of plastic, rope, and string are often used by birds for nesting materials and tangle in the baby birds. Dispose of them properly.

◇ Animals such as lizards, reptiles, and more become trapped inside bottles, cans, and yogurt containers, so don't leave them behind on a picnic.

◇ Plastic six-pack holders trap animal's heads, causing strangulation and death. As many as 1 million sea birds and 100,000 marine mammals and sea turtles die every year from getting trapped in six-pack rings.[7] Even when disposed of properly, they cause problems, so be sure to cut the rings, or, better yet, support Saltwater Brewery and other companies that are developing and using edible six-pack rings. Using wheat and barley that would otherwise be discarded from the beer-making process, Saltwater Brewery's biodegradable six-packs are completely edible for any sea creature.

◇ Small pieces of plastic are mistaken for food items and cause death. It's best if we all try not to use so much plastic or support the continued development of edible plastics by writing your congress person, liking related blog and Facebook posts, and using your dollar as a vote!

◇ Beauty products unnecessarily test their products on animals. Choose cruelty-free beauty lines. They are really great products!

◇ Even being nice humans can cause harm. Ducks and geese that are fed large amounts of bread develop wing deformities. Feed the birds appropriate grain meals.

◇ Use certified humane animal products such as eggs and milk.

◇ Toxic garden weed killers and pesticides, along with household cleaning products, leech into the environment, poisoning plants and animals. Use non-toxic products.

◇   Using poison to kill rats and mice kills more than the animal you target. Cats, dogs, fox, hawks, and even eagles can eat the poisoned animal and die. Don't use poison! It is cruel, uncontrollable, and unnecessary.

◇   Hair elastics wrap around the beaks of birds so they can't open their mouths to eat. They can also get caught around animals' necks. When throwing hair elastics away, cut them first.

◇   Support your local wildlife rehabilitation centers. The one I love in our area is A Place Called Hope (*www.aplacecalledhoperaptors.com*).

14

presence in conflict resolution

Conflict is a normal part of life. All relationships contain disagreement; after all, no two people see the world exactly the same way. In general, conflict occurs for three main reasons: conflicting needs in the same situation, competition for resources, or differences in values. An example of conflicting needs might be a child's need to explore vs. a parent's need to keep the child safe. Competition might be two people who want the same job, are fighting for the same resource, such as money, or are in love with the same person. Differing values can be as personal as whether spanking a child is considered violence or as global as political and religious orientation. No matter what the arena, feeling threatened strikes at your core and initiates a strong response. Sometimes, this response can be overwhelming.

The greater your feeling that something important to you is being threatened, the greater the emotional charge. A strong emotional charge can it makes difficult to think and respond clearly. The threat maybe real or perceived, but either way, fear or anger can drive behavior. Being able to resolve conflict constructively requires emotional awareness and the ability to reduce the stress of the conflict so that you can respond clearly. It is a perfect place to use the Eight Pillars.

Conflict is often based on differing perceptions that were developed from life experiences, family patterns and values. Perception is not easy to shift; if you were cheated in a business deal once, you are likely to perceive the next deal with distrust. Consequently, two parties in a disagreement can go over the same facts repeatedly and continue to perceive them differently. Objective facts are rarely interpreted the same way. Resolving conflict, therefore, requires willingness to self-explore. From this perspective, engaging conflict can be an unparalleled arena for growth.

The Typical modes of Addressing Confrontation

Most people don't enjoy conflict. It is uncomfortable and feels unsafe. People who do enjoy conflict, might like the energy rush or the high of winning. Your response to conflict is based on your personality and what you learned growing up in your family. The typical responses to conflict are avoidance, capitulation, fighting, negotiating or collaboration.

Avoidance is often the first response. Usually, one or both people deny that a problem or difference exists. This rarely works to resolve issues as feelings are driven deeper inside to fester until they are faced. Left unaddressed, submerged emotions can blow up in conflict over small and inconsequential events, such as not putting the cap back on the toothpaste, or leaving food to spoil in the employee refrigerator. In some instances, avoidance has a benefit in that it can provide you with time to explore your feelings and calm down before engaging someone else's challenging behavior. Using it as a tool to buy time, however, is different from using it to calm the surface while ignoring the submerged issues.

Capitulation, or submission, is another approach that doesn't actually address differences. It is a step up from avoidance in that the conflict is at least named. Instead of finding a workable solution, however, one person gives up their point of view, need or desire and agrees to whatever the other person wants. Capitulation is usually chosen out of fear of losing a relationship. In this case the relationship is considered more important than the situation. For example, you might yield to your boss in order to keep your job, or yield to your partner because you're afraid they will leave you if you don't. You might capitulate to the demands of a young child because the effort of engaging is simply too much. However, while capitulation might reduce outright conflict, it doesn't create solutions. One person can't give up who they are for someone else, no matter how much they want to keep their job, or how much they need or love another person. The differences remain unresolved and will continue to show up in various ways until they are addressed.

Fighting is certainly a classic way to engage conflict as is seen in the global politics of today. Even when one side wins, however, because the other side loses, the conflict is not resolved. It is simply delayed and the differences are usually magnified. Win or lose outcomes are part of the old paradigm of domination. When one side loses, they don't just disappear. In fact the fear, lack of security, anger and feelings of powerlessness fuel retaliation that is often violent and destructive.

Negotiation usually involves compromise in which both people give up something in order to gain something else. This is certainly better than fighting, however, because both have given something up, there's often resentment and reduced commitment to the solution. The fuel for rebellion remains present. This is especially true if one person perceives that they gave up more than the other.

Collaboration favors the best resolution with long lasting solutions. However, collaboration is difficult to achieve. It takes time and commitment and most importantly requires that the solution honors the values and motivations of everyone and aligns to values that are greater than personal gain. Most importantly, collaboration requires trust. The only way trust can be gained is through knowing what motivates another and seeking to find common ground. When collaboration is the chosen path, exciting and unexpected outcomes are possible as disparate parts generate creative solutions.

No matter how challenging, conflict is an opportunity for growth. Resolving conflict encourages looking at and evaluating values. Conflict offers a mirror for you to see where you and the other person are emotionally stuck, as it did in my experience with the ER attendant in Chapter 3. Most importantly, resolving conflict builds trust. Knowing your relationship, whether with boss, co-worker, significant other, child or parent can survive challenge and disagreement, provides a deep sense of security that builds caring behavior and commitment to shared outcomes.

The Eight Pillars and Conflict Resolution

When you feel threatened, there is a good likely hood that you will behave badly. Having your financial security, love relationship, reputation, respect or values threatened sends most people into a defensive posture. The Eight Pillars offers a path to step back and use your Presence to find the most peaceful and constructive way forward.

Presence takes you beyond personal gain to what is best for all concerned. You are linked to the other person as part of an interactive whole. If the person you are in conflict with doesn't come out of the conflict getting what they need, you don't either. Some part of you will be harmed and it will show in your life at some point. Through the practice of the Eight Pillars, you can pay attention to the needs of the other person as well as you own, stand up for yourself while honoring other people's right to the same.

Pillar of Being

Being in present time awareness creates neutrality. It allows you to respond to confrontation rather than react. By letting go of past unresolved issues as well as fear-based expectations of the future, you are able to respond to what is actually happening in the moment. Being in the present moment also helps manage stress. In confrontation, it's common to become so focused on the issue at hand that you lose awareness of escalating stress. Using present time awareness, you can pay attention to your body and maintain observation of gathering stress and discharge it before it explodes. Paying attention to your felt-perceptions keeps you informed of changes in the ambiance and alert you to hidden threat.

To practice Being, take three deep Opening Breaths and focus your attention inside your body.

Pillar of Connecting

One of the most difficult challenges to overcome during confrontation of any kind is staying connected to the person or group you are in conflict with. The first reaction is to separate yourself. Compassion is the means to staying connected. Remember, you can be angry and still care about the other person, or if it is someone you don't like, honor their right to be. Opposite feelings do not negate each other; they can both be held with respect. Through Connecting you can pay attention to the information transmitted through non-verbal communication. During the conflict with the ER attendant in Chapter 3, tuning into the attendants body language revealed his motivation. It also acted as a mirror for me to see what my body language was communicating. Understanding motivation provides connection to the needs of the other person. Holographic awareness keeps you mindful that solutions must work for all parties. Any solution that doesn't benefit everyone ultimately doesn't benefit anyone.

To practice Connecting, imagine bringing the other person into your heart. Using such visualizations changes your vibe and shifts the intensity of the situation.

Pillar of Grounding

Grounding keeps you in your body so that you can stay in present time with strength and conviction. Most of the damaging things we do during confrontation occur because we don't feel safe or powerful. Grounding connects you to your power and discharges the excess energy of stress. As stress builds up, breathing into Earth releases the muscle tension and adrenalin to relax your body and clear your mind. In addition, Grounding reminds you that there is a deeper design to life. You don't have to know all the answers, you just have to be open to allowing creative solutions made from the design of nature to form in your mind's eye.

To Ground, take three deep breaths into your body, and as you exhale, imagine you are sending your breath into the Earth. On the next inhale, imagine Earth rising inside to give you strength and support.

Pillar of Centering

Centering keeps you connected to your purpose and to what's important to your essential self. Your ability to stand up for yourself calmly and effectively depends on your ability to remain centered. Your values, core beliefs and essential truths are accessed through connection to your heart. Centering and Grounding partner to keep you focused on what is truly important in the situation with strength and calm. Through Centering you find the stillness to access deeper wisdom and find heart-centered action.

To center bring your attention into your heart-space. Inhale into your heart and exhale into Earth.

Pillar of Balancing

Creating boundaries during conflict allows you to hold your energy. Without boundaries, your energy dissipates and you lose the strength to carry out your convictions. You cannot collaborate to develop creative solutions if you can't maintain your perspective. Balancing allows you to hold your point of view together with another's point of view to find a solution that honors both.

To practice Balancing, create an awareness of the space around you and keep it clear of the other person's influence. Listen to what they say and observe their body without letting their energy into your field to knock you off your center or ground. Inhale into your heart and exhale energy into the space around you. Image the space being clear and calm.

Pillar of Aligning

Aligning brings awareness to motivation. Do you or the person you are in conflict with have an agenda or desire that isn't declared? Hidden agendas create confusion. They manipulate people. If you feel internal resistance to the process of finding a solution, you or the other person may have a hidden agenda. Stop and determine what is motivating you. Observe the other person's body language and non-verbal communication and use felt-perceptions to better understand his or her motivation. Change your perspective. Instead of you and the other person fighting each other over an issue, consider that you and the other person are joined together against the issue. In this way, you can find common ground and develop trust.

To practice Aligning, use your breath to connect with the intention of finding the highest and best solution for all people involved.

Pillar of Clearing

Limiting believes, undeclared agendas, hidden motivations, emotions of fear and anger can all sabotage your ability to find creative solutions. Whenever you notice resistance, confusion, helplessness, or other emotions that either deplete your energy so that you cannot stay centered and grounded, or escalate your feelings of aggression, you know you have encountered an unresolved inner issue that is driving this response. Although you can't take the time out for a deep inner Clearing process, you can shift yourself out of the influence of limitation and control your emotions and behaviors. When you are in control of what you feel, you can move yourself out of the need threaten, intimidate or punish the other person.

To practice Clearing, modify the Eight Pillar Process of Contact, Listen and Allow. Change it to Contact, Acknowledge and Release. Use your breath to contact the emotion you are experiencing, acknowledge its message, and release its energy. Move yourself outside of the influence of this emotion. Doing this is not difficult; what is challenging is making the decision that you want to.

Pillar of Honoring

Everybody needs respect and validation. Constructive resolution of conflict happens when both parties find something they can agree to honor. In the past, there was a saying in the USA, "I may not agree with what you believe, but I will defend to the death your right to believe it." It was agreed that everyone had a right to their own opinion. Disagreement could be tolerated and used for creative advancement because there existed universal honoring of this single idea. Today, people cannot tolerate differences. Consequently, there is more violent conflict around differences of opinion. Honoring asks that you accept everyone's basic right to be themselves. Honoring looks for what is held in common rather than what separates.

To practice Honoring, choose to see the divine within all.

Practicing the Eight Pillars brings internal peace and external peacefulness.

15

walking a path with heart

All paths lead to the same destination: an encounter with the infinite mystery. This is the view of anthropologist and author Carlos Castaneda, gleaned from his 30-year narrative journey with native shaman, Don Juan, of the Yaqui Nation.[1] Consequently, a path is chosen not because of its destination, but because it fulfills you to walk it. Don Juan refers to this as walking a path with heart. The path of developing Presence is a path with heart.

Encountering the infinite mystery is a journey inward. It is finding your connection to your heart; the spiritual center within that is connected to the heart within the center of the universe. Holographic awareness through the heart provides access to everything you need for becoming all that you are. The practices of the Eight Pillars open you to this journey and support your growth. Through developing Presence, the practices guide you onto a path with heart.

Developing Presence through walking a path with heart changes the question of what direction to take from "Is this the right path for me?" to "Does this path fulfill me?" For many people, however, there is no good measure of fulfillment. To gauge fulfillment by how much pleasure you feel or how many achievements you amass is itself unfulfilling. On the path of Presence, a path with heart, a better measure might be whether all parts of you are being used to their fullest, whether you are in service to the flow of a larger whole, and whether you feel fully alive. Changing the measure doesn't mean you shouldn't pick goals or work to achieve outcomes. Goals and dreams give you the journey; the measure of their success, however, is what you encourage within yourself along the way. Goals and dreams are the means to encounters with deeper parts of self, as well as areas that need *Clearing* to grow.

Redefining fulfillment frees your attention and releases you from being attached to outcomes; more important than what you achieve is what you experience and how you engage your inner self. David Bohm, the father of quantum physics, agrees. He says, "The ability to perceive or think differently is more important than the knowledge gained."[2] And that is the crux of walking a path with heart, the path of Presence: opening to perceive deeper layers of reality more completely.

A path with heart is alive. It brings you fully into your felt-perceptions. Whatever you encounter on the journey is not judged as good or bad; it is simply something more to explore. The journey might take you where you expect or somewhere else entirely, but wherever you are is an opportunity. The practices of the Eight Pillars can help you explore the opportunities and deepen your awareness as you develop Presence.

Being brings you fully into present time to see, hear, and feel reality, and frees you to act on what you perceive. *Connecting* facilitates energetic exchange, whereas *Grounding* in Earth brings strength and courage, and *Centering* in your heart helps you determine if the path you are on is alive for you. *Balancing* ensures you aren't pulled into a state of somnambulance, going through the motions of being alive without fully engaging life. Working, paying bills, watching TV, sleeping. Where are joy, growth, and exploration? Where are meaningful relationships and exchanges? *Aligning* maintains movement and brings you to encounters with mystery. *Clearing* ensures your shadow self brings your creative spirit forward. *Honoring* observes that what you put your attention on is what will grow. Honor and attend to what fulfills you; open to the light in everything.

Contact, listen, and allow. This is the process. A path with heart is interested in the quality of your Presence on the journey. How does your

Presence impact those around you? What awakens in the ambiance from your existence? Are you living with full engagement? These questions take you on a path with heart, a path of Presence.

Converging Fate With Free Will

One of the first internal resistances encountered on a path with heart is accepting the circumstance of your birth. Your birth was not an accident. The family you were born into, as well as the time period and culture, are all exactly where you are meant to be for the journey your soul envisioned. Time spent longing for a different life is time lost from the exploration of what is right here where you are right now. Anything you can envision, you can create. Any goal you enjoy pursuing is attainable. Go ahead and transform your life, just for the joy of it!

According to the Maya, time periods are imbued with qualities based on relationships with celestial interactions. The circumstances of life within a given time period are defined by these relationships. Whatever growth your soul has come to explore occurs through the restrictions and opportunities of the period of your birth. There is no doubt those born during the World War I or World War II had a different canvass on which to work than those born in more peaceful periods. The specific challenges of today are terrorism and the threat of ecologic collapse. Being born at this time is not a punishment meant to keep you from traveling wherever you want in the world or limiting your freedoms. It is not penance meant to bring you to your knees in pain and fear. It is a specific challenge that asks: What can you offer to this moment that adds to life? What hidden resource is waiting within you to be developed for this period?

There is a great temptation to allow anger and fear to drive the building of walls and the creation of ever larger chasms. Anger that, on the one hand, protects and helps motivate energy, on the other becomes a wildfire that imbalances the mind. Fear that is meant to provide protection becomes a destructive force that breaks the connections between people and nations. Fanning the flames of anger may feel good in the moment but rarely feels good in the aftermath of the chaos it creates. There is a different path to survive the challenges of today. You were born at this time to bring this path into being.

The most important element for change is listening with the heart: to hear the messages of anger and fear, and discharge and transmute the energy they carry before an inferno of hatred and condemnation is created. No one can speak to this more eloquently than those who have endured the pain of terrorist actions and random violence.

The parents of the young children lost in the school shooting at Sandy Hook say, "We choose love."[3] The current Dalai Lama, who has seen the decimation of his home, culture, people, and family, believes the way forward is through the development of compassion. He says, "We all share an identical need for love, and on the basis of this commonality, it is possible to feel that anybody we meet, in whatever circumstance, is a brother or sister."[4] In face-to-face meetings, differences in culture, religion, and belief give way to the commonality of being human.

Listening with the heart looks beyond differences to interconnection within a larger whole. This planet is home to everyone. Let love be the inner resource you develop to light the way on your path.

The Power of One

The first questions you might ask are "What can I do? I am only one person? How can I make a difference?" Through your Presence, you make a difference. It is the feeling of being powerless that heightens the fear and anger of this time. Remember Gandhi's message: If you believe you are powerless, the only course for self-defense is violence. If you know you are powerful, you can achieve greater results with soul-force.

Developing Presence brings your soul-force into play in the world. It's a choice whether violence closes down your heart or breaks it open. Today, you will cross the path of someone who feels desperate, maybe in a grocery line or on a bus. What if you are the person who, by reaching out a friendly hand, changes the course of that person's life? Today, decide to overcome isolation in the world by reaching out to one other person. Today, cross the lines of us and them.

Social media offers avenues of change with unlimited influence. Consider Marie Forleo, who describes her reaction to the Syrian refugee crisis as yelling at the TV asking, "Why isn't anyone doing anything?" When she realized she was the "anyone" she was questioning, Forleo went on to join a group of everyday people and entrepreneurs in the creation of the Compassion Collective.[5] This group is raising millions of dollars used to clothe, shelter, and feed Syrian refugees. Their motto is *"There's no such thing as other people's children."*[6]

In truth, there are a million ways to create positive impact. But first, you must believe your Presence makes a difference. You are more powerful than you can possibly know. In opening to the path of Presence on a path with heart, you become conscious of your impact. The message of today's crises to the individual is that how you go about fulfilling your dreams influences the larger whole. What you do matters.

Engaging the Mystery

Astonishingly, many scientists and skeptical people still imagine the tiny fragment of reality we experience through the narrow range of our senses represents all-that-is. Yet astrophysicists at NASA tell us that energy and matter that we can't see, feel, or measure, dark energy and dark matter, make up 95 percent of the universe. What is termed normal matter constitutes only 5 percent of all-that-is. This 5 percent is "everything on Earth and everything ever observed with all of our instruments."[7] Dark matter and energy, like subtle energy, cannot be directly observed or measured. Their existence is inferred based on the observations of their effect. Yet dark matter is thought to create the structure for normal matter. Scientists say the "normal matter flows gravitationally into dark matter scaffolding."[8]

Even with this great ambiguity, many people can't seem to make room in their minds for anything outside known limits. One hundred years ago, people were just beginning to use radio waves. The idea of cell phones and Wi-Fi would have seemed magical, and we know this is a mere step in what is to come. Technology continues to expand human reach, and yet the size and scale of the mystery continue to be denied. Perhaps what can't be accepted isn't the existence of things outside our awareness, but the idea that what is out there might be conscious and interactive.

Presence is the part of you that interacts with mystery, with the light basis of reality. Your Presence calls forth something different from the ambiance than does mine. As you develop Presence, what you call forth changes. Your inner force is magnified and your interactions with the mystery become more palpable. This is a natural process of awakening to your essential self. Don't worry if you feel unprepared for the journey; all you need is an open heart. You are where you are meant to be and at exactly the right time.

If the reason for being alive is to experience and all paths go to the same infinite mystery, why not choose to walk with heart on a path of Presence?

CONCLUSION

Erin and Emerson

Erin is released from the hospital directly to home since she exceeded the progress goals of a rehab facility. Despite repeated offers, she declines to stay with us at the farm. She wants the familiarity of her own home and the company of her dog. She wants to discover her limits and take control. Mostly, she wants to find normal. We try to convince her otherwise, but my beautiful daughter is stubborn. She walks her path resolutely. There is no arguing.

The car ride home is perilous. Her head, enclosed in the halo device, barely fits into the passenger seat and every bump or curve jostles her against ceiling and door. She would fit better in the back where Colin sits, but when we try, her body panics. Although she has no memory of the accident, of hurtling through space from the back seat of the car, her body remembers all too well.

Erin hobbles into her living room and looks around with hungry eyes. Her dog, a rescue of uncertain heritage, certainly boxer and probably some pit bull, barks excitedly from the porch.

"Jake!" she exclaims joyfully as she maneuvers into a chair. Hearing her voice, Jake leaps against the glass slider, his barking escalates to a fever pitch.

After so much time in the care of others, no doubt he imagined she was never coming home.

I pull back the curtain and slide open the door. Colin prepares to intervene if Jake's 90 pounds of excitement threaten Erin's well-being. He needn't worry. One look at Erin in her head gear drops Jake, cowering, to the floor. His worried eyes watch her, looking as though he thinks her injuries and odd attire are somehow his fault.

Erin encourages him forward. He slinks on his belly to where he can reach her, then shyly performs an examination by smell: sniffing the leg brace, the halo, the blood still matted in her hair. It takes nearly a quarter of an hour before he accepts that yes, this is Erin, and no, he did nothing wrong.

Now begin the long months of Erin's housebound recovery and extensive physical therapy. There is no way to describe what it takes for her to get up each morning after a sleepless night to face yet another day of pain. Jake is the one constant companion, the caring witness to her exhaustion, anguish, and courage. He repays her rescue of him a thousand times over in his rescue of her.

It is Halloween, 10 weeks after the accident, when the halo device is removed. We arrive at the neurosurgeon's office for a CAT-scan, expecting that, if all looks good, a date will be set for that event. Much to our shocked surprise, after reviewing the results with us on the big viewing screen, the neurosurgeon pulls a screw driver from his pocket, and he and his team set to work removing screws and rods. Erin takes deep, slow breaths to overcome her sudden panic and to subdue the trembling of her body. Astonishingly, there is little pain and no blood. Erin is assured that although the four holes in her head will leave scars, they will heal. She is sent home in a neck brace, her bones 75 percent healed. Another CAT-scan is scheduled in January, after which she will be able to drive and resume a nearly normal life.

She limps out of the office wearing the neck brace. Without the defined and protected space of the halo, she is exposed and vulnerable. There is no holding back the world and all of its demands. We drive directly to a hair salon where her tangled mop is cleansed, cut, and styled. It is a new look, one she would have never chosen. This final adjustment to her identity is somehow the most challenging. Sweet victory arrives, however, when she steps into a shower for the first time in two and a half months.

In January, the CAT-scan shows Erin's neck is completely healed. The neurosurgeon smiles as he shows her the images: There are no healing lines in the bones. It's as though the breaks never occurred. Nature's design successfully executed.

When Erin first came home, Emerson's health rose and fell, paralleling her up-and-down progress. Then, at some point, their mirror images separated. Now Erin continues uphill, and Emerson, perhaps because his job is finished, begins a slow decline. My horse, Gabriel, constantly stays within feet of him, caring diligently for his friend of 14 years. Earlier, in November, a new horse, Annie, a gorgeous Clydesdale—the type of horse that pulls the Budweiser wagon—came to the farm as a boarder to be Gabe's companion once Emerson passes. Annie's sweet nature and mothering Presence boosts Emerson's spirit. With her arrival, his health bounces back. Even though Emerson is an older horse, well into the time of life to die, I stop thinking that he will.

In the evenings, the horses come into the barn for dinner then, weather permitting, are let back out for the night. One night in March, Gabe and Emerson playfully gallop around the paddock after dinner, bucking, kicking and having a grand time. I laugh as I watch them frolic while Annie tries to stay out of their way. Emerson doesn't act like a 30-something horse; he gives no indication he has another place to be.

In the morning, Annie and Gabe come in for breakfast, leaving Emerson's empty body lying under a tree.

Erin kneels by Emerson and strokes his muzzle. Gabe stands beside her. It is a poignant moment, watching the two who love Emerson best saying good-bye. Gabe noses Emerson's neck and blows his breath along Emerson's face. He turns and nuzzles Erin's check, consoling her tenderly. I struggle not to cry. Annie walks across the paddock to put her nose on my shoulder. I lean against her solid warmth, touched by how perceptively the horses take care of us.

Erin grows immensely through what she endures. This doesn't mean she has no further growth to undertake or that she won't slide into areas that are still driven by unconscious conditioning. In the months of recovery she makes many self-negating decisions as unresolved emotional pain drives her choices. Unlike before the accident, however, now she can't escape into ignorance. She is witness to something greater in herself and in the world. She answers to an inner directive as well as to awareness of unconditional love, the substance of life. She can and at times probably will resist growth, but nonetheless, her soul has decided to awaken.

The Journey Continues

Through the awakening of Presence, like Erin, you have embarked on a journey of self-awareness. Once begun, there is no turning back. Once you know something, you can't un-know it. This doesn't mean you will always do the right thing or never behave in ways you later regret. It doesn't mean you won't let pain cause you to lose mindfulness of what is important. Developing Presence is not about creating a perfect human; it is thinking differently from the ways you have always thought before. The path of Presence is the creation of your own path with heart as you inter-act with deeper layers of consciousness.

Pain cannot be avoided. It is part of life. You can use pain for growth or you can give it an internal harbor and let it grow without being pro-cessed and understood. When you use pain to fuel growth, it stops driv-ing unconscious behavior. When you harbor pain, it is projected outward into a "me and them" mentality. "You are bad and I am good. You are wrong and I am right." Projection automatically causes division. It cre-ates an unbalanced ego, thus robbing ego of the strength to support soul-force. Everyone has the potential to be both conscious and unconscious. Everyone is part of the problem and part of the solution.

There is no end to a path of Presence, no point where you will be per-fect. You will always be growing, and you will always encounter pain. You will also be able to reach for an experience more joy, fulfillment, curiosity, and creativity. With the commitment to Presence, life becomes an exquisite adventure. Rather than letting your inner self be dictated to by external circumstances, external circumstances develop your inner resources that you can use to create different external circumstances. This is the flow between internal and external reality. It is the spiral of the evolution of consciousness.

Final Thoughts

In his book, *The Undivided Universe: An Ontological Interpretation of Quantum Theory*, physicist David Bohm, father of quantum physics, writes that the notion of separate organisms with boundaries between them is an abstraction. "Underlying all this is unbroken wholeness even though our civilization has developed in such a way as to strongly emphasize the separation into parts." He adds, "Indeed, the attempt to live according to the notion that the fragments are really separate is, in essence, what has led to the growing series of extremely urgent crises that is confronting us today."[1]

It is commonly thought that scientific concepts open people's minds and shape the direction of society. However, the truth might be more the reverse: that, because humanity is evolving into the experience of wholeness, science is able to define the theory and discover its proof. The ability to conceive a new thought is born from first perceiving or experiencing its reality. Rather than leading the evolution of consciousness, science validates the path.

The perception of wholeness unveils the flow between internal and external reality, the flow that carries your ability to manifest your dreams in the external world. Bohm also says, "There is a difficulty with only one person changing. People call that person a great saint or a great mystic or a great leader, and they say, 'Well, he's different from me—I could never do it.' What's wrong with most people is that they have this block—they feel they could never make a difference, and therefore, they never face the possibility, because it is too disturbing, too frightening."[2]

What about you? Are you willing to accept that what you believe and how you live your beliefs through your choices, relationships, and treatment of the natural world makes a difference? If you are, you have taken a leap into the deep end of the pool of consciousness. You are not alone. Earth is shifting out of the existing paradigm of separation. You are part of this awakening. Practicing the Eight Pillars opens your senses to the light-basis of reality where your Presence is already established.

Here is the bottom line: You have extraordinary abilities you have only begun to tap. Everything you need is already inside you. You are connected within to all-that-is. Now is the time to wake and embrace the journey. You were born for this time. You are here on purpose. Love is your natural state of being.

APPENDIX:
EMOTIONAL MEANING CHART

Adapted from *The Path of Emotions*

Emotion	Function
Anger	Essentially for protection, anger directs you to assess your boundaries. Are they as strong as you need them to be? Do they balance your needs? Are they respectful of the needs of others?
Anxiety	This emotion tells you something is out of alignment. Look for what isn't congruent. Are you trying to hide your fear of not being good enough? The Pillar of Clearing may be helpful.
Apathy	Apathy tells you that you aren't connecting to something in yourself or others. It's often due to not feeling valued and seen. Value and see yourself.

Boredom	This is another emotion of disconnection. Boredom suggests you aren't engaged in the world or using your creative spirit. You aren't being recognized for you. Start with recognizing yourself. The Pillar of Centering is a good place to start work on what you might have lost.
Contentment	Contentment is the result of flow and alignment. It represents well-balanced Pillars all round!
Denial	Denial protects your core. What is under attack and what are you afraid of seeing? Use the Pillar of Centering.
Depression	Depression can be asking you to take the time to assess the elements in your life. Have you left part of yourself somewhere along the way? Depression may be telling you to step back and take some time to just be.
Desperation	Desperation tells you what you've done so far isn't working. Creativity and a new approach are needed.
Disappointment	When illusion clouds your vision, disappointment is the outcome. Dispel false ideas. What are you afraid to see?
Discouragement	This emotion is reminding you everything is a learning experience. Disappointment suggests there is a deeper motive that you haven't addressed. Find and address it. The Pillar of Clearing may help.
Envy	Envy suggests that you haven't clearly assessed what you have and who you are. It motivates you to use your potential and overcome your fear of failure.

Excitement	Excitement is a motivator. It moves you forward and asks whether you can you believe in your dream.
Fear	Fear warns you that you are unsafe, physically, emotionally, or otherwise. Assess your situation and see where danger is coming from. Then act.
Grief	Grief is the response to broken connections. If you can reestablish the connection, do so. Otherwise, allow the repair the time needed. Working with the Pillar of Connecting may be helpful.
Guilt	Guilt tells you when you've over stepped another person's boundaries and caused harm. Receive the message, let it go, and then act.
Happiness	This is the reward you give yourself for being you.
Hatred	The nuclear bomb of self-protection, hatred tells you that your core is in danger and you're afraid you won't survive. The attack can be from outside self or from your priorities being misplaced. Either way, is nuclear war your best option?
Inspiration	Inspiration is your interaction with deeper forces within and without. Inspiration demonstrates connection.
Jealousy	You are alerted to losing your center and not valuing what you have to offer. Find your essential self-expression and relax.
Joy	You are in the flow of creative self-expression.
Love	This is the unity emotion that brings you into alignment with the sacred light with all.
Obsession	Obsession reveals you have lost your balance. Reevaluate priorities and create boundaries.

Passion	Passion feeds your growth and connects you to your path.
Sadness	You are reminded of what is essential.
Shame	This emotion, although difficult, helps you restore your integrity. It asks you to forgive yourself and others.
Wonder	Wonder is the emotion of awakened potential. You can see the limitless nature of reality.

GLOSSARY

Action versus movement: action is motion fueled primarily by willpower to fulfill an intention; movement is motion inherent in an event that moves an intention forward using less effort.

Active imagination: a technique first developed by Carl Jung to access subconscious information primarily through images that can be personified as separate entities. Additional types of active imagination include visualization and shamanistic therapy.

Affirmations: positive statements used in self-talk to affirm inner strengths and improve commitment to outer goals.

Alchemy: the process of taking something ordinary and, through some type of transformation, turning it into something extraordinary.

Allowing: the act of reducing your internal resistance to an idea, intent, action, and so forth.

Ambiance: the palpable mood, quality, atmosphere, or character of the environment you are in.

Amorphous: something that is formless, insubstantial, or without definition.

Art of not doing: the ability to allow the inherent movement within events to produce results rather than exerting excess will power.

Attention: the focus of the mind; selective concentration on a specific object, person, or aspect of information.

Aura: the ambiance, atmosphere, or quality that is radiated from a person, thing, or place.

Authentic, essential, core self: your true self distinct from social and family conditioning, usually related to your spiritual nature.

Balancing: the ability to find the fulcrum of opposing forces and establish equilibrium; paying equal and simultaneous attention to internal and external stimuli.

Being: living in present-time awareness, awake to what is happening in the moment, and open to inner potential.

Biochemical communication network: the body's internal communication system made up of nerves, neurotransmitters, hormones, and cytokines.

Body awareness: the ability to maintain awareness of information received through the body in the form of sensation, feelings, and emotion; the ability to split attention between internal (body) and external stimuli.

Body-mind: integration of physical, mental, emotional, and spiritual parts of self into a unified perception.

Bow wave: the wave formed in water or other mediums that is displaced forward as a boat or other object moves; the faster the movement and the larger the boat or object, the larger the bow wave. Energetically, as first defined by Dean Radin, a bow wave is the displaced energy that precedes an event; the more emotionally intense the event, the larger the bow wave.

Bracts in pinecones: the modified leaf that spirals along the outside of a pinecone.

Cardinal points: in a compass, the four directions of north, south, east, and west.

Centering: bringing one's attention to the internal core, where it is easier to access your basic values, truths, and desires. Physically located in the center of the chest or the solar plexus.

Centering breath: consciously using the breath to bring one's attention into your center while using your awareness to access feelings, sensations, and inner knowings.

Cervical collar: a medical device worn around the neck to stabilize the vertebrae.

Charisma: personal charm that can influence others.

Circadian rhythm: a 24-hour biological cycle geared to light and dark that controls sleep patterns, eating patterns, and hormonal balance.

Clearing: reducing the influence of past situations or limiting beliefs on your actions and feelings.

Cohesive thought field: a unified and focused field of energy generated by your mind during times of concentrated attention.

Coincidence: chance happenings.

Colin Andrews: present-day consciousness researcher; part of the first team of people to investigate crop circles in the 1980s.

Concept: abstract idea, basic understanding, or guiding principle.

Congruent: two or more things that are consistent with each other; energetically, when two or more things are congruent, there is better communication and flow of energy between or among them.

Connecting: the act of placing one's attention on the natural links between people, plants, animals, objects, and so forth.

Conscious breathing: using awareness of your breath to guide your attention into the body or to specific areas within the body to access the sensations and felt-perceptions in the area.

Core: the center of your being where your true beliefs and inner truth are found.

Cosmology: a culture's idea of the nature of the universe.

Crop circles: patterns in crops made by the flattening of plants into geometrical designs. The making of them seems to involve spontaneous interaction with humans, Earth energy, and spiritual energy.

Crux: a crucial, central, or deciding point.

CAT-scan or CT-scan: a type of diagnostic X-ray involving cross-sectional imaging.

Cymatics: the study of the effect of sound waves on matter.

Discernment: the ability to select the important pieces of information in an array of stimuli.

Disembodied: mental activity that is separated from awareness of the body, emotions, or feelings.

Divine timing: the timing of events to a larger plan and purpose than what is easily seen and understood by humans.

Divinity awareness: observing the sacred within all; seeing from a larger perspective than purely personal self-interest.

Duality: the philosophical belief in opposing and separate forces that represent good and evil.

Dynamic: growth-oriented movement that expresses vitality, purpose, and enthusiasm.

Ecosystem: the environment and organisms within an environment that form an interdependent whole.

Ego: a conscious part of self that maintains self-worth and supports the enactment of inner truth; an imbalanced ego has lost awareness of self-worth and often compensates with exaggerated self-importance.

Egotistical: a person with an unbalanced ego that has become inflated with self-importance.

EKG: electrocardiogram; a machine that measure the electric function of the heart.

Electromagnetic field: physical field of energy produced by electrically charged objects that influence the behavior of other electrically charged objects within the field.

Electromagnetic frequency: the rate of vibration of a particle or the number of repeating waves in given period of time as measured in hertz units (Hz).

ELF: extremely low frequency; usually below 30 Hz.

Emotional awareness: the ability to pay attention to emotions and use the information and energy they contain to understand self and the world in order to interact more meaningfully.

Emotional intelligence: the capacity to recognize emotions in self and others and to understand emotional information to guide your thinking and behavior.

Emotional patterns: a set of repeating feelings triggered by specific events that are responding to old trauma and beliefs rather than current information.

Emotions: part of the body's sensory system receiving, emotions are translations of subtle energy information that communicate between the mind and the body.

EMT: emergency medical team; first responders at an accident.

Energetic attack: using the force of one's intent powered through destructive emotions with the purpose of causing harm to another person.

Energetic boundaries: the personal space around a body that reflects the emanation of vital life-force.

Energy awareness: the capacity to pay attention to body sensations and/or visual images that are responding to the flows and fields of life-force energy.

Energy center: locations in the body and in Earth that gather and process vital life-force energy.

Energy field: in physics, an area of electromagnetic radiation; energetically, the area around a person, animal, plant, or object that transmits its life-force—often called aura.

Enmeshed: two or more things tangled together and difficult to separate.

Entangled: two separate things bound together in some fashion; in quantum physics, it refers to quantum particles continuing to affect each other from a distance; energetically, it refers to the desires and intent of one person impacting another.

Essence: the identifying quality or nature of something.

Essential nature: the quality that makes something what it is.

Essential self: your true self; the part of you that makes you who you are.

Everyday awareness: the usual state of awareness in which the mind is occupied primarily by plans and things that have to be done and less aware of information received through the body.

Expectation: a mental image of something you hope will happen; standard of conduct.

Felt-perceptions: awareness based on the combination of mental insight with body sensations, emotions, and feelings. Felt-perceptions are the basis of intuition, gut feelings, hunches, and deeper insights that reveal your inner truth.

Felt-senses: another word for felt-perceptions.

Fibonacci sequence: a series of numbers where the next number in the sequence is found by adding up the two numbers before it. Starting with 0 and 1, the sequence goes 0, 1, 1, 2, 3, 5, 8, 13, 21, 34, and so forth. Geometrically, the sequence approximates the growth spiral or logarithmic spiral found in galaxies, pinecones, and sunflower seeds, and is part of the foundational geometry of creation.

Flower of life: a geometrical figure composed of multiple evenly spaced, overlapping circles that are arranged such that they form a flower-like pattern with a six-fold symmetry. Another of the foundational geometries, this symbol is found in every religion throughout the world.

Four-fold process of emotional healing: a process for finding the information held in an emotion and releasing the energy in positive action. Found in the book *The Path of Emotion.*

Full engagement: accessing all parts of self and bringing your full self to the situations you encounter in life.

Giveaway: giving away your center, purpose, or intention to another, sometimes for the purpose of emotional or physical survival, or misplaced belief in another person's right to control you.

Golden mean spiral: a logarithmic spiral also called equiangular spiral or growth spiral that is approximated through the Fibonacci sequence and part of sacred geometry.

Grounding: the ability to focus your attention into Earth, bring your awareness more fully into your body, and experience the connection between you and Earth.

Habituated response: a conditioned or patterned response to a specific situation; in general, habituated responses do not take new information into account when generating a response.

Halo device: a medical device to stabilize a broken neck.

Heart-based intention: an intention that takes into account the needs of your true self alongside the needs of others.

Heart center: the energetic center located in your chest that is home to your spiritual center and core, essential, authentic, or true self.

Heart-centered action: an action based on the needs of your true self and the true self of others.

Heart-centered awareness: paying attention to the inner and outer world through the feelings of your true self.

Hologram: a three-dimensional image of an object made from the interference patterns of coherent (laser) lights such that each piece of the picture contains all the information held within the entire picture.

Holographic awareness: paying attention to the interconnection of each individual piece with that of the whole.

Honoring: respecting the divine within all.

Intentional attention: the act of using your attention with intent.

kHz: kilohertz; 1,000 hertz or units of frequency of one cycle per second: 1,000 cycles per second.

Land art: artwork using land as a canvass, such the Nazca Plains in Peru, crop circles, the Sri Yantra mandala found in the Oregon desert, and so forth.

Life-force: subtle energy that forms the matrix for physical matter providing the animating, motivating, and enlivening force of life.

Manifesting: the creative act of turning something from an idea into an object, situation, or event.

Metatron's cube: sacred geometric pattern made from 13 equal circles that in three dimensions contains all five platonic solids.

Mind's eye: the imaging center of the brain often located at the energy center of the third eye.

Non-action: see wei-wu-wei.

Path: the personal journey you take in life to uncover the unique expression of your true self.

Personal power: your ability to direct life-force toward positive expression of your true self and manifestation of your path and purpose.

Personal space: the space one arm's width around you that is the projection of your energy field; also the psychological distance you require to self-reflect on your actions, your motivations, and the events in your life.

Pillars: the eight energy practices that uphold Presence.

Platonic solids: five three-dimensional shapes formed with multiple equal sides that form the basis of how matter is constructed. First discovered by the Greek philosopher Plato, born in 428 BCE.

Precession of the equinox: the movement of the 12 constellations across the sky over the course of a 26,000 year cycle.

Present time awareness: focusing your attention on what is happening the in the here and now.

Projecting: taking your thoughts or feelings and ascribing them to the thoughts and feelings of others.

Psyche: the center of thought in the human mind.

Pythagoras: Greek mathematician and scientist from the sixth century BCE who illuminated many aspects of sacred geometry.

Quantum physics: a branch of physics based on the principle that matter and energy have the properties of both particles and waves, and that studies energy such as light as small separate units (quanta) of energy.

Resonance: sympathetic vibration, often used to mean being in synch with a person or idea.

Right-timing: the timing of events that includes all elements of a situation, seen and unseen, to produce the best possible outcome; often outside of human control.

Sacred geometry: the repeating mathematical principles underlying the design of nature.

Sacred light of life: the divine spark within everything that unites all into one whole.

Sacred space: an area recognized for having unique properties that can bring you closer to your spiritual nature.

Schumann resonances (SR): a set of peaks in the extremely low frequency (ELF) portion of the Earth's electromagnetic field.

Semipermeable: the quality of a boundary to allow certain substances to pass through while blocking others.

Shadow self: the part of you that holds all the negative feelings you are afraid to express.

Solar plexus: an area in the upper abdomen that holds one of the energy centers of the body and for some is their spiritual center.

Solfeggio harmonics: an ancient six-tone musical scale used in sacred music such as Gregorian chanting.

Soul-force: a term coined by Gandhi to represent a person's full spiritual strength.

Source: the divine, God, universal consciousness, singularity, all-that-is, and so forth.

Spiritual essence: the element of the divine within all, your primary nature.

Subtle energy: life-force energy; vibrational wave-lengths outside the known electromagnetic spectrum that are thought to correspond with the dark energy of physics.

Synchronicity: a person's experience of two or more events that are unrelated by cause and effect but that occur in a significant manner.

Tai Chi: a form of martial art exercise from China that develops body, mind, and spirit.

Tan Dien: an area in the lower abdomen that is the physical center of the body and is also one of the body's energy centers.

Torus/toroid: a three-dimensional donut-shaped geometry that is part of the repeating structures in nature termed sacred geometries.

Transcendent emotions: emotions that lift you beyond personal self-interest.

Vibrational essence: the identifying vibration of a person (animal, plant, or human), place, or thing.

Visualization: creating a vivid and positive mental picture of something in order to promote a desired outcome.

Wei-wu-wei: the art of not doing; the ability to go with the flow and use the energy of a situation to move you forward rather than your will power.

Witnessing: giving testimony to integrity and truth in the face of social injustice; acknowledging that fair and honest social dealings come from personal wholeness.

Yantric paintings: symbolic representations of the vibrational energy with the energy centers of the body.

NOTES

Chapter 3

1. Dalai Lama XIV, *The Compassionate Life* (Boston: Wisdom Publications, 2003).

Chapter 5

1. http://www.onbeing.org

Chapter 6

1. https://whatis.techtarget.com/definition/superconducting-quantum -interference-device
2. Gary E.R Schwartz and Linda G.S Russek, "Registration of Actual and Intended Eye Gaze: Correlation with Spiritual Beliefs and Experiences," *Journal of Scientific Exploration* 13, no. 2 (1999): 213–229.
3. http://groups.google.com/forum/#!topic/holistic-quantum-relativity-hqr /vl4g8zeATTM

Chapter 7

1. *Andrews, Synthia and Colin, 2012,Wiley Press, 2008 pg.*
2. Jonathan Haidt and James Morris, "Finding the Self in Self-Transcendent Emotions," *Proceedings of the National Academy of Sciences* 106, no. 19 (2009): 7687.

Chapter 8

1. Candace Pert, *Molecules of Emotion: Why You Feel the Way You Feel* (New York: Scribner, 1997), 179.

2. Alexander Lowen. *Bioenergetics* (New York: Penguin Books, 1976).
  3. http://www.thework.com

Chapter 9

  1. http://www.thefreedictionary.com/honoring
  2. Paul Williams, *Remember your Essence* (New York: Harmony Books, 1987), 62.
  3. Haidt and Morris. "Finding the Self in Self-Transcendent Emotions," 7687.
  4. http://www.earthbreathing.co.uk/sr.htm
  5. Mellen-Thomas Benedict, *Spirit of Gaia*, video series. Accessed at http://www.mellen-thomas.com
  6. Meredith Young-Sowers, *Inner Circle*, video series. Accessed at http://www.stillpoint.org
  7. http://www.azquotes.com/author/44493-Nicholas_Roerich

Chapter 10

  1. http://www.dictionary.com
  2. http://www.merriam-webster.com/dictionary/authentic
  3. http://www.oxforddictionaries.com/us/definition/american_english/authentic

Chapter 13

  1. Maryann Mott, "Did Animals Sense Tsunami Was Coming?" *National Geographic News*, Jan. 4, 2005. Accessed at http://news.nationalgeographic.com/news/2005/01/0104_050104_tsunami_animals.html
  2. Pert, *Molecules of Emotion.*
  3. http://www.henrybeston.com/quotes.html
  4. http://www.exopermaculture.com/2013/06/22/bill-witherspoons-oregon-desert-land-art/
  5. http://www.artheals.org/ahn-awardee/bill-witherspoon.html
  6. http://www.sacredarchitecture.org/
  7. http://www.digitaltrends.com/cool-tech/edible-biodegradable-six-pack-rings-save-ocean/#ixzz4CgSy00sL

Chapter 15

  1. Carlos Castaneda, *The Wheel of Time: The Shamans of Ancient Mexico, Their Thoughts About Life, Death, and the Universe* (New York: Pocket books, 1998), 19.

2. https://www.goodreads.com/author/quotes/9809.David_Bohm
3. http://www.facebook.com/SHWeChooseLove
4. Dalai Lama XIV, *The Compassionate Life*, 37.
5. http://www.marieforleo.com/2016/05/the-compassion-collective/
6. http://thecompassioncollective.org/
7. http://science.nasa.gov/astrophysics/focus-areas/what-is-dark-energy/
8. Richard Massey, Jason Rhodes, Richard Ellis, et al., "Dark Matter Maps Reveal Cosmic Scaffolding," *Nature* 445 (2007): 286–290. Accessed at http://www.nature.com/nature/journal/v445/n7125/full/nature05497.html

Chapter 16

1. David Bohm. *The Undivided Universe: An Ontological Interpretation of Quantum Theory*, Kindle edition (New York: Routledge, 2006).
2. http://www.goodreads.com/author/quotes/9809.David_Bohm

INDEX

Abandonment, 103-104
Action, 36
    authentic, 217-222
    forced, 145-147
Agitation, 145
Alchemy, 88-89
Aligning, Pillar of, 24, 139-157, 205, 208,
    210, 221, 225, 232-233, 255, 258
Allow, 207, 211, 212
Ambition, 71, 142, 184
Anger, 259
Animals, 237-248
Approval, 103, 131
Attachment to outcomes, 90
Attention, 27, 69, 85, 130-131, 224
    dual, 49
    free, 44-45
    intentional, 240
    lack of, 38-40
Authentic self, 213-222, 227
Authenticity, 66-67, 250, 251-253
Avoiding pain, 81-83
Awakened perception, 21-32
Awareness, 19, 22, 25, 27-28, 63, 91, 207
    cyclical, 143-145
    divinity, 185-187
    Earth-centered, 79-81
    emotional, 163-164, 166
    energy, 123-125
    heart-centered, 101-102
    holographic, 58-61, 65, 71
    present-time, 35-51

Balance, 15, 63, 81, 100-101, 112, 253
Balancing, Pillar of, 24, 117-130, 204, 208,
    209, 221, 225, 233-234, 255, 258
Bearing witness, 169-170, 174
Becoming authentic, 216-217
Behavior, 162
Being, core of your, 23
Being, Pillar of, 24, 33-51, 204, 208, 209,
    218-219, 225, 229-231, 255, 258
Beliefs, 123, 162
    false, 23
Bioenergetics, 165
Body signals, 26
Body, physical center of, 86-88
Body-mind, 25, 67
Boundaries, 121-122, 124, 125, 126-127,
    132-134, 233-234, 253, 267
Breath, 21, 27, 47, 48-51, 133
Breathing, 75
Broadcasting, 225, 234-235
Burn-out, 122, 250, 253-254
Carelessness, 187, 188-189
Center of gravity, 87
Center, 100-101, 105, 111
Centering, Pillar of, 24, 97-116, 204, 208,
    209, 220, 225, 226-228, 255, 258
Ceremony, 84-85
Charisma, 28-29
Choices, 66, 267, 204, 236
Clearing, Pillar of, 24, 159-179, 205, 208,
    210, 221-222, 225, 234-235
Commitment, 251

Communication, 190
Compassion Collective, 261
Compassion, 65, 67
Competition, 32
Conditions, 104
Conflict, 130
Conflicting needs, 122
Confusion, 28-30
Connecting, 60-62
Connecting, Pillar of, 24, 53-74, 204, 208, 209, 219-220, 225, 231-232, 255, 258
Connection, 85, 124, 125, 194-195
Conscious breathing, 27
Conscious living, 19
Consciousness, 21, 36, 87-88, 102, 186, 193, 237, 249, 268
Contact, 207, 211, 212
Contentment, 188-189
Contribution, 128
Control, 90
Conviction, 22
Core of your being, 23
Creating a link, 225, 231-234
Creating your vision, 223-236
Creativity, 168, 267
Criticism, 194
Crown, the, 191
Culture of confusion, the, 28-30
Curiosity, 266
Cycle of growth, 232-233
Cycles, 143-145
Cyclical awareness, 143-145
Dark matter, 261
Death, 40-41, 44
Delays, 151
Dependency, 125-127
Developing presence, 22, 25, 30, 32
Disappointments, 151
Disharmony, patterns of, 90
Distortions, 23
Divine timing, 233
Divinity awareness, 185-187
Dominance, 32
Double standard, 250-251
Doubts, 228, 234
Dual attention, 49

Duality, 187-188
Earth, connecting to, 75
Earth-centered awareness, 79-81
Ease, 205
Ego, 62-64, 71, 214, 266
Eight Pillar Process, the, 203-212, 225, 268
Eight Pillars of Presence, the, 24-25
Emotional awareness, 163-164, 166
Emotional intelligence, 163
Emotions, 25, 65-66, 82, 103, 107, 109, 120, 152, 227-228, 238
    processing, 165-166
    suppressed, 164
    transcendent, 191-192
    unprocessed, 162-163
Energetic boundaries, 132-133
Energy awareness, 123-125
Energy link, 68-69
Energy, 89, 131, 261
Entrepreneurship, 249-255
Envy, 103
Essence, 30, 67, 69-70, 185
    spiritual, 130, 187-188
Essential self, 104-106
Excessive force, 233
Exhaustion, 122
Expectation, 133
Explore the Sacred Through Geometry, 245
False beliefs, 23
Fate, 144, 145, 185, 259-260
Fear, 40, 92, 103, 161-162, 259
Feelings, 19, 25
Felt-perceptions, 25-27, 28, 46, 190, 206
Fibonacci sequence, 243, 245
Flexibility, 253
Force of your spirit, 22
Force, 204
Forced action, 145-147
Forgiveness, 162, 196-197
Forming an intention, 225, 226
Free attention, 44-45
Free will, 144, 145, 259-260
Fulfillment, 257-258
Future, 39-40

Genuineness, 71
Goals, 82, 142
Gratitude, 81, 85
Gravity, center of, 87
Grounding, 106, 154
Grounding, Pillar of, 24, 75-96, 204, 208, 209, 220, 225, 228-229, 255, 258
Growth, 266
  cycle of, 232-233
  spiritual, 71
Guilt, 93
Hardships, 100
Healing, 85
Heart center, 106-108
Heart, path with, 257-262
Heart, the, 191
Heart-centered awareness, 101-102
Hierarchies, 144
Holographic awareness, 58-61, 65, 71
Honoring, Pillar of, 24, 181-200, 205, 208, 210-211, 222, 225, 235-236, 255, 258
Imagery, 150
Imbalance, 29
Imperfections, 23
Indecisiveness, 89
Infinite mystery, the, 257
Inner self, 22
Innocence, 205
Integration, 161
Integrity, 204
Intelligence, emotional, 163
Intention, 27, 68, 152, 154, 224, 240
  forming an, 225, 226
Interaction with light, 45
Internal guidance system, 65
Intuition, 19, 107
Irritation, 122
Isolation, 61-62, 70
Jealousy, 103
Joy, 122
Judgment, 67
Lack of attention, 38-40
Lack of love, 196-197
Life-force, 82-83, 189-190
Life, sacredness of, 184
Light, interaction with, 45

Limitation, 61
Link, creating a, 225, 231-234
Listen, 207, 211, 212
Listening, 91
Living, conscious, 19
Losing authenticity, 250, 251-253
Love, lack of, 196-197
Love, unconditional, 105, 187
Manifesting, 223-236
Maya, time and, 148-149
Meaning, 16
Meditation, 46
Memory, 38-39
Mind-body split, 42-43
Mindfulness, 164, 266
Mistakes, 100, 101
Molecules of Emotions, 163
Mother Earth, 83-86
Motivation, 226-227
Movement, 81, 142-143, 144-145
Muscles, 87
Mystery, the infinite, 257
Nature, 58-59, 71, 75-96, 237-248
Needs, conflicting, 122
Nourishment, 120, 192-194
One, power of, 260-261
Oneness, 58-61
Opportunity, 142
Outcomes, attachment to, 90
Outermost House, The, 239
Overwhelm, 89
Pain, 61, 196, 266
  avoiding, 81-83
Paradigm of separation, 268
Paradigm of wholeness, 31-32
Path of Emotions, The, 16, 39, 163, 172
Path of Energy, The, 16, 27
Path with heart, 257-262
Patterns of disharmony, 90
Patterns, 143-145
Paying attention, 46
Perception, 37, 164
  awakened, 21-32
Perceptions, 25, 60, 150, 186
Perceptiveness, 43
Perfection, 64

...sonal power, 130
Personal space, 123-124, 129, 133
Phases, 143-145
Physical body, 41-44
Physical center of body, 86-88
Pillars of presence, the eight, 24-25
Planetary, 85
Platonic solids, 243
Power of one, 260-262
Power of presence, the, 22-24
Practice of aligning, 152
Practice of balancing, 131-135
Practice of being, 45-47
Practice of centering, 109-112
Practice of clearing, 171-173
Practice of connecting, 67
Practice of grounding, the, 89-93
Practice of honoring, 194-197
Prana, 49
Present time, 35-51
Prioritization, 122
Processing emotions, 165-166
Projection, 266
Purpose, 108-109, 125, 206
Pythagoras, 243
Qualities of presence, 30-31
Rationalization, 153
Regret, 266
Relaxation, 205
Remembering, 38-39
Resistance, 17, 145, 186
Resistances, 259
Responsibility, 127-128, 129, 134, 135
Revenge, 103
Sacred geometry, 80, 242-245
Sacredness of life, 184
Scarcity consciousness, 90
Schumann resonance, 80, 193
Self, authentic, 213-222, 227
Self, essential, 104-106
Selfishness, 126-127
Self-awareness, 245, 266
Self-care, 120, 122, 229
Self-compassion, 64
Self-doubt, 103, 161
Self-importance, 29

Self-reflection, 24
Self-sabotage, 168
Self-trust, 100
Separatism, 57-58, 124, 126, 268
Shadow self, 166-168, 170, 173, 174, 214
Signals, body, 26
Solar plexus, 129
Soul-force, 170-171
Sound, 80
Space, personal, 123-124, 129, 133
Spirit, force of your, 22
Spirit-matter rift, 83
Spiritual essence, 130, 187-188
Spiritual growth, 71
Split, mind-body, 42-43
Stability, 75, 81
Stillness, 204
Strength, 75, 81, 204
Struggle, 70
Suffering, 61, 196
Suppressed emotions, 164
Synchronicity, 142, 150-151, 154-155
Tan Dien, 86-88, 92, 107
Third eye, 149-150
Thoughts, 123
Thrill-seeking, 40, 41
Time, 147-149, 154
Timing of movement, 144-145
Timing, 233
Transcendent emotions, 191-192
Transformation, 186
Truth, 22, 26
Unbalanced ego, 266
Unconditional love, 105, 187
Undivided Universe, The, 267
Unknown, 36
Unprocessed emotions, 162-163
Vision, 152-153
Vision, creating your, 223-236
Visualization, 150
Voice, the, 169-170
Wei-wu-wei, 146
Wholeness, 31-32, 99, 167
Wildlife, 237-248
Witherspoon, Bill, 244-245
Witness, bearing, 169-170, 174